LIM CHONG YAH

An Autobiography

Life Journey of a
Singaporean Professor

LIM CHONG YAH

An Autobiography

Life Journey of a Singaporean Professor

Lim Chong Yah

NUS, Singapore & NTU, Singapore

with the assistance of

Tan Chung Lee

WS Professional

NEW JERSEY • LONDON • SINGAPORE • BEIJING • SHANGHAI • HONG KONG • TAIPEI • CHENNAI • TOKYO

Published by

WS Professional, an imprint of
World Scientific Publishing Co. Pte. Ltd.
5 Toh Tuck Link, Singapore 596224
USA office: 27 Warren Street, Suite 401-402, Hackensack, NJ 07601
UK office: 57 Shelton Street, Covent Garden, London WC2H 9HE

Library of Congress Control Number: 2016057147

National Library Board, Singapore Cataloguing-in-Publication Data
Name(s): Lim, Chong-Yah, author.
Title: Lim Chong Yah : an autobiography : life journey of a Singaporean professor /
Lim Chong Yah.
Description: Singapore : WS Professional, [2017]
Identifier(s): OCN 965783399 | ISBN 978-981-32-0304-4 (hardcover)
Subject(s): LCSH: Lim, Chong-Yah. | Economists—Singapore--Biography. |
College teachers—Singapore--Biography.
Classification: DDC 330.092--dc23

Desk Editor: Shreya Gopi

Typeset by Stallion Press
Email: enquiries@stallionpress.com

CONTENTS

DEDICATION

This book is dedicated to my wife See Nah Nah for sharing with me my life since our marriage on 11 May, 1957.

Lim Chong Yah
11 May, 2016

OPENING POEM

Human is human

Divine is divine

Mix not the two

If do

Disillusionment.

Lim Chong Yah
Singapore, 1952

PREFACE

This book chronicles my life as I see it, as I recall, as I reflect and as I reminisce. It is an autobiography. It thus has many I and I.

There are five extraordinary blessings I am particularly grateful for in my life.

One, my beloved family: My dear wife, my gifted children and their supportive spouses, and my seven adorable grandchildren.

Two, the rare Senior Professorship appointment followed by the Emeritus Professorship in the National University of Singapore (NUS), and subsequently, the inaugural Albert Winsemius Chair Professorship, followed by another Emeritus Professorship in Nanyang Technological University (NTU).

Three, as the founding Chairman of the National Wages Council of Singapore and also as the founding Chairman of the Skills Development Fund Advisory Council.

Four, my life-long research publications, the list of which is at the back of this autobiography.

Five, as the founder or co-founder of regional economic institutions like the Federation of ASEAN Economic Associations (FAEA), the East Asian Economic Association (EAEA), and the Pacific Economic Cooperation Conference (PECC), besides heading for a long period of time: The Economic Society of Singapore (ESS) and its journal, the *Singapore Economic Review* (SER).

Much of this book describes my life's journey connected with and arising from the above five important events or undertakings. Other important aspects of my life, especially my role as an educator, are also events that have contributed to make my life more interesting, more challenging, and more enriching. They fill up the other pages of this book.

Two lines in the immortal poem of William Henley, "Invictus", run thus: "In the fell clutch of circumstance, I have not winced nor cried aloud." I must confess that in my case, particularly in my growing up years, I had on some occasions cried privately, in sorrow, in desperation and in helplessness. As I grew older, I turned to God for solace, comfort, support and guidance.

Life, however, as my life shows, has much, very much, more hope, more joy and more happiness than sorrow, sadness and despair. Even in the worst of circumstances, there was always hope, hope for a better tomorrow, hope for the breaking of dawn, after the dark midnight was over.

Lim Chong Yah
20 May, 2016

ACKNOWLEDGEMENTS

My wish in this autobiography is to share my life's journey with my readers. This, however, was not my original intention. The book was first meant only for the information of my children and grandchildren and probably their offspring. The readership target, however, was soon enlarged to include my relatives and friends. The scope later developed to become wider and wider to include all interested readers. Being an autobiography, the self-centeredness of the approach, however, remains, and I hope it will be understood and tolerated.

I would like to express my grateful thanks to Ms Doris Tan Chung Lee for her invaluable help in the preparation of this book, particularly for transcribing my first long-winded autobiography in oral form to written readable manuscript. As the scope and orientation of this book changed with time, important revisions to the transcript had to be made. Dr Sng Hui Ying, my academic colleague in the NTU Division of Economics, volunteered the onerous repeated typing of revisions. I have suffered from typing ineptitude, and would like to thank Dr Sng for patiently and efficiently helping me out. I would also like to thank her for checking the correctness of the Chinese words and quotations.

My thanks and gratitude must go to my gifted journalist younger daughter, Lim Suet Lynn (Lin Xueling), for helping me with the selection of, and the captions for, the photographs.

I would also like to thank NTU for the invaluable office support. The secretarial staff in the Division of Economics, Ms Shida Baji, my former long-serving secretary Ms Christina Seet, and the Economic Growth Centre project officer, Ms Youjin Cecilia Kim, have been most helpful in providing secretarial support to this project.

My gratefulness must also go to the globally well-known distinguished publisher, World Scientific, for agreeing to publish this book, including the part played by

Ms Shreya Gopi as the coordinator and desk editor and Ms Vanessa Sundrasagar, this book's marketing executive.

Most of all, I must thank my dear wife for allowing me in my retirement as an emeritus professor still to take so much time off from her and our family, and for the support she has given me in one form or another.

Of course, I take full and complete responsibility for the content and the style of presentation of my autobiography. None of my invaluable helpers should take any blame for whatever remaining inadequacy, inelegance, or subject omissions and inclusions.

Lastly, I am thankful and grateful to everyone mentioned explicitly and implicitly in this book for the time spent together, the relationship and fellowship made, whilst life existed for me on earth. Many dear souls mentioned in this book have passed on. I would like to record my thanks and gratefulness for their memory, and for making my life's journey richer, more meaningful and more fulfilling. To those I have inadvertently left out in this book due to limited space, I must confess that I cherish their dear memory, their fellowship, and their friendship, all the same, and there are many, many in this group as well.

And lastly, I must thank God for life itself, and for the challenging and unpredictable journey made from birth, childhood, adulthood, marriage, family formation, career, old age, and now at 84, still healthy enough to research, to reflect, to recall, and to write this autobiography. Thank you, O God, from whom all blessings flow. The reader can see a surfeit of blessings in this autobiography.

Lim Chong Yah
June, 2016
Singapore

TIMELINE

1932	Born, Malacca, Straits Settlements
1940	Mother died
1941	Japanese occupied Malaya
1945	British returned to Malaya
1948	Malayan Emergency declared
1951	Joined University of Malaya (in Singapore) as Malacca Straits Settlement Scholar
1954	BA in Economics, English and Statistics
1955	BA Honours in Economics
1955	Singapore Administrative Service
1957	Independence of Federation of Malaya
1957	Married See Nah Nah, in Singapore
1958	First child Fern was born, Singapore
1959	Second child Wun was born, Singapore
1959	Assistant Lecturer, University of Malaya (UM), Kuala Lumpur Branch
1962	MA in Economics (UM)
1962	British Commonwealth Scholarship to Oxford
1963	Third child Lynn was born, Oxford
1964	Doctorate degree, Oxford University

1965	Founding Head, Division of Applied Economics, University of Malaya, Kuala Lumpur
1965	Independence of Republic of Singapore
1968	Fourth child Ron was born, Kuala Lumpur
1969	Reader and Acting Head, Department of Economics, University of Singapore
1971	Elected Dean, Arts and Social Sciences, National University of Singapore (NUS)
1972	Professor of Economics, NUS
1972	Chairman, National Wages Council, Singapore
1977	Confirmed Head, Department of Economics and Statistics, NUS
1979	Chairman, Skills Development Fund Advisory Council, Singapore
1983	Promoted to Senior Professor, NUS
1989	Quintuple heart by-pass surgery, National University Hospital (NUH)
1992	Retired as Emeritus Professor, NUS
1992	Appointed Professor of Economics, Nanyang Technological University (NTU)
2005	Promoted Albert Winsemius Chair Professor of Economics, NTU
2012	Retired as Emeritus Professor, NTU

LIST OF PHOTOGRAPHS

ROYALTY STATEMENT

All proceeds from the royalties of this book will be paid to the NTU Professor Lim Chong Yah Bursary Fund established in 2007. So far, 1,655 individuals and institutions have contributed to this Fund, and 111 NTU undergraduates have benefitted from it.

CHAPTER 1

CHILDHOOD YEARS

A bolt from the blue

It was a bright and beautiful morning; I was barely eight years old and I was in the Primary 2 class in the Bandar Hilir English Primary School in Malacca. I was listening to our teacher telling our all-boys class the story of Aladdin and the Forty Thieves.

Then I saw a completely unexpected person. Uncle Cheng, my father's brother-in-law, who had married his younger sister, suddenly appeared standing by the side of the classroom. The teacher hurriedly went out to talk to him. They spoke in whispers. The teacher came back and said quietly to me: "You have to go home, your mother has passed away."

It was a bolt from the blue.

Although I was dazed by the news, at the same time, I wondered how Uncle Cheng, who could not speak a word of English or Malay, was able to obtain permission to take me home. As far as I knew, he could only speak Hainanese, the family Chinese dialect spoken in our home.

We walked silently the 400 metres from my school to get home. We were careful to enter by the back and not the front. It was considered inauspicious and disrespectful if we were to go in by the front. Ours was a long house, distinguished by its two wells; one, the bigger one, in the front courtyard and the second, in the back courtyard.

All my siblings had gathered, seated in the back courtyard, their feet immersed in a separate pool of water. I did not understand the significance. I just followed suit; I did what I was told to do and did what they did. All of us were sobbing.

My family comprised an elder sister, Chong Tee, who would soon assume the role of matriarch of our household at the tender age of 12; myself as the eldest boy, my second brother, Chong Lian, a third brother, Chong Wah, and my youngest sister, Chong Fong, who was barely two years old. I recall having a sibling every two years.

The loss of our mother (Quek Ah Mooi) was a blow to all of us and especially to me, as I was her favourite. I tried to find out what had taken her away from us. It was tuberculosis which was rampant and a scourge at that time. My mother was slender and petite in appearance and quite reticent in temperament.

Looking back, I noticed that whenever she was ill, she would keep herself completely apart from us. So we were not really aware of her suffering as she was in another room. It must have been tough for her. We had been kept ignorant of her illness and because we were so young, we also did not notice much as we were more interested in playing.

My eldest sister was quite precocious. She slipped into her new role as matriarch with ease, preparing food for the table at the appropriate times. Our house had many other residents; one family comprised distant relatives; the others were tenants, some of whom had very colourful backgrounds.

The mixed residents

The house we lived in comprised 10 rooms, shared bathrooms and a big kitchen where all the residents would take turns to cook and often giving each other food as well in the true community spirit of *gotong royong* commonly practised then.

Our family shared the well in the front courtyard, from which we drew water for cooking, bathing, and washing; for drinking we relied on potable tap water. The well in the back courtyard was for emergency use. Each well would have a fish, a fairly sizable fish. I was told that should the fish be dead, we should not take water from the well, especially for cooking and drinking.

There was one household whose occupants spoke only Malay even though they were ethnic Chinese. They were Peranakan or Straits Chinese, descendants of intermarriages between migrant Chinese men and local Malay women in the British administered Straits Settlements of Malacca, Singapore and Penang. In Malacca, the Peranakan called themselves *baba* (for men) and *nonya* (for women). They were kind and helpful; the lady of the household taught my eldest sister how to cook Peranakan dishes which are rich in spices and chilli. She also liked to talk to me and from her I learnt to speak Malay.

In that rather hotchpotch group of tenants was a man from Shandong, China. He was tall like most of the people coming from that province. His job was to sell baskets made of soft pliable wire; he did this in the garden at the back of the house. I loved to watch him using his hands to make the containers during the weekends.

He went out during the week to sell them. He ate *mantou* (Chinese steamed bun) instead of rice.

There was another family with a special interest to me, for they were Hainanese like us. The man of the household would go to sea — I was told that he worked in a lighthouse where apart from his duties he would spend much of his time fishing and salting his catch. He came back once a year to his family.

I noticed that every time he came back the wife would be in the family way. His return was looked forward to not only by his wife but by the other residents for he would bring with him all kinds of fruits like berries and his prize catch of salted fish, which he would distribute to every household.

There were about 20 people living in the Bandar Hilir house. They were all ethnic Chinese but of different backgrounds; how they all managed to get along was a marvel and everyone was happy to help each other out.

I have fond memories of our house in Bandar Hilir and the residents who shared it with us. I still think of them and wonder about their families.

Apart from the three families I have mentioned, there were some other single tenants.

One of them, a pretty young woman in her 20s, I noticed, occupied the best room in the house and every evening, she would come back with a different man. Sometimes, she would come back with two men. I was curious about her. I found out later that she worked as a cabaret girl in a nightclub. I guess my father would simply rent out his rooms to any law-abiding person who could pay the rent. The pretty woman was the only one who did not mix with the rest of us.

Growing up in Malacca

There were two other single women, both sisters of Portuguese descent. They were not among our residents; they lived next door but enjoyed coming over to our house to chat. There was nothing much by way of entertainment in those days and it was common for neighbours to drop by.

Bandar Hilir was a well-established settlement with many people of Portuguese descent. The majority were Chinese *baba-nonya* and the rest comprised all kinds of other Chinese and Malays. But all groups lived harmoniously together.

The Portuguese sisters, who were in their 20s, worked as teachers and would insist on teaching me English. They told my mother to let me go to their house next door so that they could teach me English.

They also taught me nursery rhymes. The only thing I did not like was their bread; it was too salty; whenever I returned home I had to drink lots of water.

Years later, when I was appointed a lecturer in the University of Malaya in Kuala Lumpur in 1960, they came to see me one day. It was a welcome surprise; they said they had read about my appointment in the newspapers. I was delighted to see them and at dinner that night they could see how fruitful their efforts had been as we conversed entirely in English!

Our neighbourhood of Bandar Hilir was very peaceful. We never saw a beggar and we harboured no feelings of insecurity. As young children, we could go everywhere safely by ourselves in the whole neighbourhood and even beyond in rural Malacca.

Malacca was, and still is, rather cosmopolitan thanks to its history. It was a Malay sultanate in 1400 before being colonised by the Portuguese in 1511 and the Dutch in 1641. In 1826, it came under British rule and was part of the Straits Settlements together with Penang and Singapore, before it joined the Malayan Union with Penang and later the Federation of Malaya in 1948. All this has imbued Malacca with a rich cultural heritage. Little wonder it was given UNESCO World Heritage status in 2008. On reflection, living and growing up in Malacca must have affected my international global outlook.

So it was in this kind of harmonious environment that I was brought up. All my younger siblings were born in the house in Bandar Hilir. I was born in another part of Malacca and our family had moved into the house when I was still a baby. I was told that I was born in a coconut plantation in Bachang, Malacca. That was how I came to have the name 'Yah', which means coconut palm.

Years later, my younger sister, the youngest in the family, would say to me, "You know why you are named after a coconut tree? Coconut trees stand out tall, majestic and elegant and I think you were and still are my coconut tree." I was moved to hear that.

My father, like many Hainanese, owned a coffee shop which was moderately profitable. He had two workers to help in the daily operations. I found it fascinating to watch them at work, to see how they prepared *kaya,* a breakfast spread made of egg and coconut milk that people relished at that time and even now.

I would also watch them preparing coffee for the table. Before serving, they would dip the cups and saucers in hot water to sanitise them and keep them warm. I liked to help them too, if circumstances permitted.

My first rebellion

Because of my father's hands-off attitude in child upbringing, my siblings and I were left largely to manage on our own. We loved the outdoors and spent much of our free time camping out. We did what we liked, mostly flying kites, climbing trees and catching birds and fish. We also did kite-fighting, which involved trying to down your opponent's kite in mid-air by cutting his string. To do this, we would grind glass and coat our kite strings with it to give them a cutting edge.

We enjoyed catching fighting fish and other species such as *ikan arowan*, *ikan botol* (so-called because it is shaped like a bottle) and *ikan sepat*, all of which thrived in the paddy (rice) fields and wetlands or *sawah* of Malacca. We would hunt for these types of fish and after scooping them place them in water-filled tanks. So we had many fish tanks in the house. We learnt to dig for earthworms to feed the fish and ensure there was oxygen in the tanks to keep the fish alive.

Thanks to this childhood pursuit, I still have a fish tank in my Caldecott home in Singapore today brimming with arowan, botol and sepat fishes.

One afternoon, my brother Chong Wah, who was just four years old, came home crying, with a broken arm sustained when he fell off a tree. Someone carried him back. Fortunately, we knew of a Chinese physician in Bachang, 10 kilometres from our home, who was able to mend broken bones.

Another incident not long after involved my other brother Chong Lian, who went missing. We searched for him everywhere in the neighbourhood but could not find him. It was only at night, about 8 pm, that he turned up; he said he had gone off with Jack, a Eurasian neighbour, to visit the island of Pulau Besar, just off the coast of Malacca.

After these episodes, fearing for our safety and presumably well-being, my father decided to get a stepmother for us. One day — it must have been Saturday or Sunday — I looked out of our house and saw a trishaw with my father in it next to a woman roughly of his age-group. I was stunned.

We were introduced to her; however, we found out she could speak only Cantonese so our communications with her were very limited.

When she cooked, it would only be Cantonese dishes which we were not familiar with, having grown up eating mostly spicy Peranakan food — because of which I cannot eat without chilli to this day — or Hanainese chicken rice and mutton soup, our family favourites.

Our stepmother was not able to cook any of these. We did not like her cooking and complained that she used too much ginger. (Ironically, I now like ginger very much!)

I was a picky eater as a boy and thus could not grow. There was nobody to coax me to eat. When my mother was alive, I was her pet. When people cooked special dishes such as double-boiled chicken soup for her she would not eat them but would reserve them for me. I had a special place in the family.

My eldest sister, who used to cook before the arrival of our stepmother, was the one who started to sow the seeds of rebellion. To me, she was strong in mind and spirit and a very healthy-looking "young lady", though only 12 going on 13. She went to a Chinese school, where the teachers would sing nationalistic songs and rebellious anti-Japanese songs. This was in 1940 and the second Sino-Japanese War was then raging on. Japan had invaded China earlier in 1937. One of these songs was March of the Volunteers, which later became the official national anthem of the People's Republic of China in 2004:

Arise,
Ye who refuse to be slaves!
With our very flesh and blood,
Let us build our new Great Wall!
The peoples of China are in the most critical time,
Everybody must roar his defiance.
Arise! Arise! Arise!
Millions of hearts with one mind,
Brave the enemy's gunfire, March on!
Brave the enemy's gunfire, March on!
March on! March on! On!

The song was a battle cry of the anti-Japanese resistance movement. (To understand the Chinese, one must delve into their past to fathom their response to situations whenever they were greatly humiliated).

So my sister already had a rebellious streak; she could not stand my stepmother and asked my father to let her go. She was strongly supported by me, her oldest younger brother. The rest would just follow us, the ring-leaders.

All of us went on a hunger strike. It proved successful. It was the first and only hunger strike of my life. However, it also marked the first of more rebellions and industrial strikes to come later in my life.

So my father had no choice but to send our stepmother away.

Later on, there were times I regretted our childhood actions especially when times were hard and tough. Maybe my father could have got someone else to help us, especially to look after our younger siblings.

Chinese New Year is traditionally a time when children would have new clothes, shoes and even new hair-dos. The Chinese New Year immediately after my mother's passing saw Uncle Cheng's wife, my aunt and my father's youngest sister, visiting us a week before. To her horror, she found out that we had nothing new to wear for the coming festive season. I remember her bringing the four of us to the only Bata shop in Kampong Java Road to outfit us with new shoes.

I was delighted to get a new pair of Bata canvas shoes and was grateful to my aunt for this. Her simple gesture reinforced my feeling that an adult woman was necessary to look after us.

I still remember my stepmother with kindness; it was a pity she could not relate to us.

A propensity for mathematics

At around this time, my father got me involved in his coffee shop operations. He discovered that I was quite precocious, particularly in mathematics.

It started when he got me to accompany him to buy provisions for the coffee shop such as coffee beans, butter, sugar and cigarettes.

Later, he would send me alone to buy the goods. I would walk the three kilometres to the wholesale suppliers and return in a trishaw with the provisions in the right amounts and with the correct change. My father told me that he was glad that I could be of some help to him.

My first house moving

But alas, things did not go well for my father's business in the year after the passing of my mother. Perhaps he lost his entrepreneurial drive or maybe his spirit was broken.

Uncle Cheng would come to our coffee shop often to have beer and *kachang* (peanuts) with my father. Both of them were often in deep discussion and it was decided one day that our family should move in with my uncle's family to their house located on Bona Vista Road in the district of Bachang, which was about 10 kilometres away from Bandar Hilir at the other end of Malacca town. The move was made so that my aunt could keep an eye on us apart from alleviating my father's financial situation.

In those days, most street names in Malacca were either in Portuguese or Dutch; in later years, under the process of "Malayanisation", most of the names were changed to Malay names and Bona Vista Road is now known as Jalan Hang Tuah.

The decision to move was traumatic. It was our first house moving and we were very much attached to our Bandar Hilir house. After all, this was where we grew up. Bandar Hilir was, and still is, next to the heart of Malacca town, home to historical attractions such as the Portuguese fortress and the Dutch church built in colonial times, right beside the limpid meandering river that flows across and into the township.

Our stay in Bandar Hilir nurtured in me a deep love for the outdoors. We would go to the sea, in front of present-day Hotel Equatorial. That was my paradise. It was here that we would catch fish and fly kites. I remember flying a kite that looked like an eagle. It attracted other birds of prey but later they flew off when they realised the kite was a fake. We would also watch women wading into the sea, when the tide was out, to prise oysters off the rocks to sell. Till today, I love to eat oysters and I love seafood.

We had two lorry loads of possessions when we moved to our new house. We took everything along — even our fish, all kinds of fish — and our birds; we had black and white *burung kochi*, *burung berabak* and our favourite — *burong pipit pinang* that would roost in the pinang trees near our Bandar Hilir house. Even today, I have planted many pinang trees in the garden of my house in Singapore hoping to attract these small lovely birds.

Although the change in our circumstances were challenging for us, little did we know that a tougher and even more challenging era was soon to unfold in our lives — the march of Japanese soldiers into Malacca in 1941. The British were defenceless.

1.1 My father, Lim Tee Chee, at about 48 years old. Sadly, I do not have a photo of my dear mother.

1.2 Picture of me at about four years of age, together with my elder sister. Interestingly, each of us is carrying a book. My father was always very concerned about education.

CHAPTER 2

DARK CLOUDS OVER MALACCA

Japanese occupation

At that time, until the Japanese arrival, I did not know much of Malaya of which Malacca was a part. My world then comprised only Bandar Hilir and Bachang where my family lived.

But my life as told in the first three chapters of this book shaped and built my temperament, character, attitude and aptitude until I came to Singapore at the age of 19.

Might is right?

Prior to the Japanese invasion, which led to the outbreak of World War II in Malaya, the Japanese Imperial Army had made a sweep from North-east China all the way down to Beijing, Shanghai, Canton and Hong Kong. They even had soldiers trained in the foothills of the famed Five Finger Mountain of Hainan with a view to invade Southeast Asia.

The British, who were the colonial masters of Malaya, which included Singapore then, had been expecting the Japanese to attack via the sea but history proved them wrong.

The Japanese Imperial Navy bombed and sunk the British battleships *Repulse* and the *Prince of Wales* in the South China Sea on 10 December, 1941. Thailand finally agreed to let the Japanese Imperial Army march through southern Thailand — what is today Pattani, Narathiwat, Songkhla, Satun and Yala — down to the south towards the Malay Peninsula.

These provinces had been apportioned to Thailand under the Bangkok Treaty of 1909 which had divided northern Malaya into two parts. Thailand would give up its claims to Kedah, Trengganu, Kelantan and Perlis which were integrated into the

British sphere of influence as protectorates and later together with Johor became known as the Unfederated Malay States.

So, the Japanese troops were able to make their way down into Peninsular Malaya almost without much fighting. Well-trained and toughened by their war in China, they actually came in on bicycles!

The British were no match. As they progressed southwards, Malacca also fell. To ensure compliance and obedience from the local populace, the first thing they did was to chop off a few heads, putting them up prominently on traffic islands and instituted a law that if any person stole anything, his hands would be chopped off.

The British currency was quickly replaced by Japanese 'banana' notes. Each general was apparently given a printing machine to print up to a certain amount of these notes. After a few years, the Japanese generals reached their maximum allocations and were simply told to use their discretion in printing as they liked. Hyperinflation soared; I was taken in by all this and thus began in my childhood years my fascination with monetary economics. Indeed, although I was just a little boy, I knew how to quickly exchange whatever banana notes I had for durable goods for myself and my family.

The war in Malaya had the effect of cutting off the country from the outside world. There was an international blockade, and the twin pillars of Malaya's economy — rubber and tin — took a beating as they could not be exported while imports were not possible either. So the local population, caught up in all this, had to find different ways of feeding themselves and earning a living.

In Malacca, some local entrepreneurs began to harvest salt from the sea for sale. Others built impressive-looking *tongkangs* (boats). I marvelled at their ability, their enterprising spirit.

Life in Bachang Simpang

With the move to Bachang Simpang and having had to give up his coffee shop business, my father had bought over the provision shop previously owned by Uncle Cheng as his new line of business.

My father must have known war was coming, as he made sure that his shop was well-stocked. There were plenty of rice packs, oil, tinned food, dried noodles, salted fish and sugar. In fact, the whole shop was so full of goods that it was difficult to find a place to sit.

The house belonging to my aunt and Uncle Cheng was a thatched-roof semi-detached house. It was also sold to my father. We all however lived together, all in all nine of us under one roof: six Lims and three Chengs, as my aunt had only one son, Cheng Suet Ming.

Behind the house was an air raid shelter, which had been specially built during the war, but I don't remember ever having used it. We, the children, did go inside to play though.

What was more memorable about the house was its back garden, which provided us with a welcome supply of fresh vegetables during the difficult war years.

Uncle Cheng managed the garden extremely well, even building a sort of irrigation system. It was full of a wide variety of vegetables — two of which stood out — *chye sim* (mustard greens) and loofah which grew profusely. During the war, I took up gardening. As Uncle Cheng was tired of gardening by then, he left the garden to me, an ever willing hand. What a privilege for a little boy.

Uncle Cheng concentrated on his thriving coffee shop business, located obliquely in front of our attap house. When he died, his wife (my aunt) took over, and ran it most ably. My cousin, Suet Ming, went to a Chinese-medium school and conversed with me throughout in Mandarin. He was a brilliant boy. He helped his mother run the coffee shop.

I must confess that I did not know my aunt's name. In accordance with the tradition of the time, I only called her by a Hainanese honorific, Youngest Aunt, meaning she was my father's youngest sister.

Escape to safety

One day, we received news of the Japanese invasion of Malacca. Bombing had started and we were told to evacuate.

All nine of us would go to another place that belonged to another relative. This was in Bukit Rambai, about 10 kilometres from Malacca town. We travelled by road along the coast by way of Tanqueriah and took a detour inland for another five kilometres to our "hide-out" which was strategically placed. It was owned by Ong Min Keet who was the Malacca head of the clan from the district of Wanning (Baning in Hainanese) in Hainan. He had invited us to stay in his home until it was safe to return to Bachang. We were there for two weeks and during that time I had more lessons in agriculture.

Behind our safe haven in Bukit Rambai was a huge garden where I observed, every morning, an elderly man pulling out monkey nuts (peanuts) and harvesting *mang kuang* (Chinese sweet turnip, also known as yam bean).

These were usually grown in sandy areas, in the tin mining districts of Ipoh in Perak in the north of Malaya but in Malacca the sea with its sandy coastline was close by so such crops were able to thrive there in Bukit Rambai.

I just sat and watched the old man go about his tasks as I was curious about what he was doing and wanted to learn.

Beside the garden was a *kolam* or pond. It had plenty of fresh water fish such as the bottle-shaped *ikan botol, ikan sepat* and *ikan arowan* and lots of water hyacinths. It was a beautiful and tranquil setting. This was long before I was able to appreciate the same kind of scenery in the lake districts of England and north Italy and that of Suzhou and Hangzhou in China later in life. For little me, that *kolam* represented the beauty of life at its best.

My elder sister, who was 13 years old, slept in one side of the dwelling with the other grown-up women of the house, while my little brothers and I occupied another part of the building. But I could listen to what the women were telling my sister — about healthy foods and matters of hygiene. They said one should eat steamed food as it is healthier and they constantly talked about the wonders of soya bean and black beans which would influence my own future diet.

They also talked about boys and men. But I had no interest in that kind of chatting. But when they talked of war, my antenna went up, as my "fear adrenaline" began to take over.

Return to Bachang

When the bombing had stopped and Malacca town was captured, it was deemed safe to return home to our provision shop in Bachang Simpang. I still remember the address: 175, Bona Vista Road.

The store was intact although some food items were missing. Some people probably had pilfered them. We tried to make good with what was left. But Malacca — and Malaya — was cut off from the outside world and it was difficult to get new supplies.

Food became more and more scarce. We resorted to serving tinned food for meals. Medicines also were in short supply; neither was there toothbrush nor toothpaste — we had to make do with wood ash. Sadly, it was because of the lack of suitable alternative tooth-cleaning materials that I later lost half of my teeth.

Without medicines available, we turned to using herbs as cures for illnesses. Thank goodness, I had a herbalist aunt. I was told that knowledge of herbs as medicines ran in my family. A long time ago, one of my Lim ancestors, Lim Mo Niang was and is still worshipped as the Goddess of the Sea. She lived by the seaside in Putien in Fujian Province. She learnt how to use herbs for medical purposes and passed that knowledge down the generations. Thus my herbalist aunt knew what to use to cure headaches and other not very serious illnesses. One of the common herbs she used was duck grass. She would pound it with curry leaf and steep it in water as a sort of tea to drink. She made me her assistant. I learnt from her how to use different herbs for different purposes. She would often mix various herbs as well. Many from the village came to seek her help.

From all this I learnt that knowledge is important. In economics, the key to human civilisation is knowledge.

Economics through agriculture

As the war went on, the food shortage was so acute that we had to forego eating rice and turned to sweet potato, millet and tapioca instead.

Subsistence farming became a necessity, and at the age of 10, I took over the garden at the back of our house. I learnt to cultivate, *inter alia*, tapioca and sweet potato, becoming so good at it that I was even able to sell any surplus in the market. My family's two female ducks would each dutifully lay an egg before roaming the wide marshy space further behind the house every morning. They would return in the evening without fail. I adored them.

Despite the many deprivations we had to endure during the Japanese Occupation, it was a period that provided my first grounding in real economics. For instance, when it came to planting vegetables, I discovered there were different lengths of gestation. I preferred growing crops with short maturation periods. I found that growing *kangkong* (water spinach) was great since it flourished quickly with little or no maintenance. I also learnt the importance of learning from others; in tending to my garden, I learnt from neighbouring adult farmers by watching them.

The Japanese Occupation taught us to put to good use whatever available land there was. In other words, make full use of your resources. I picked up a precious skill in market gardening, or euphemistically termed, horticulture.

Till today, I am very fond of gardening. I have planted trees along the roads outside my house in Singapore, drawing much appreciation from my neighbours, other than attending pleasurably to my own garden.

Apart from planting your own vegetables I discovered how fruits from the nearby Bachang forest, such as attap seeds, could be harvested for food. Then there was a variety of local fish that was available from ponds and the nearby drainage system.

Indeed, my father utilised another plot of nearly empty land, about two acres. We grew mainly sweet potatoes and rice. I was his assistant. To prevent birds from eating the rice in the paddy fields just before harvesting, we used scarecrows and bells to frighten them off. My job was to set off the alarms.

Not only did we grow plants for food, we also reared poultry. We had chickens and ducks. We even reared pigs in my father's brother's homestead about five kilometres away.

Every day, after working in the fields, at 6 pm, the bells of a nearby Catholic church at Gaja Berang would ring. To me, it was the sound of music since it meant the time had come to pack up and go home for our meals. I was always so hungry; without any food to eat in the fields, those bells were a welcome peal. Many decades later, when I was a Visiting Fulbright Professor at Ohio University in the USA, the church bells too would ring for my lecture to end for lunch break and they reminded me of my paddy-field childhood days in Malacca.

Meat in those war years was so rare that when you invited someone over for dinner and you had meat to offer you would say: "We will be serving you chicken, please come."

We also had a goat; I took her to feed on grass but not in the morning because of dew. She would have diarrhoea. To cure that, I would give her a *bawang merah* — red onion — to chew and it would be all right. Goats are passionate; the goat gave us two kids, they were very playful and joyful. I became a goat-herd, I would bring them to the fields not too far away to feed on grass each day. I spent quite a great deal of time with them; it was one of the best times in my life as a goat-herd.

So during those difficult years we learnt the importance of taking care of animals as well as people, and making full use of whatever land resources that were available.

One late afternoon, my father asked me to accompany him to the police station. Apparently, a man had been caught trying to steal our sweet potatoes and the authorities wanted to find out if my father wished to have him prosecuted. My father simply asked the man why he had tried to get the sweet potatoes. His answer: "I was very hungry." So my father told the authorities that he would just make a required report, as it was an offence to steal, but that he would like to give the man some sweet potatoes and tell him not to steal again. I learned from my father to be compassionate and to be helpful to the poor and needy.

As you can see, food was always a concern in those days. Scarcity — not obesity — was the problem then.

In the grips of poverty

Apart from growing our own crops for survival, I did a bit of buying and selling to try to earn some extra money for the family.

I had observed people selling Japanese cigarettes in the market. They would buy them in bulk and resell them in smaller quantities at a higher price. They seemed to be making money. My second brother and I decided to hawk them as well.

At the Malacca wet market where we sold cigarettes, I often saw people going through garbage to pick out whatever vegetables or fruits that had been discarded and could be salvaged. They would bring them home for their families. I also noticed there were many vagabonds without a roof over their heads; they were often wandering aimlessly.

The vagabonds were mostly Indians who had come from the rubber estates where they were previously working, or Chinese who were in town who had lost their jobs and had nowhere to go. The vagabonds of both communities had bloated stomachs; because they had not enough to eat, many ended up dead on the streets. I recognised several of them as having worked in a shop in town. As I witnessed their pitiful, pathetic and helpless condition I told myself, "I must grow up fast. I must be strong. I must be able. I must not fall into the pit as they did. I have a family to look after."

What I saw influenced me later in life. When I began studying economics, I was determined to make sure that people should not die of starvation. I became interested in eradicating poverty and starvation.

The Japanese Occupation was a brutal one. People were constantly worried that the girls and women in their families might get raped by Japanese soldiers. To prevent such a fate befalling my elder sister, my father decided to marry her off when she turned 16. When my sister left our house, it became my task, *inter alia*, to cook.

I had to learn cooking by trial and error. The first time I cooked fish with coconut oil in the *kwali* or wok, I used high heat; the fish was burnt on the outside but was still raw inside. My aunt taught me how to fry a fish, cooked inside as well. Years later when I read what Lao Tze, the great Chinese philosopher, once said about how not to over-govern, "Governing a large country is like cooking a small fish. Do not overdo it." it reminded me of my cooking misadventure.

However, when it came to cooking *kangkong*, high heat was important. You put oil in the *kwali*; as soon as it gets very hot you throw in the vegetables, stir quickly and take them out immediately. The best cooked *kangkong* is on the table.

I sold cigarettes in the evenings in an amusement park frequented by an almost all-Chinese crowd, some of them would head for a nearby theatre to watch a Chinese variety show at 10 pm. The show was in *min nan hua*, or *min nan* dialect, as the actors and actresses came from south of Min River in the province of Fujian.

I would sometimes watch Taiwanese variety shows showing in the amusement park with my brother Chong Lian and at midnight, we would return home to sleep.

Up to today, it has become a habit of mine to read on my iPad till midnight before going to bed. I would need a siesta in the heat of the afternoon though.

In those days, there was not much by way of entertainment, even in the kind of movies shown in cinemas. There were only two in Malacca — one was named Capitol and the other Savoy.

I remember a movie with a song '*Mai Tang Ge*' about selling sweets to opium smokers. This was a propaganda film the Japanese produced in their efforts to drum up anti-British feelings. Their message was: "We are Asians — down with the Westerners who forced you to smoke opium to enslave you." They called for East Asian unity.

In those days, I enjoyed going to the movies as there was little else to do for entertainment. But I had no money. So how did I get in to see the movies? I would simply look for a family to attach myself to, entering the hall as they did when ushered; the ushers never checked — sometimes I marvelled at my survival "ingenuity".

However, sometimes if a movie was popular, I would buy a ticket and tout it, making a little profit. Should touting be banned? I would have missed making a few more important cents.

Thrown into Alor Gajah jail

In the process of hawking I met a rather hefty boy by the name of Ter Kia (Piglet). He was several years older than I was. He had a smiling face, was extremely cheerful and lived in a slummish area. He called me Hai-nam Kia (Hainanese boy) and both of us became good friends.

One day, Piglet suggested going to Tampin, a small hamlet, about 40 kilometres from Malacca town. He said we could take a bus. Why? I asked. His answer: "The cigs are cheaper there and we can make some profit when we sell them here."

From him, I learnt arbitrage — buying in one market and selling in another, profiting from the difference in price.

I accompanied Piglet to Tampin where there was also a flowing stream in which he and I would swim. As children, that naturally took priority before business.

We ended up going there every week to swim and buy cigarettes.

It was on one of our visits that I saw something which bothered me.

I saw a group of Malayan People's Anti-Japanese Army (MPAJA) personnel, an armed branch of the Communist Party of Malaya, in the streets of Tampin.

All were ethnic Chinese, and very young. The MPAJA was formed by the Malayan Chinese to fight the Japanese; later they fought against the British too. However in Tampin, the MPAJA was also involved in another kind of warfare — with the Malays in the government. They were seeking vendetta. In fact, I was told that throughout Malaya there were many such incidents.

I became frightened: what if a racial war among ourselves were to break out?

One day, after our usual swim in the Tampin river and purchase of cigarettes, we were arrested by a Chinese detective.

We were taken to the Alor Gajah prison, 27 kilometres from Malacca town. The next day we were brought into a courtyard and a burly Malay sergeant gave each of us four strokes of the *rotan* (cane). There was no court trial. We did not know where we had gone wrong.

Later, I found out what we were guilty of. Malacca and Tampin had different customs zones. Tampin was a border town with its customs department coming under the jurisdiction of Negri Sembilan which was part of the Federated Malay States. There was, however, no sign separating the two sides of the one-street Tampin hamlet. That incident provoked my interest in free trade areas and customs unions in later years.

So, when we were buying cigarettes in Tampin and bringing them into Malacca, we would have had to pay customs duty. We had not done so hence we were jailed for the offence. The year was 1944 and I was only 12. There was no customs office in Tampin. Piglet told me the Chinese detective wanted some money and he did not give it to him. So, we were locked up.

We shared our cell with a Malay man. We asked him why he was there. He said his wife had betrayed him and she had a boyfriend who was powerful and got him put into jail.

Sadly, might appears to be right; in later life, when people say 'Free the prisoners,' they have my sympathy.

In prison, we were given tapioca cooked with salt — that was the diet for each day. As for water, we had to drink from the tap in a toilet. Next door, there were some 20 other young men — Chinese and Malays — who told us they were considered Communists and subversives when we asked why they had been jailed.

One Malay guard was nice to me, perhaps because he also came from Bachang, Malacca. He said he would take us out to dinner but we had to pay for the meal. He said he could pass a message to my parents. I gave him my father's address.

I was in prison for one week. In that week, I thought of my family. There were no telephone lines at all and there was no means of communication. I wondered if my family members knew I was still alive.

Then one day, I heard my father's voice; he had come to Alor Gajah to get me out. When I left the prison, I was so happy. I wanted to walk the 27 kilometres back to Malacca town. I felt as free as the birds in the sky and as happy as they were.

It was my greatest joy to taste freedom. That's why I like the song "Born Free". Since then, I value freedom so much that I have on many occasions, tried to speak out for it. That is why I love to roam God's good earth. Being free to roam is the greatest privilege of all.

Piglet came out with me. He was the best friend I ever had. With his rotund figure, he was like a miniature Friar Tuck. But alas, after we were released from prison, we never met again. To this day, I have always wondered how he has fared over the years and where he is now.

Till this day, thanks to the prison guard, I also realise how cherished the *kampong* (village) spirit is among our Malays. The guard who *kesiang* (took pity on) me did so simply because we hailed from the same place, Bachang. He told me so.

This episode of imprisonment and freedom inspired me later in life to connect with the poor, the underprivileged and labourers who had to work very hard, in often very trying conditions, to survive and eke out a livelihood for themselves and their families.

This is best exemplified in the Song of the Volga Boatmen, one of my favourites. Some lines are:

Sing, boys, sing, songs give courage, sing, boys, sing
Trust the mighty father's care, he shall make all labour fair
Man shall labour ever more, ever more

I learned this song when I was a school boy in Malacca High School. It was taught to me by a school girl, a classmate.

To school or not to school

When the Japanese occupied Malacca, English-language schools were banned. Only Japanese schools were allowed and in these, some Chinese would also be taught. The Chinese community found themselves in a dilemma: Should they send their children to school at all? Those who were English-educated were reluctant to do so as they were afraid their children would not be able to cope with lessons being taught in Japanese and Chinese.

My father was one of those caught in two minds. Initially, he refused to let me go to school as he thought the Japanese would soon be defeated and there was no point in learning Japanese. Later, he changed his mind.

In school, I learnt to speak some Japanese; I even sang Japanese songs and could sing the Japanese national anthem. I also learnt some Chinese.

What I liked most of all was that we had to do half an hour of physical exercise each day. I still remember the steps involved and continue to practise these; it's akin to today's pilates.

The Japanese then had felt that the local community did not pay enough attention to physical exercise and good health so they introduced these.

I was in school for two years before my father pulled me out when there were sure indications that the British were coming back.

My growing up years during the Japanese Occupation would be what I call "the university of hard knocks", with attendance forced on me. I learned my economics lessons the hard way. I also learnt what it means to be a good human being, the attribute I cherish most in my life. Under the circumstances, I grew up fast, very fast. Thank God, under the bludgeonings of circumstances, my head was bloody but unbowed.

Gambling as an opiate

Gambling and opium smoking were allowed by the Japanese as they wanted to make the population subservient and compliant.

The Indian community was permitted to continue to make and drink toddy as the Japanese figured that if they got drunk on it, it would encourage complicity.

My father, however, was quite puritanical. He forbade us to try toddy and made sure that opium was out of reach too. So was gambling, a strictly forbidden activity.

Gambling was rampant though. Everywhere you went in Malacca, there would be thousands of people gathering to take part in all forms of gambling.

Years later when the government in Singapore wanted to introduce casinos, I was infuriated as it reminded me of my childhood days in Malacca when people were reduced to being compliant, subservient and despondent.

I have never believed in the game of chance, so becoming a Methodist Christian later in life suited me.

The new dawn

One day, when I was working in the paddy fields I saw 20 to 30 adult Malays wearing beautiful clothes walking along Bona Vista Road; they were happy and shouting. They shouted: "The British are coming back, we are liberated."

My father declared: "At long last, I am going to have my toast of bread with butter. I have missed it for four long years!"

I realised then what an anglophile my father was, although he did not speak a word of English.

I asked him why he was so happy, he said he liked British rule; "that's why we migrated from China to British Malaya in the first place."

He related an incident I had not known before. "There was law and order in British Malaya. Your third uncle was giving out tracts spreading Communist propaganda saying we would have our own independent communist state of Malaya; he was arrested and put on a slow boat back to China." My father added that the British were fair, "In China we would all have been arrested." That was the China he knew, ripe for revolution.

In Singapore, in later years, I realised that we too inherited this British sense of individual justice and fair play.

For instance, in Malaya, when Chin Peng and his comrades were fighting the British in the jungle, their families were left alone in the town of Sitiawan, Perak, even though he was actively sought out.

The new dawn with the return of the British marked a time of liberation for Malacca and Malaya. I considered this to be the start of a new life for me and for my family.

Malayan Emergency

However, in 1948, the Malayan Emergency was declared. At the height of the Emergency, in 1951, Sir Henry Gurney, the British High Commissioner to Malaya, was gunned down by the Malayan Communist Party (MCP) in an ambush in Fraser's Hill, Pahang. Nearly all the members of the MCP were ethnic Chinese, so was the allied MPAJA, the Malayan People's Anti-Japanese Army, set up to fight the Japanese invasion of Malaya.

During the height of the Malayan Emergency, thousands and thousands of ethnic Chinese in the rural areas were rounded up and placed in barbed-wire New Villages to protect them from being forced to supply food and other help to the armed communist insurgents in the nearby thick Malayan jungles. Prior to this, on 12 December, 1948, it was reported that in one village at Batang Kali in Hulu Selangor, one whole village of ethnic Chinese, old and young, males and females, were gunned down by British soldiers (Scots Guards) simply because they were ethnic Chinese.

I grew up in the relatively safe Malacca town during the Malayan Emergency, though the head prefect of my school, a Methodist School, was detained by the Government. I lived on hope and prayer that peace would return to Malaya, to my country and my people.

I would like to end this chapter with two lines from a famous poem in Chinese, similar in meaning to the following lines from the hymn Whispering Hope.

If in the dusk of the twilight, dim be the region afar

Will not the deepening darkness brighten the glimmering star?

山重水复疑无路,

柳暗花明又一村。

CHAPTER 3

A NEW CHILDHOOD LIFE

Back to school

As soon as the war was over in 1945, all the pre-war schools in Malacca that had been shut re-opened. However, as I had now moved to a new neighbourhood — Bona Vista Road in Bachang — I had to find a new school nearby. I was then 13 years old.

My sister's husband (Khoo Kian Teng), who was almost twice my age, insisted on accompanying me to be properly registered as he knew my father was fussy about education. He got me enrolled in the neighbourhood Methodist Boys' School, opposite the Tamil Methodist Church, not far away from my home.

But two days later, on my first day at school, I discovered, to my horror, that the school was a "*sekolah kambing*" or "school for goats" meant for those lagging behind academically.

I might not have been able to speak much English then, arising from the four years of Japanese Occupation, but I had no wish to be in such a school for academically handicapped pupils.

My new class teacher advised me to enrol at the Anglo-Chinese School (ACS) at Tranquerah instead, if I wanted to study in a "proper" school. So I did, starting in Standard 2, the same level as four years ago, before the outbreak of war.

I was weak in English but could manage mathematics and Chinese. Indeed, I found maths to be far too simple, and was often solving equations immediately after the teacher completed the questions on the class blackboard.

However, I had to try very hard to master English. Each week, we were given 20 new words to learn and spell and I made sure I would score a perfect score in spelling. I did not know then that I was a little dyslexic. We also had recitation classes in which we would be given poems that we had to learn by heart and recite.

I enjoyed this very much and till today can recall many poems that I learnt at school. One of my favourites is one entitled "I saw a ship a-sailing".

I saw a ship a-sailing,
A-sailing on the sea;
And, it was all laden,
With pretty things,
For you and for me.

This poem conjured images of foreign ports and exotic lands, sparking off a life-long fascination with ports and ships. At that time, however, the most intriguing port for me was Singapore, south of Malacca and the Malay Peninsula.

Another poem that I have always cherished is one by William Wordsworth. Only two stanzas out of four are reproduced below.

I wandered lonely as a cloud
That floats on high o'er vales and hills,
When all at once I saw a crowd
A host of golden daffodils;
Along the lake, beneath the trees,
Fluttering and dancing in the breeze.

The waves beside them danced, but they
Outdid the sparkling waves in glee:
A poet could not but be gay
In such a jocund company:
I gaz'd — and gaz'd — but little thought
What wealth the show to me had brought:

Because of this poem, I developed a close affinity with flowers, lakes and nature, and years later, when I went to England for the first time as a student, I was overwhelmed by the beauty of the countryside around Oxford University. I saw beautiful fields of daffodils and crocuses and was able to appreciate the extraordinary beauty and tranquillity of the English Lake District.

I loved poems because in some situations only in verse can feelings and emotions be tersely and beautifully communicated.

Learning English

As ACS is a Christian institution, Sunday School classes were also conducted, and in English. That helped me greatly. A classmate of mine, Ah Shi, gave me a Chinese-English dictionary which also proved most useful in improving my English.

We were told stories from the Bible, of Joseph and the pharaoh's dreams and how he interpreted them, and how he helped the Egyptian pharaoh to solve problems of good years and lean years, its ups and downs, its booms and troughs…familiar topics in later years when I studied economics at university.

It was partly because of Sunday School that I became a Christian later in life.

As my grasp of English improved, I sailed through school easily enough and was promoted each year. In fact, I was double promoted twice. I thus missed Standard 3 and also Standard 5.

The year when I was due to start Standard 5, our school principal Goh Choon Lim, who also taught Sunday School, turned up in our class to find out who were deserving of a double promotion.

One of them was Rashid, who had topped the class and could skip Standard 5 to go straight to Standard 6. I do not know what emboldened me to put up my hand to declare that I had topped the class too. I explained that Rashid did not have to study Chinese or Religious Knowledge whereas I did. I had a higher average mark if these two subjects were included in the calculation. Instead of feeling that I was perhaps too forward with my plea, the principal was impressed with my explanation and gave me a double promotion too.

With the double promotion, I finished school in five years, obtaining my prized school leaving certificate in December 1949 with several distinctions to boot.

In those days, anyone educated up to Standard 9 would become a clerk, considered then to be an elite position in Malacca.

But I did not wish to be a clerk; I aspired to be a branch manager of a bank. As a child, when accompanying my father to the bank, I had observed these managers at work, dealing with money and signing cheques; it all looked very impressive.

The path to a bank manager's job was via university and so I set my sights on going to the University of Malaya which had just opened in 1948 in Singapore at Bukit Timah. Little did I know that I would one day serve there as a Dean and a Senior Professor of Economics.

School life at ACS

It was good to be back in school after the war. It was here that I spent some of the most carefree years of my life and made many life-long friends.

One of them was Ah Shi, a tall thin boy who had tuberculosis. I recounted how my mother had died of TB and told him to take care of his health. His father had a thriving antiques shop at Wolleston Road. He would walk several miles to see me at my home. We became great companions and friends. He also gave me a book in English on idioms and proverbs, which I cherished. To this day, I am fond of quoting proverbs.

My absorption capacity at school was great. I loved to study, probably as an escape from other lifestyles described in the previous chapter.

This phase of my life in school marked an amazing transformation for me, allowing me to go on to university after only five years of schooling. I owed a debt of gratitude to my school teachers and principals.

We were fortunate to have another energetic principal in Reverend Charles Shoemaker, an American who had worked as a missionary in China before arriving in Malacca in 1947.

He was young and resourceful. He believed in instilling in us leadership qualities. For instance, he got rid of the old method of having teachers appoint prefects, introducing instead a system of election with prefects voted in by the student population.

I was one of those elected; to ensure that I would get in, I had to learn how to campaign and canvas for votes. Among ourselves, we selected a head prefect.

One of our tasks as prefects was to produce a school newsletter. The teachers were unsure if we were capable of doing so but our principal had faith in us. We were also told we would have freedom of expression and that there would be no censorship.

It was in such an atmosphere that I formed the Chinese Literary Association in school. I also formed the Popular Science Club.

I founded the Chinese Literary Association amid a debate on whether one should study Latin or Chinese. I said Latin was a dead language but those who supported it decried it as "nonsense". But our nurturing and liberal environment meant that we could debate and discuss these opposing attitudes.

Another notable element about my school life then was our social gathering every Wednesday at the Methodist Girls' School nearby. The purpose of the get-togethers was to have the boys and girls of both schools know one another. We did this through games, songs and hymns, many of which I still sing today. Among my favourites were "Oh master, let me walk with thee" and "What a friend we have in Jesus".

No dancing or drinking was allowed though as the Methodists were quite puritanical then but these weekly gatherings introduced me to a new world and gave me the opportunity to meet girls and boys of my age.

Aside from the school texts, which then included the New Testament Bible, two most favourite books of mine that must have some important influence on my life were Dale Carnegie's *How to Win Friends and Influence People* and *Aesop's Fables*. The Chinese newspapers, all from Singapore, which I read as my daily bread were Ming Seng Daily, Nang Chao Daily, Sin Chew Jit Poh, and Nanyang Siang Pau. The first two dailies were rather leftist inclined with a lot of news on the then raging civil war in China. The Chinese dailies were then available at my aunt's (later my cousin's) coffee shop obliquely opposite my house at Bona Vista Road. In my father's generation and among my siblings, none spoke English. So I was the first and only English-speaking member of the family in those early days. I had no access to The Straits Times until I became an undergraduate of the University of Malaya, then in Singapore. I read mainly the Editorials in The Straits Times. They were quite opinionated then.

High School in Malacca

The path for most school leavers in Malacca after completing Standard 9 was joining the work force or going to university for which you needed to enrol in the Malacca High School to prepare for the entrance examination.

I entered Malacca High School in 1950. It was there that I got to know very well Singapore's future health minister, Chua Sian Chin and Malaysia's best-known poet, Ee Tian Hong.

There were around 15 students in our class. Unlike the more *laissez-faire* system of Anglo-Chinese School, the British-run government High School adopted a more top-down approach with teachers appointing school prefects, for instance.

Yet, the school introduced mock elections to give us a taste of politics. This was a time of political awakening in much of Asia then, led by India and China.

KC Dutt, a science student, represented the Conservative Party while Sukomari Nair, who came from a prominent family and who later married the head of the Malayan Rubber Research Institute (RRI), ran for the Progressive Party. Her brother, the well-polished Dr Raja Kumar was to later become a prominent leader of a political party (Labour Party) in Malaya. I stood for election as the representative of the Labour Party. All three of us were given a platform to put forth our arguments for our causes, appearing on stage to speak before the student body.

Chua Sian Chin was my campaign manager and among my greatest supporters was Ee Tian Hong.

I suppose my sympathies for the common man during my time as chairman of the National Wages Council (NWC) in Singapore had its beginnings in my High School days in Malacca.

In my campaign speech, I advocated fighting for freedom declaring that in an independent society such as ours, all citizens should be treated as equals.

I raised the question of why Malacca's only swimming pool then was open only to whites with Malayans banned from using it.

The pool and all other facilities, I argued, should be open to all — whites and locals alike. I also urged for some of Malacca's narrow roads, built for bullock carts, to be widened. I did not know then of the value of heritage.

I was cheered; my stance won me many votes especially among the Malay students who admired my guts to speak up. I won the election, though I was a new High School boy, hailing from ACS, Malacca. KC Dutt had been a High School boy from the beginning.

However, the following day, the organiser of the mock elections KT Joseph, who was also my teacher, was afraid that my extreme views would offend the British school principal. He was unhappy with my outspokenness.

I assured him that it was only a mock election and that if it were real I would be more tempered in my approach. Years later, his son and I were to become good friends and were together in the academic staff union of the University of Malaya in Kuala Lumpur.

The governor has wisdom

Immediately after completing my university entrance exams, I applied for a Malacca Settlement Government Scholarship. Only four were awarded each year. I knew of the scholarship through school. I was determined to get it as it was my only passport to a better life. There was no other means of going to university as my family simply did not have the money.

The interview was conducted in the Stadthuys or City Hall built by the Dutch in 1650. It still stands there today next to the distinctive clock tower in the historic heart of Malacca town. Some towns in today's Netherlands remind me of my own town in Malacca in architecture and in architectural layout.

The chairman of the interview board was the resident commissioner of Malacca named GEW Wisdom.

I was prepared for a gruelling interview but mid-way Mr Wisdom simply said, "Young man, you can prepare to go to Singapore." Astonished, I asked, "So you are giving me the scholarship?" Mr Wisdom just smiled and nodded. I was ecstatic! For me, being able to go to university was better than striking a million dollars in a lottery. Nothing would give me greater happiness and joy.

Unlike the *babas* and *nonyas* who were more settled in their lives perhaps because they had established roots in Malacca over a longer period of time, I was a typical example of the children and grandchildren of the more recent immigrants and so was very achievement-oriented.

I was very grateful to Mr Wisdom, who had a street named after him in Malacca town. Alas, after Malayanisation, this street no longer bears his name, which was the name of the last British Governor of Malacca. Malacca too sadly demolished the iconic beautiful Rest House at the height of Malayan nationalism.

A double life

My determination to go to university was born of a strong desire to improve my lot. I knew I had to go for further studies, otherwise I would remain stuck in Malacca, probably as a clerk.

During my post-war school years, I led two parallel lives of which very few people knew of, even my best and closest school friends.

Each day, I would get up at 5am. I would then cycle to a bakery about 12 kilometres away to collect freshly baked bread to deliver to various coffee shops in town, recording my sales in a small booklet. After that was done, I would return home to take a short rest before getting ready for school. Later in life, I have at times wondered why my two sons and my younger daughter developed a keen interest in long-distance cycling. They were doing it for leisure of course while I did it out of necessity.

After school finished at 1 pm, there would be some time to revise my homework before helping out my father in his dwindling provision shop business. At night, after dinner, I would be off to the amusement park to sell cigarettes with my beloved younger brother Chong Lian.

So life at an early age for me was a tough one. Having to make ends meet by hawking cigarettes, I was terrified of seeing my class teacher or other students from school.

I did not want them to know that I was so poor that I had to work so hard while attending school. I liked to preserve the image that I was a normal pupil.

In the early morning when I had to cycle for miles to the bakery, I at times fell into self-pity and would sob while cycling. I would cry for my mother. At times, I would sing revolutionary songs in Chinese. One of my favourites was "The Mid-Night Cry". When at night I had to walk back with my little brother for eight or nine kilometres, I would pray for courage, and for hope for my two little brothers and my little sister; "Dear God, please do not abandon us. Please."

It was because of my experiences as a boy that during my years with the NWC I was determined to let rank-and-file workers know that I would deliver on my promise each year to ensure that they would be paid justly as long as I was chairman. I was worried about the extreme poverty of people, and of my own Singaporeans in particular. Since God had given me some ability to help, I would not shirk my responsibility.

I have been quick to respond to injustices and unfairness. Someone once said to me, "You have a great soul," to which I replied that I simply love life and treasure it and if I could help to correct injustices for others when encountering them, I would do so.

My father's legacy

My father had a rather hands-off approach when it came to raising children as was typical of many Chinese heads of households in those days. The long hours my father had to work in his coffee shop and later in his provision shop just to eke out a living were perhaps a contributory factor.

I was, however, grateful that when occasions permitted, he instilled in my siblings and me some moral values that we all practise to this day. He believed firmly in walking the straight and narrow path, which meant being honest, no gambling, not getting drunk or mixing with bad company.

He would quote proverbs in Hainanese to convey his message. He was fond of saying: "One who mixes with red ink will turn red; one who mixes with black ink will turn black."

Like most Chinese of immigrant stock, he believed in hard work and thrift. Saving for a rainy day and avoiding sloth and laziness were principles he ingrained in us.

He taught me how to use the Chinese abacus which helped me greatly in my ability to handle mathematics in school. For him, knowing our family background and ancestry was very important as he felt we needed to have a sense of history. Our Chinese roots can be traced to a place called An Yang in Henan province about 3,000 years ago. From there, my ancestors moved to the coastal province of Shandong, then Zhejiang and south of it to Fujian province. Later, they moved even further south by boat to the island of Hainan, dubbed the Hawaii of China because of its semi-tropical climate.

It was from Hainan that my father made his way to Singapore and Malacca. In the process of the long migration in China, there were intermarriages with other non-Lim Chinese from Henan to Hainan. Marriage within the same surname group was considered to be incestuous, and strictly forbidden.

Yes, I must not forget the family middle-name generational poem in Chinese my father left with me as his eldest son. From the middle-name order, we know who are related to us, male-line that is, and the generational matrix of the relationship, especially if the dialect group and the geographical location of the residents are also known. I did use the poem to name my four children and the four Lim grandchildren. The poem, in classical Chinese, also depicts the historical antecedents of the Lim lineage. It runs thus:

元 君 居 廷 国
青 春 必 登 朝
盛 世 崇 学 士
联 宗 冀 奕 峤

I will pass the poem to my Lim grandchildren, and whether they will continue the tradition of naming their children 林联__, and their grandchildren 林宗__, will be left completely to their discretion and free will. I have discharged my inherited traditional duty, passed down by my dear father.

Now, we must move on to my leaving Malacca for higher education in Singapore, which was then part of Malaya — British Malaya.

First teaching job

Before my arrival to Singapore in 1951, I had to help out an Anglo-Chinese School schoolmate in Malacca, Chua Leng Kee.

He was an English teacher in a Chinese school in Muar, Johor, but decided to take a better-paying job as an inspector in the police force in Kuala Lumpur. He asked if I could take over the remainder of his contract as a school teacher.

The school was called Cheng Kuo (Jiang Guo), located in a rubber estate in Muar's Bukit Gambier district. I was expected to board there as commuting between Muar and Malacca town would be too tiresome a prospect.

What attracted me to take over from Leng Kee was the fact that Cheng Kuo School used Mandarin as a medium of instruction and I saw it as an opportunity to hone my skills in the language. It was also a chance to earn some badly needed money.

But there was the darker side to the school. It was in what was considered a "black area", where Communist sympathisers were known to lurk. This was during the time of the Malayan Emergency which had begun in 1948 when the British colonial government was caught up in a guerrilla war waged in the jungles of Malaya against the Malayan Communist Party (MCP), an outgrowth of the anti-Japanese guerrilla movement which had emerged during the Second World War.

So, unlike the "white areas" in towns such as Malacca and Singapore where you could move freely, Bukit Gambier, an area of rubber estates, was subject to a nightly curfew.

I shared a big room with another teacher, who came from Singapore. One night we heard gun shots and for some time after that, my room-mate who was scared out of his wits resorted to sleeping under his bed. When he woke up the next day, his trousers would be wet with urine. He was that frightened.

I was determined to find out the reason for the gun shots at night. As it turned out, contrary to what most of us had thought, the shots did not come from the Communists, then branded as terrorists, but from the local police who were trying to frighten small traders in the area into paying protection money!

My first strike

I was expected to work at Cheng Kuo for a term of four months. I received regular payment in the first two months but nothing for the months that followed; none of the other teachers were paid either. We complained to the principal but he said there was little he could do as the school board controlled the purse strings. He told us to be patient and wait. I could not afford to wait, I said, as it was time for me to start my university term.

While teaching in Cheng Kuo, I would, on weekends, travel to Muar and stay overnight with a fellow teacher in his home. I had an idea and shared it with my colleagues. We should all go to Muar for the coming weekend and simply let the very conscientious but helpless principal know that we had no intention of returning to school.

One of the teachers asked: "Are you suggesting that we go on strike?"

I replied: "I am telling you how to get our money back."

So all of us got together and went to Muar. Before leaving, I went to the principal to tell him where we would be, giving him the address of where I had always stayed in Muar. Before the weekend was over, someone came to look for us and told us to go back to school.

The following day, the chairman of the board of governors appeared in school to apologise for not paying our wages on time. He said there was money in the coffers but due to a "technical error", we had not been paid. We accepted the oversight and most happily came back to work.

So we got our money back. That was my first successful strike. When it was time for me to take my leave, the school gave me a fond farewell. All the pupils would line the street leading to the school to bid farewell to me. I missed my fellow teachers and the school children as much as they missed me. But it was time to move on to the next chapter of my life — as a university undergraduate. It was the start of a new dawn.

I would like to end this chapter with a quotation from Alexander Pope:

"*Hope springs eternal from the human breast.*"

CHAPTER 4

JOURNEY TO UNIVERSITY

Singapore, here we come

In June 1951, I took an express coach of the Sin Lian Bus Company from Malacca to Singapore. It arrived at Beach Road from where I took a taxi to the Telok Ayer Methodist Church which is located at the junction of Telok Ayer Street and Cecil Street. The church has a 125-year history and still stands today; it has been declared a National Monument.

I was to meet Chia Teow Kin, my classmate from Anglo-Chinese School, Malacca. I used to visit him at his home in Malacca to study together. He became one of my closest friends and was instrumental in introducing me to my future wife. Sadly, he passed away at the age of 85 in July 2014.

Teow Kin had arrived earlier in Singapore to begin his three-year course in teaching. Since I had no relatives to stay with in Singapore, Teow Kin arranged for me to stay with him on the church premises which had some accommodation on its upper-most floor. I spent a week there before moving to the then Bukit Timah Hostels of the University of Malaya. Most of the students from upcountry lodged at the Bukit Timah campus. Later, we moved to the Dunearn Road Hostels nearby.

The Bukit Timah Hostels housed about 250 students in two-storey apartment blocks set in spacious grounds in the Oxbridge tradition with quadrangles in-between. In 1981, the university was moved to Kent Ridge after it merged with Nanyang University to become the National University of Singapore. The Dunearn Road Hostels reverted to its original role as student digs when they were leased by the Lee Kuan Yew School of Public Policy which opened in the former Bukit Timah Campus.

There were only a few students in the Bukit Timah Hostels who came from Malacca. Most of the students hailed from elsewhere in Peninsular Malaya — Kedah, Perak, Selangor, Johor, and particularly from Penang and Kuala Lumpur.

At the Bukit Timah Hostels, first-year and second-year students were accommodated in dormitory blocks. Third-year students could enjoy the comparative luxury of double-room accommodation. I remember meeting one of them, Ong Pang Boon, who shared a room next to my dormitory. He later became Singapore's first Minister of Home Affairs.

Another that I recall sharing the dormitory with me was Tan See Peng from Batu Pahat, Johor who later became the first local Auditor-General of Singapore.

The early 1950s produced a sterling crop of students who went on to make a mark on the political scene in Singapore. They were a product of the post-world war movement that had stirred a political awakening among the local people in British Malaya and the subsequent rise of anti-colonial and nationalist sentiments. The failure of Britain to defend Singapore and the Japanese Occupation were also contributing factors. The two events showed that the British were not the supreme power they had projected themselves to be then. There was a big crack in the world of Pax Britannica.

In my second year, considered a "honeymoon" year as no year-end examinations were held, I decided to stand for election to the Student Council of the University of Malaya Students' Union (UMSU). Others who were also elected included Poh Soo Kai, Shen Nam Chin and Lim Hock Siew who all later qualified as medical doctors but because of their leftist leanings spent many years in political detention. Elected as chairman was Wang Gungwu who went on to become a pre-eminent academic and historian and Vice-Chancellor of the University of Hong Kong.

The hostel grounds of the Bukit Timah campus were dotted with impressive tall tembusu trees which provided plenty of shade. However, getting to the Bukit Timah campus from Dunearn Road Hostels was another matter altogether, as the long road had few trees to provide shade. So we would feel hot when making the daily trek to and from classes.

More worrying though were the floods along Bukit Timah Road and Dunearn Road. The floods were frequent whenever it rained heavily. Sometimes, cars would stall on both Dunearn Road and Bukit Timah Road and we would help to push them out of the water. Some grateful owners would even give us a tip!

In 1952, I was elected to be the founding secretary of the University of Malaya Debating Union (UMDU). Among the memorable debates we organised was one on why the University of Malaya should establish a law faculty as soon as possible. One of the speakers we invited to speak on the subject was Lee Kuan Yew, a young lawyer who had just returned from Cambridge University in the United Kingdom. Together with the president of UMDU, I had gone to his law practice that he had set up with his wife Kwa Geok Choo in Malacca Street to help persuade him to consent to participate in the debate.

It was the first time I had met Lee Kuan Yew who later became Singapore's first prime minister in 1959. I was struck by his charisma and eloquence when he spoke in the debate held at Oei Tiong Ham Hall. The University of Malaya did eventually set up its Faculty of Law in 1956. The student population voted unanimously for the proposal.

Oei Tiong Ham Hall was the focus of many intellectual activities and was also the venue for the university's convocation ceremonies. It hosted many debates on politics, which were well-attended. The Federation of Malaya was moving towards independence then and many of the university students were naturally keen to know more about what was happening. Oei Tiong Ham Hall was renamed Oei Tiong Ham Building in 1966, housing the University of Singapore's administrative offices. Today, it is home to the Lee Kuan Yew School of Public Policy.

At the debates held at Oei Tiong Ham Hall during the time I was there from 1951 to 1955, two people in particular stood out. One was Han Su Yin who later became a renowned author, famous for her novel *Love is a Many Splendored Thing*. She was an icon to male students especially; she was attractive, elegant and very eloquent. And she spoke first-rate English and Mandarin.

The other speaker who captured our imagination was Lee Kuan Yew who participated in several political debates. Many of us regarded him as our leader, the Malayan leader. Although I listened carefully to the political debates, I avoided taking part in any politically motivated activities. This probably stemmed from memories of the time when one of my uncles was asked to leave British Malaya to go back to China because he had been distributing pro-China and pro-communist pamphlets. Besides, the village in Wanning, Hainan where my parents came from had been embroiled in the mutually-destructive civil wars from the overthrowing of the Qing Dynasty down to the establishment of the Peoples' Republic of China. Incidentally today in 2015, Wanning can boast of being voted as having one of the very best golf courses in Asia, and Asia has some of the best golf courses in the world. What a metamorphosis!

Ended up with economics

Apart from the medical school and the science faculty, there was only one other faculty — Arts — offering courses. So, it was Hobson's choice for me then, when it came to studying at the University of Malaya. I was not qualified to enter the science faculty or the medical faculty. My school in Malacca only taught us General Science. The medical school only took in students with full science qualifications.

When I first started at the university, other than the compulsory English Language course, we had to pick three subjects to study. I chose English Literature, History and Economics. In the second year we were limited to two subjects and one subsidiary; I chose Economics and English Literature which by the way kindled my interest further in poems and novels. The subsidiary I picked was Statistics. In the third year, I was able to study the same courses. However, in the fourth year we were told to specialise in one subject. I enjoyed literature, but found that we often had to do a lot of reading which was very time-consuming. I remember when we studied Milton's *Paradise Lost*, instead of reading the book in its entirety, I took to reading reviews of it and still managed to score well. It was paradise regained.

The long vacations

One hallmark of student life was the long vacation or "long vac", as it was called, which lasted from three to four months. The question was how would we fill up our time during this period? I was brought up as a workaholic.

For upcountry students like me, the question was whether we should go back to Malacca or stay on in the hostel in Singapore which would incur additional expenses apart from the fact that it might be very lonely because nearly all of the other students would not be there.

I decided to do part-time teaching, in neighbouring Johor, as a chance to earn extra pocket money. An opening was available in Pei Hwa Primary School located in an essentially rural area between Kukup and Pontian Kechil.

It was a Chinese language school, so I was again immersed in the Chinese school culture. I taught English and mathematics. All the other teachers, including the principal, were from Singapore and would go home for the weekend.

So, I was often left alone. We were lodged in wooden huts and these were located in a "black area". I hardly ventured out because of the possibility of getting shot by security forces in the area.

I stayed in and read many of Bernard Shaw's books to broaden my horizon. I also read up on the then widely publicised and controversial Barnes' Report and the Fenn-Wu Report on our future school education system. I was not totally alone though, as at night I would hear the symphony of croaking frogs, and sometimes the frightening roar-of marauding tigers.

On my second "long vac" I stayed on in Singapore to work part-time for the Geography Department to conduct surveys on farms most of which were located in Lim Chu Kang and Ponggol. The objective of the surveys was to gather various statistics such as what the farmers were rearing by way of livestock, and the kind of crops they grew.

Although most of us diligently went around the farms to collect facts and figures, there was one instance when a fellow student refused to get involved with pig farms. As a Muslim for whom pigs are considered unclean, he felt it was not appropriate for him to go among the hogs to make a physical count. So, he gave an approximation which was accepted without the Geography Department knowing any better. From this episode, I learnt that sometimes field surveys may not be as reliable as we believe them to be.

In my third year, I decided to go back to Malacca. I had been experiencing severe migraines and so I thought it was more prudent to return home. The university doctor I saw said it was probably a psychological problem (I had been worrying about whether I would be able to obtain my degree) or linked to my diet which had been lacking in fresh fruits and vegetables and which was possibly also the cause of boils erupting on my buttocks. I should have used whatever little extra money I earned during my vacations to improve my diet but I would always send the extra money to my family in Malacca.

As if to prove the point, the moment I left university and landed a job with the Singapore Civil Service, earning a steady income, all my boils and migraines vanished.

Another reason for going back to Malacca was the fact that I managed to clinch another scholarship in my third year to tide me through so there was no need to work. I had seen an advertisement published by the Hua Yue Society in Singapore. This was a Hainanese clan association that is still located on Seah Street. A one-year scholarship was available to university students of Hainanese origin. So, I applied and was granted an interview. I was told that I already had a scholarship from the Malacca government, so why was I applying? I explained that the money was not enough, hence my need to work at part-time jobs during the long vacations.

I was given a grant of $1,000. That timely help was to influence me in later life to help students in similar circumstances, prompting me to set up a bursary fund at the Nanyang Technological University (NTU).

When I went home to Malacca that year, I went back with Ee Tian Hong, Chua Sian Chin and Tong Teck Eng — all fellow students from Malacca. We would get together often during our vacation back home, going to places such as St Paul's Hill and discussing our future. We even joked about the possibility of one of us becoming the first local governor of Malacca!

Soon boredom set in, and I decided to go back to Singapore. When I turned up at Dunearn Road Hostels, I met another Malayan by the name of James Puthucheary, a political activist, who had been released in 1952 after an 18-month detention. Before his arrest, he was a student at Raffles College and so was allowed to re-join the Economics Department. He seemed to know my examination results. He said that I had topped the list in my BA in Economics and that I was second in English. I wondered where he got his information, but was flattered by his disclosure, which of course I hoped was true.

I later learned from Dr You Poh Seng, my statistics lecturer, that I came out first in Statistics. He did not believe it himself, as I had often failed in his tests. I said, "I spotted your questions correctly." He replied, "Then, you deserve to top the list."

The brilliant Jamit Singh also studied Economics and English but failed to graduate. I remember meeting him one bright afternoon just after I had finished an examination. I was in a joyous mood. He asked, "Do you know that we have an exam on Shakespeare taking place in half an hour?" Bewildered, I replied, "I just came back from there!" He had his time-table mixed up again. He thus failed his BA exam twice. As a result, he found it difficult to find employment until he was offered a position as secretary of the Singapore Harbour Board Staff Association.

Jamit went on to become a distinguished trade unionist in Singapore, uniting port workers in their fight against unfair treatment under the colonial government.

For the rest of us who graduated, the natural route to employment then was via the civil service or education sector. There were hardly any job opportunities in the private sector then.

Campus life

I have fond memories of campus life, especially the camaraderie that prevailed among students. Campfire nights were a staple at the Dunearn Road Hostels enabling us to bond.

Classes were small; there were 12 of us studying economics in the Honours Year so we were able to get to know one another quite well.

We had dedicated and first-rate teachers and researchers. Our History Department, for instance, was headed by Professor CN Parkinson who gave us Parkinson's Law.

The head of the Geography Department was Professor EGH Dobby. At a time when geography was skewed to British syllabi, he was the first man to write authoritatively about Southeast Asian geography and also on agriculture in Malaya. I benefited enormously from reading some of his impressive publications before joining the University as an undergraduate.

Most of the teaching staff in the university were expatriates, mainly British.

One of them was Professor Thomas Henry Silcock (Tom Silcock for short) without whom my life would have been very different. He was head of the Economics

Department; the other was Professor Lim Tay Boh who was one of the first locals to go to Cambridge for his doctorate degree; he later became Vice-Chancellor of the university.

The retirement age was 55 then. Most of the expat professors would either return home or go to Australia; most Malayan staff would return to Peninsular Malaya. One of them was Ungku Abdul Aziz, who was later appointed the Royal Professor of Economics of the University of Malaya (at Pantai Valley) and its Vice-Chancellor, and a very distinguished one at that.

There was some rivalry among staff and departments. Professor Dobby, despite being a great academic, somehow had a dislike for the Economics Department and I was told that there was some discrimination in the granting of the Queen's scholarships when he was Dean of the Faculty. Those from the Geography Department could be awarded the scholarship even if they only had a class two upper whereas those of other departments in the Faculty had to have first class honours as a prerequisite.

That made me wary of discrimination according to academic specialisations in later years and I was determined not to practise it when I became an academician and Dean in the university.

In those days, professors were very much looked up to in our society. But they had their own rivalries and conflicts.

However, many of the other professors were genuinely warm and friendly; they would invite us to their homes for dinners. We were grateful especially those of us not from Singapore.

It was nice to have a lovely meal in a home and we could relax and get together. So, we students knew each other rather well and also our professors.

Changing times

Alas, when I returned to Bukit Timah Campus in 1969 to begin work as a Reader in the Economics Department in the University of Singapore, I found that the camaraderie I enjoyed as a student was no longer there.

Classes had become too big and there was less rapport between students and teachers. Where we had two to five students for each tutorial, now there were 20 or more.

There was less emphasis on tutorials and the writing of essays. Instead, multiple-choice answers to questions became the norm. As professors today we have learned to cope with large numbers of students.

Tolerance in hostel life

As residential students, we were encouraged to share the same room regardless of race or religion which helped to foster mutual tolerance and understanding.

It was only in the fourth year that we could choose our room-mate. Mine was Pang Tee Pow who later became the first permanent secretary of the Ministry of Defence; he was handpicked by the then defence minister Dr Goh Keng Swee.

Tee Pow studied economics but alas, died young of cancer. I did make a point to visit him at the General Hospital before he passed away.

In campus and in the hostels, we all spoke in English. The sense of community was strong.

However, the university did a disservice by putting older girls in Dunearn Road Hostels. The custom then was to court girls two or three years younger. But the girls staying in the hostels were older as they already had their degrees and were pursuing diplomas in education so that put a dampener on our getting to know the fairer sex.

There were other girls staying at Mt Rosie, another hostel. But the students of both sexes did not have many natural opportunities to mix.

The most popular pastimes were football with matches held in Bukit Timah and debates at the King Edward VII Medical College. All in all, we had an all-round education.

When I was a student, we had a lot of discussions on politics. I remember Tan Cheng Lock, then chairman of the Malayan Chinese Association coming in to give talks. He warned the Malayan students of Chinese origin that if we carried on as we did, we would end up playing second fiddle to the Malays. To me, our society had already fractured on racial lines, the result perhaps of colonial rule, and of our political parties built on racial lines.

Later, he invited me to his house in Malacca. His motive was to persuade me to get interested in politics with a view to joining his party.

I had no such inclination. For me, my priority was to get a good job and to get out of poverty, get married and raise a family.

And most of us in the university then had no fear of communists taking over Malaya because we knew they would not succeed. Despite the battle being fought in the jungles of Malaya between the communists and the British forces, many of us as undergraduates did not discuss the situation much.

First convocation

After three years, I was to be conferred a degree — it was one of the most important points of my life. The year was 1954 and I would receive my degree scroll in Oei Tiong Ham Hall, after which there would be a reception on the Quadrangle.

We needed to wear a suit for the occasion. Since I could not afford to get a suit done, my brother-in-law loaned me a white suit. But white was not appropriate according to my fellow students who said people wore white when serving in hotels.

Luckily, one of them, Wong Lee Hoon, who later became the second local Postmaster-General of Singapore, said he had a grey suit to spare. I wore it for my convocation.

The ceremony was presided over by Malcolm MacDonald, who was the university's Chancellor and the British Commissioner-General in Southeast Asia. He was a most impressive orator. His father, Ramsey MacDonald, was at one time the prime minister of Great Britain.

My father was proud of what I had achieved but he could not attend the ceremony. Neither did the parents of most of the other students from north of the Johor Causeway.

On my part, I was just thrilled to find out that I was able to get into the honours class that same year. I was given the option to read Economics or English Literature. I chose Economics.

CHAPTER 5

LIFE AS A CIVIL SERVANT

After graduating with an honours degree (2nd class, Upper) in 1955, my first job was as assistant warden at Dunearn Road Hostels. Siew Nim Chee, who was my lecturer on Labour Economics, was the warden there. He knew that I needed to work to save up enough money to fund my post-graduate Master of Arts (MA) course which I had already signed up for with Professor Tom Silcock as my supervisor.

The Malacca government, which had awarded me my scholarship, had earlier indicated that they had no position for me in Malacca, so I was free to do whatever I pleased, hence my decision to go for a higher degree.

Towards Malayanisation

However, several of my Malacca friends urged me to apply to work in the Singapore Civil Service, declaring that it was better than pursuing an MA. It was a period when the British were preparing British Malaya for independence and so the Federal Civil Service in Kuala Lumpur and the Civil Service in Singapore were in a state of flux with many positions gradually being transferred from British expatriates to locals. In Singapore, there was even a high-powered and highly-publicised Malayanisation Commission for the civil service take-over.

I applied for the Audit Department, the Postal Department and the Singapore Administrative Service. Competition was very keen particularly for the Singapore Administrative Service. Much to my pleasant surprise, I was successful in all the three applications. I was probably quite good at interviews.

Discrimination against locals

I chose to work for the Singapore Administrative Service. I thus left the university. I was to work in the Financial Secretary's office at Empress Place, which was then the headquarters of the British administration in Singapore.

So, one early morning in 1955, I climbed up the wooden steps of the grand Empress Place Building, which today houses the Asian Civilisations Museum, to begin my first day of work. I was made to share a room with Oon Khye Kiang. He had come from Penang and was the most senior of the local officials. It was he who had urged the British government in 1937 to consider creating a university and introducing subjects such as economics to equip graduates for the business world. He was the president of the Raffles College Union then and had lamented that no local businesses employed Raffles College graduates who could find work only in the Civil Service or Educational Service. He was 50 then, while I was 23.

I was very surprised that he had not been given a room of his own despite his seniority. I sensed serious discrimination against him, because he was a local. As a newbie and the youngest I held the lowest rank of Acting Third Assistant Financial Secretary. Mr Oon only carried the title First Assistant Financial Secretary. Our room overlooked the Singapore River. In colonial times, only the British were given individual rooms, even junior officers without tertiary qualifications.

Not far from Mr Oon's room was George Bogaars, the Second Assistant Financial Secretary. He later went on to head the Singapore Civil Service. Being Eurasian, he was given an office of his own even though he was much junior in rank to Oon. The British tended to treat their own kind as first class citizens, Eurasians second class, while all other locals were considered third class citizens.

I became good friends with Oon. He gave me useful advice such as the need to be more reticent about my work and not to speak too much of the Civil Service when he overheard me speaking freely to my friends about my job. In general, he became my civil service mentor, and a good one at that.

The work that I did was uncomplicated. One of my responsibilities was to approve car loans. The maximum loan amount was $4,000 which was interest-free. I had an experienced administrative assistant to help me vet the loans. He was familiar with all the rules regarding loans. He would give his recommendation on whether an application should be approved or not. One of the rules was that the loan could be used to buy only a British-made car. If I was unsure of whether a loan application should be approved, I could send it to a more senior official like the principal assistant secretary to make the decision with my view stated.

Another of my duties concerned foreign exchange controls. We had to buy from the sterling area wherever possible. Although experienced and well-qualified foreign exchange officers would handle the actual deals, my job was to ensure that regulations were followed.

I also had to conduct surprise checks on the cash balances of various departments within the Civil Service. My task was simply to order the checking of their accounts to ensure that money was being used and kept properly. As I was so new, I was expected to get the support of a more senior officer before acting. I learned quickly that the Treasury had a significant control over the finances of the public sector.

Cadet training

All new recruits to the Civil Service were regarded as cadet officers and we were given appropriate training to ensure that we would fit into our jobs. We attended training classes twice a week in the afternoon.

Since much of being an administrative officer would involve attending and recording meetings, part of our training consisted of how to conduct meetings properly, how to record minutes and how to write papers and reports for presentation to the Cabinet.

What I learned about the writing of reports came in handy during the time when I served as Chairman of the National Wages Council (NWC). Being clear, lucid and concise was the key in the presentation of reports and I put that into practice whenever I had to write to then Prime Minister Lee Kuan Yew on the NWC recommendations made every year.

For cadet administrative officers, one of the more important courses that we had to undergo and for which there were examinations were several courses on basic law which we had to be familiar with. These laws consisted of the Criminal Code, the Law of Evidence, the Criminal Procedure Code and a thick document called Colonial Rules and Regulations. Passing the law examinations was mandatory, if we wanted to be confirmed in our post as administrative officers. We also had to learn a second language — Chinese, Malay or Tamil. I was assigned to Chinese and I had a Chinese tutor who came to my home on weekends to conduct lessons.

In three years, I was a confirmed officer in the permanent pensionable service. Although I was elated, I was at the same time none too happy not because of the work *per se* but because I knew that however hard I worked or was good at my job, I would never gain an accelerated promotion or bonus.

What's more, whoever served ahead of you would always be your senior. It was a seniority system, not a meritocratic one.

Perhaps because of this experience, when I was with the NWC, I sought to do away with lengthy time scales and promotions based only on seniority and introduced payment schemes for which workers would be rewarded for being productive and working hard.

I also decided to do something more productive with my time as a means of earning extra cash. So, with permission from my superiors, I taught evening classes at Cairnhill under the auspices of the Adult Education Board. The students were all working adults keen on bettering themselves. I gave a series of lectures on Singapore economics. One of them was on income inequality. Later, when the Singapore Polytechnic was set up at Shenton Way, I became a "Visiting Lecturer", teaching a very popular course of "Money and Banking" in the evening. I was delighted that my name appeared in the first Prospectus of the Singapore Polytechnic as a Visiting Lecturer.

These evening classes and the study of law and the exposure to public administration were to have a positive effect on my life later.

My second posting

In 1955, David Marshall was elected as Singapore's first chief minister. His administration was faced with many challenging issues, one of which was the economy. On the advice of the local British government, an economics advisory unit was set up. It was headed by Sir Sydney Caine who was vice-chancellor of the University of Malaya (in Singapore). Caine had gained a reputation as an economics wizard in the West Indies before he took up his university appointment. He would be the economic advisor to Marshall and he appointed as his assistant Paul Wilson.

They both wanted to have a young local economist in their unit. I was thus transferred to work in the Chief Minister's Office as second assistant economic advisor. In the process of working with these two gentlemen I learned a great deal about the actual workings of the Singapore economy.

Caine had a unique way of doing his reports. He would dictate to his secretary with blanks which were meant for me to fill. One of the blanks in a particular report eluded me. It was about the total capital accumulation or capital stock of Singapore.

I was at a loss, so I went to seek Paul Wilson's help. He told me to simply refer to the Bukit Merah business directory that was published annually and add up the stock of the companies featured. The problem was that they only featured companies of the private sector and there was no information on the public sector. Besides, only listed companies were shown, and most of them were Pan-Malayan in orientation and content.

I then hit on a solution. I could get some information from ECAFE (Economic Commission for Asia and the Far East). The organisation was founded in 1947 in Shanghai, China, to assist in the post-war economic reconstruction of countries in Asia. In 1949, it moved its headquarters to Bangkok, Thailand and was renamed ESCAP (Economic and Social Commission for Asia and the Pacific) in 1974 to reflect both the economic and social aspects of development and the geographic location of its member countries.

I took the available capital-output ratios of the East Asian countries and obtained an average and used this average ratio to derive Singapore's capital stock. It turned out to be fairly accurate and the two economic advisors were amazed when they found out how I arrived at the capital stock figure for Singapore.

Several months later in 1956, the International Economics Association (IEA) decided to hold a meeting in Singapore to which young economists from Southeast Asia were encouraged to attend. The IEA is a non-governmental organisation formed in 1950 under the auspices of UNESCO. Its aims were to promote international understanding and ties among economists through meetings, research and publications. I was invited to take part by Professor Tom Silcock, who had taught me in university. He asked me to present a paper.

I was also able to meet economists from Indonesia, Thailand and the Philippines with whom I have forged important connections over the years. Some of them became dear friends. I guess my interest in economics was entrenched at this meet.

It was at this conference that I met several globally eminent economists. One of them was the British economist and national incomes expert Dudley Seers, who was famous for his view that "the focus on national income as a target for achieving poverty reduction avoided the real problems of development." The other was Harry Johnson, a Canadian economist who held professorships concurrently at the University of Chicago and the London School of Economics.

Harry Johnson was larger than life. He had served before as the external examiner of economics at the University of Malaya (in Singapore). He was a prolific writer with some 500 papers to his name. He enjoyed travelling to conferences and delivering papers. Whenever he was in Singapore, he would often go to Johor Bahru to feast on curry and satay. He was very much at home here and was fond of showing off his dexterity with chopsticks.

I was intrigued at how he gained the comparative advantage of using chopsticks. He breezily replied that he often ate at Chinese restaurants in his native Toronto where he picked up the art of using chopsticks and unhesitatingly added that one's comparative advantage could change.

One day, several decades later, when I was in Toronto to present a paper at an international economics conference, I met up with Johnson. He had been caught up in a controversy when he declared that "No Canadian economist worth his weight should remain in Canada." At the conference, he was very critical of the papers of the participants, nearly all of whom were from developed countries. He was asked why he did not criticise me when I was presenting my paper. He answered that he had been my external examiner and if he had criticised me, he would be criticising himself! Most of us thought his health had deteriorated too much at this stage, explaining his unusual criticalness.

The unsociable me

The IEA wrapped up its programme with a social event — a beach picnic at Sisters' Islands off the mainland of Singapore.

I did not attend as I was courting my future wife. Sir Sydney Caine did not know this. He was disappointed at my failure to attend.

He said, "If I, as Vice-Chancellor and Economic Advisor, could find the time to attend such an event, you should make the effort to do so as well. You need to have better time management. There were many people of your age, and the picnic offered a chance for you to get to know them better and establish ties which might come in useful one day."

I apologised, and from then on I made sure that I would participate in more work-connected social activities. And he was right that good time management was important in life. I did not tell him I was courting, and courting had no time limit.

One day, when Sir Sydney had a bit of a drink and was in a more open mood, I asked if I could apply to do a master's degree in economics on a part-time basis with the ultimate aim of obtaining a doctorate degree. He was aghast, arguing that there was no need to do so.

He asked me to name five top British economists with a doctorate. I could not. He reeled off the names of distinguished British economists without a doctorate: Sir John Hicks at Oxford University, his wife Lady Ursula Hicks, Professor Joan Robinson of Cambridge University, and also at Cambridge, Nicholas Kaldor, a Hungarian refugee who went on to become an economic advisor to the Labour government and was noted for mooting the idea of having an expenditure tax, the forerunner of today's goods and services tax (GST). Then there was James Meade, who in 1997 was co-winner of the Nobel Memorial Prize in Economic Science.

"Not a single one of them possessed a PhD!" exclaimed Caine. So, in his view there was no need for me to consider getting one. He himself had sat on many PhD awarding committees with only a first degree — a first class honours from LSE (London School of Economics) though.

But my mind was made up. I wanted to leave the Civil Service for the academic world but did not wish to tell him that. I needed a PhD to be accepted as an academic economist. I am not Hicks, Kaldor, Meade or Caine.

Adult education classes

As the name implies, adult education classes are aimed at adults, some of whom may be working and are seeking to advance themselves in their careers or are studying for personal enrichment. Those who are not working hope enrolment in these evening classes might give them an edge in their job search.

In the mid-1950s, Singapore was going through a political transition towards self-government. The times were chaotic and there were many fears of unemployment and job losses. Thus, it was no surprise that the evening classes held at the Adult Education Board premises on Cairnhill Road would be well-attended.

Of the students who attended my class, three in particular stood out. One was Sir Han Hoe Lim, a medical doctor who entered politics and held a number of high offices. He was an unofficial member of the Legislative Council of the Straits Settlements in 1933 and was a member of the Executive Council in 1940. After the war, he was an unofficial member of the Singapore Advisory Council from 1946 to 1948 and the senior unofficial member of the Executive Council of Singapore from 1948 to 1951.

He had helped found the University of Malaya (in Singapore) and when he was attending my class in 1956, was serving as a member of the Public Service Commission. He was knighted in 1946, the second Malayan Chinese to receive the honour.

I wondered why a man of his stature would sit in my class. He explained that with the prevailing uncertainty he needed to make sense of the economic scene. I was highly flattered by his attendance.

The other memorable attendee in my class was Janet Lim Chiu Mei, who had written *Sold for Silver*, the first local autobiography and book to be written in English. It recounts her life in China where she was sold into slavery and brought to Singapore to be resold to a wealthy family in the 1930s.

The book documents her lot in life as a *mui tsai* (domestic servant) from which she finally managed to escape. She went on to acquire an education and training as a nurse in St Andrew's Mission Hospital before being sent to Sumatra to work as a nurse during the war years. When she attended my class, she was the hospital matron of St Andrew's Mission Hospital. She was the first Asian to be appointed in 1954. I too was flattered by her attendance. Above all, I was most impressed by the achievement orientation of my Singapore audience.

The third unforgettable attendee was my childhood neighbour in Malacca, Johnny Loh. He was then the estate administrator in the Port of Singapore. Johnny Loh and I had great times together when we were little kids in Bandar Hilir, Malacca.

His family had an elegant house by the sea and I used to go there to play at the huge well-kept empty land beside the house. We pretended to be boy scouts and would camp on the beach or play with guns fashioned out of coconut trunks. I was pleased to see him again. I was also flattered that he would find it worth his while in attending, like Sir Han Hoe Lim and Ms Janet Lim, the entire course in the evening class.

The presence and participation of these prominent adult attendees were a great encouragement to me to switch jobs to be a lecturer from that of an officer in the much coveted administrative service.

Brush with the law

My civil service training in law came in useful when I had my first, unintentional, brush with the law.

I had been working for three years and had just acquired a car, a Ford Prefect, made possible by a government car loan — the same kind of loan I had been processing for others in my first job!

I was courting my future wife then; she was a newly qualified school teacher. In the late afternoons after work, we would meet for tea and curry puffs at the then popular Polar Café on High Street, which was within walking distance from my Empress Place office. On weekends, one of our favourite spots for breakfast was Merdeka Bridge, beneath which we could sit quietly to have our corned beef sandwiches while enjoying the view. Note that Merdeka means Independence, and Singapore was then still a British colony.

The bridge, which spans Kallang Basin and later expanded to form Nicoll Highway, had just been built in 1956 but not commissioned for use yet so the area was empty and I could park my car in a little bay just above the flight of steps leading to our picnic spot.

A week later, I received a summons from the traffic police charging me for illegal parking. I was informed that the offence would be compounded if I agreed to pay the fine, or else I would have to appear in court. I opted for the latter.

I was told in writing that I had parked along a double white line along the road. But I pointed out to the learned magistrate that I was wrongly charged, as my car was actually in a parking bay meant for buses but as the road had not been opened yet, there were no buses, so I had not caused any obstruction. Besides, the traffic rules then did not mention about two white lines, only one white line, but I was charged for parking along a road with two white lines. The training in the basics of the law in my days in the civil service made me aware of my rights and I intended to stand up for that.

The magistrate let me off. He also told the traffic officer to add as an offence parking against double white lines. One colleague in the civil service thought I was cheeky to have challenged the traffic police.

Years later, I was confronted with a similar situation during my student days in Britain. I was charged with parking my car illegally beside a white line on St Aldate's Street in front of Christ Church College in Oxford. I called the Oxford Automobile Association for help but I was advised to pay the fine. I knew the charge was wrong since I did not see any white lines in that area. Appearing at the magistrate's court, I argued that when I had parked the car, there was no white line in sight.

I said I just arrived from Malaya, I would not want to break any British law. What was more disturbing for me was that the owners of four other cars that were parked on the same road were not charged. "Could it be that I am a newcomer or because I am not white that I am charged?" I asked. The police admitted to the polite lady magistrate that they had charged me for the offence and not the others because students from Malaya then had a reputation of being trouble makers. One Malayan student, who came from Singapore, was often seen speeding around in an open-top car with British girls, the police said. The police officer too admitted that at the time of the alleged offence, no visible white line was there, and that the police had re-painted the white line only after the summons was issued.

The good lady magistrate apologised, squashing the case and got the police to apologise as well. I continued to have faith in British justice and fair-play, like my father before me.

Lecturing stint at polytechnic

Apart from the classes at the Adult Education Board, I also took up an evening teaching job at the Singapore Polytechnic in 1957. As usual, money was the main motivator as I wanted to remit some money to my family in Malacca. I had also just got married and the extra cash would come in handy. But the short stint also helped to nurture my desire to become an academic.

I was appointed visiting lecturer, teaching money and banking. Two of the female students, who came from England, told me they were grateful for my lectures as they learnt a lot about monetary economics, which they could not get in attending similar classes in London.

Another was a student whom I would meet again some years later in Hong Kong when he approached me at the old Kai Tak airport. I was en-route to Tokyo for a conference but he asked if he could invite me to dinner.

He said he had been my student in the Poly and even after graduating he kept up with my articles that I had published in the local newspapers. One of them was on rubber replanting. He learned the ropes of the trade from my articles. He had been working in Standard Chartered Bank and decided to buy rubber estates for replanting. He became so successful that he went on to acquire a bank in Hong Kong. He owned a fleet of four out of only six Rolls-Royce cars in the colony. When I went for dinner, he had invited 20 others in my honour. Many of them were prominent in business.

Frederic Benham

In 1957, Sir Sydney Caine resigned to return to Britain to take up a post as Director of the London School of Economics. Mr Paul Wilson followed shortly after. Before he left for Britain, Wilson was given a farewell dinner by the then vice-chancellor, Professor Lim Tay Boh of the University of Malaya. This was at Chequers Hotel. I was invited as well. Eager to let Wilson have a taste of local food, I brought along some durians; the poor man nearly threw up!

Years later, I found out that Wilson was the best man at the wedding of my Oxford PhD supervisor Professor Sir John Hicks and his wife Lady Ursula Hicks. It was a small world after all.

Taking over from Sydney Caine was Dr Frederic Benham, a very eminent British economist. He is best known for his 1938 textbook, *Economics: A General Textbook for Students* written for first-year British university economics students. Prior to this appointment, he was the Economic Advisor to the British Commissioner-General in Southeast Asia, based in Singapore.

During his tenure as economic advisor, Dr Benham published the pioneering book *The National Income of Singapore* in 1956. He had researched and written an earlier pioneering book *The National Income of Malaya* in 1951. He was probably also the first person to compile the national income of Australia and Jamaica. His books and articles on the subject of economics had a profound impact on me.

Dr Benham had noticed tension developing between Singapore and the Federation of Malaya at a time when the latter was preparing for independence while Singapore would be effectively cut off and left on its own as a British colony.

He was concerned, and wrote about the consequences of the Federation of Malaya casting itself adrift from Singapore.

For him Singapore was the metropolis of British Malaya. The natural catchment area for the southern states in the Malay Peninsula such as Johor, Malacca and Negri Sembilan was Singapore. He argued that this southern zone would also be cut off from its conduit of goods via Singapore's port since the Federation's Port Klang was not well-developed yet. Inflation, unemployment and falling income would set in, if the Federation were to terminate the use of the Singapore port.

I was convinced he was right. In fact, years later when I was working in the University of Malaya in Kuala Lumpur, this issue of isolating Singapore kept cropping up in discussions.

When Dr Benham left Singapore in 1959, the Economics Advisory Unit was shut down and I was moved to the new Ministry of Local Government, Lands and Housing.

Before his departure, Dr Benham acted as my sponsor at my wedding on 11 May, 1957. He introduced me as the groom at my tea reception held at the Robinsons Department Store on Raffles Place. I saw him off at the airport when he left. I knew it was unlikely that I would ever see him again. I missed another good mentor.

Land registry

By the time I started work at the Ministry of Local Government, Lands and Housing, the Civil Service had been more or less Malayanised. The permanent secretary of the Ministry was Mr Hon Sui Sen, his deputy was an able middle-aged Briton called Mr Meadows while I was the assistant secretary.

I was the front man dealing with all the correspondence to the office. Matters of greater import would go to the deputy secretary to handle while the permanent secretary would be kept in the loop.

One of the biggest issues of the times was the supply of water pipes. Most households in Singapore lacked running water. This was available only at public water pumps and it was a daily chore for household dwellers to make their way to these pumps with pails to fill up with water.

I was now dealing with giving approvals no longer for car loans but for the installation of water pumps. We were inundated with requests for water pumps in various locations. Before giving approval, I would write to the Public Utilities Board and other concerned departments to check on the feasibility of the request and if they endorsed it, I would inform the deputy secretary Mr Meadows accordingly. He in turn would consult the permanent secretary, Mr Hon Sui Sen, who would then issue a directive for the pump to be installed.

The other big issue that the Land Office of the Ministry had to deal with concerned the clearing of slums. There was a dire housing shortage in Singapore with the majority of the population living in squatter settlements in the suburban areas or in densely packed shophouses in the central area such as Bukit Ho Swee.

The Land Office found it difficult to get the slum dwellers to move so that the land they occupied could be freed for redevelopment.

It was only when the next government formed by the People's Action Party came into power under the tough leadership of Lee Kuan Yew with its promise of providing cheap housing for all that the slum clearance scheme was able to take off.

Trade and industry

Before 1959, when I was still a probation officer, I was transferred to the Ministry of Commerce and Industry (now known as Ministry of Trade and Industry). The newly formed government, headed by Mr Lee Kuan Yew as the first prime minister, took office in June 1959.

I remembered Mr Lee dropped in to say "hello" to some of us after assuming office. He casually asked me what were the most serious economic problems facing Singapore. I replied, "Strikes and lock-outs". Our workers were restive. Our employers were fearful.

I made some friends working as administrative officers in the same ministry.

One of them was Hugh Savage who was recruited to set up Singapore's first tourism office. I worked closely with Hugh, as I was an assistant secretary then and working files sent to the Ministry came to me first. Hugh had been editor of the Malayan Tribune. He had also been a member of the high-powered Malayanisation Commission in Singapore.

Hugh and I kept in touch over the years. When I was working in Kuala Lumpur at the University of Malaya in Pantai Valley, Hugh would visit me from time to time, bringing with him his favourite roast duck from Kuala Lumpur for a meal together with my family. Incidentally, Professor Victor Savage of the National University of Singapore is his son whom I had the privilege of recruiting when I was dean of the University several decades later.

Another officer with whom I developed a close friendship was S Ramdas who went on to become a lawyer. He went to England to study law during the time when I was at Oxford and we would meet up often.

During our days at the ministry, he invited me to his house several times for South Indian curry and on several occasions, I met S Jayakumar, his kid brother, who later became our distinguished foreign minister and deputy prime minister. Ram took his brother to visit me at Oxford. At that time, Jayakumar was a law student and honorary secretary-general of the Students' Union.

There was also Harry Chan Keng Howe, who rose to prominence in the Civil Service holding various important appointments including ambassador to Cambodia and Egypt and high commissioner in New Zealand. Harry revisited the United Kingdom when I was there and I would take him to revisit Stratford-upon-Avon,

Shakespeare's birthplace. I also purposefully went to town to buy crumpets, which he liked, for him.

When we were at the ministry, all three of us — Harry, Ramdas and I — were asked to accompany OHR Beadles, who was the deputy secretary to Kuala Lumpur for an ECAFE meeting. We were to be part of the Singapore/British Borneo delegation together with representatives from Sarawak and British North Borneo.

This was in 1957 and the Federation of Malaya had just become independent with the much-loved Tunku Abdul Rahman as founding prime minister.

Hotels were scarce then in Kuala Lumpur, so we had to share accommodation. We were there for three weeks. We were put up in the historic colonial Station Hotel. My room-mate was Mustapha bin Harun who was to become the first governor and later chief minister of Sabah (the new name for British North Borneo) when the Federation of Malaysia was formed in 1963. Harry and Ram shared a room whereas Beadles, as a Briton, had his own room elsewhere. In the Federation of Malaya as well as in Singapore, Caucasians were to enjoy privileges denied to locals during the time of the Colonial administration.

I remember a British lady complaining about how when she went to the Anglican church in the Padang (now called Merdeka Square) in Kuala Lumpur, she was refused entry to the church just because her accompanying husband was a local Chinese.

In between our meetings we would all play canasta. Once, Mustapha invited me to go with him to a *joget* nightclub. I declined as I could not dance but he said I would be able to pick up the steps just by watching him. He was a good dancer and no, I was unable to follow his steps!

Mustapha told me that the Tunku had asked him whether he wanted to be in politics. Although he was keen because he felt he should contribute to his state, he felt that he was constrained because he did not speak English well. Six years later, Malaysia was formed, and he served as the first Chief Minister of Sabah.

Once coming back from a trip to Japan, I decided to pay the newly titled Tun Mustapha a courtesy call and wrote him in advance of my intention. I was surprised to find a car waiting for me at Sabah's airport to pick me up. We had tea and Mustapha asked about Harry Chan and Ramdas. He chided me for still being an academic. He said: "Why not come to Sabah? You can help me in my correspondence in English and I can give you land to develop."

I declined, saying that I would have no clue on how to develop it — the land would probably turn into *sawah* (marshland)! He retorted that academia was dull to which I added "and poor too".

I noticed a map in his office which showed part of the Philippines as belonging to Sabah. When I pointed this out he said he hoped to claim back these parts someday. They belonged to his ancestors.

Years later, friends said that I should have accepted his offer. But I know my limitations.

Alas, I guessed I was destined to be rich only in learning and scholarship were I to succeed in academia. Malcolm Forbes has been reported to have said, "The biggest mistake people make in life is not trying to make a living at doing what they most enjoy." I have enjoyed my life as an academician.

5.1. At a retreat for Southeast Asian economists organised by the International Economic Association held in Singapore c. 1957. Front row on the far left with a tie is my old professor at the University of Malaya, Professor Thomas Silcock. On the extreme right is Professor Harry Johnson from the London School of Economics and the University of Chicago. Professor Johnson was the external examiner at the University of Malaya. I am in the second row, third from the right — a young economist in the Singapore Administrative Service.

5.2. Induction training of Division One civil servants c. 1955. I am seated in the front row, third from right. Standing third from left is my Anglo-Chinese School (Malacca) classmate, Tong Teck Eng. He died most unfortunately very young in an accident at home. Standing, second from right, is Pang Tee Pow. He was my university roommate. He later became the first Permanent Secretary of the Ministry of Defence.

5.3. The famous economist, Dr Frederic Benham, congratulating me at my wedding reception at Robinsons, Singapore. Dr Benham wrote the seminal book on the national income of Malaya; he was also the pioneer in compiling the first national income of Singapore. Dr Benham was the head of the Economic Advisory Unit to the Singapore government around 1956–57. He was one of the key figures who inspired me to take up economics as my life-long profession and passion.

CHAPTER 6

FAREWELL TO THE CIVIL SERVICE

Minimum Standards Committee

Before Sir Sydney Caine left, many meetings were conducted to map out concrete plans for the comprehensive development of Singapore for the next four years — a kind of unannounced four-year plan.

These included the reclamation of Singapore River, containing the floods in Kallang Basin, the rejuvenation of Kallang Basin itself, and all kinds of flood-prevention and flood-relief projects across Singapore. Most of the people involved in the proposed development project were engineers from the Public Utilities Board. All were British, except me, the least capable and youngest local member.

When Sir Sydney, Mr Wilson and I returned to our office, which was just next to the Chief Minister's Office in the same building, Wilson told Sir Sydney that they would not be around to witness the implementation of the plan. Sydney replied, "Yes, but Lim would be here to witness the outcome."

The plan was submitted to the Lim Yew Hock government but, as far as I know, it came to nought.

Another committee set up by the Economics Advisory Unit that scored some success was the Minimum Standards Committee. It was chaired by Sydney himself; Wilson was secretary and I was assistant secretary. Another member was S Rajaratnam, then a left-of-centre journalist who later became Singapore's Minister for Culture and, later still, the most distinguished Minister for Foreign Affairs and Deputy Prime Minister.

The committee looked at the minimum standards of living and how these could be met although no minimum wage was recommended. However, it submitted a report endorsing the setting up of a Central Provident Fund (CPF), which was established in July 1955, as a compulsory savings scheme to allow workers to save for their retirement. This was at a time when many people were struggling to survive. It was a sobering experience being part of the committee and it probably influenced me in my conviction in later years that one cannot leave behind important sections of people in the name of progress. At age 23, I was by far the youngest member. I merely sat there silently but attentively, without the will or ability to participate in the deliberations.

First meeting abroad

Working in the civil service presented me the opportunity to visit foreign lands. The first was in 1958 to Thailand where an ECAFE (Economic Commission for Asia and the Far East) trade meeting was to be held in Bangkok.

I went there as secretary to the Singapore delegation. Among the delegates was Mr Tan Siak Kew, President of the Singapore Chinese Chamber of Commerce, who was advisor to the committee. He was a prominent member of the Teochew community in Singapore and had many links to Thailand, thanks to his business dealings with Teochew rice-millers there.

My superior, Mr OHR Beadles, who was the Director of the Trade Division at the Ministry of Commerce and Industry, was there too. The meeting was just after the Federation of Malaya was granted independence in 1957.

I was very impressed with my first glimpse of Bangkok. It had posh hotels like Erawan where we stayed and we travelled everywhere in air-conditioned cars. That was the first time I came across air-conditioned cars.

That visit opened my eyes to the economic and social backwardness of Singapore then — unbelievably so.

Today, however, the picture is different. Singapore is now so well-developed having undergone a complete transformation especially where the architectural and economic landscapes are concerned.

In Bangkok, we were taken on a tour of the city's attractions by Mr Tan Siak Kew's contacts. We sailed on the Chao Phraya River and toured the Botanic Gardens which were more impressive than ours. They also introduced us to the city's business elite. Among them was Dr Puey Ungphakorn, the Governor of the Central Bank of Thailand.

Little did I know that, decades later, I would be the public orator during his conferment of an honorary doctorate from the University of Singapore. The honorary degree recognised Dr Puey's contributions to the development of Thailand and the regional development of Southeast Asia.

On my visit, Bangkok seemed to be more developed than Singapore was in so many ways. The Thais also spoke well and were confident of themselves in international meetings. While ferrying us around and during mealtimes, I got to know Mr Tan well and developed enormous respect for him. He was a gentleman and we discussed on a variety of issues from education and society at large to the gap between Singapore's and Bangkok's development.

He was kind of a mentor to me. When I was asked to write a speech for Beadles to deliver at the ECAFE meet, I showed it to Tan first. He was supportive. Beadles, on the other hand, was disappointed with my draft, as he felt I was touching on policy changes which were outside the purview of our mission.

He said that we were taking part in the ECAFE meeting as a colony. As such, it was out of his reach to be propounding solutions for a better world. He said that as a civil servant, he was expected to talk about the need to support free trade and how this allowed us to survive. So, I had to tweak the speech accordingly. As an aside, decades later, the ECAFE appointed me as its Senior Economic Advisor. I contributed little to this appointment, as nearly all my time was taken up as Head of the huge Economics Department of NUS (National University of Singapore).

For all our meetings, we were ferried around individually in separate chauffeured cars and Beadles wondered whether we should accept such hospitality. Tan Siak Yew told us not to worry, as he had accorded the Thais the same treatment when they visited Singapore.

In May 1966, nine months after Singapore's independence, Tan Siak Yew was appointed ambassador to Thailand — the first of our pioneer ambassadors. He served well and without pay. But he had to deal with a very tight-fisted Ministry of Finance which would question all requests for expenses "to the point of absurdity," as former president SR Nathan noted in his memoirs. So when he managed to finally secure suitable premises for a permanent embassy for Singapore, instead of dealing with the Ministry of Finance, he decided to take care of all the entire furnishing of the embassy himself. He never asked to be paid back. He was a remarkable man; one of our most respected and well-loved pioneer Singaporeans.

Second overseas mission

My second departure from Singapore was again in connection with ECAFE. This was in 1959 when another meeting was scheduled to be held in Broadbeach on the Gold Coast of Queensland in Australia. As in Bangkok, I was amazed by the development I saw in Queensland. We stayed at The Hilton; we had no such deluxe hotels in Singapore then.

Two things I remember from that visit: We had as part of our delegation some representatives from Sarawak and British North Borneo as Sabah was called then. One of them was a Haji Mohammad Sulaiman. His name was registered as HM

Sulaiman and when we arrived, the Australians were calling him His Majesty. He told me to keep it up. The Australians were not so exposed to Asia in those days.

I said I would, except that if he was HM, I would be thought of as his staff! He promised to buy me lunch if I acted along; we spoke in Malay. He was being naughty and playful.

There was a Chinese restaurant near a river in the area of Broadbeach where all the Asian delegations would flock to. Our delegation too decided to go there for dinner. I met the cook and noted that he and his assistant were Hainanese, so I spoke to them in Hainanese. They knew Singapore well, having lived there before. They were sailors who were marooned when they were shipwrecked on the way to Australia. They ended up living in Queensland for the past 20 years. They spoke nostalgically of places they knew such as Beach Road and Middle Road and of people they knew.

They were grateful, they said, to have met a fellow Hainanese and speak in their dialect. They flatly refused to bill me my dinner when the time came to pay for our meal much to the amusement of the rest of the Singapore delegation.

Fond memories of Civil Service days

Although I was keen to leave the Civil Service in pursuit of my goal to obtain a PhD to eventually join academia, it was a painful decision to make, as I had very fond memories of my working life spent in the service and the people that I had met.

In any British town, High Street is the centre of town and it was no exception in Singapore in colonial times. High Street was an important place for me. Located here was the Polar Café, famous for its curry puffs; it was where my wife and I would rendezvous as we would meet here almost daily after work.

There was also another café along High Street, the GH Café, nearer the Singapore River, where civil servants liked to go for lunch. Tay Seow Hwa invited me for lunch there. We were undergraduates together, but he was one year my junior. He sought my advice on whether to join the Administrative Service or the Police Force. I said he would do well in both. He chose the Administrative Service and was years later a permanent secretary.

But, alas, High Street as I knew it then has gone today, taking along with it some of my fondest memories there. But, thank goodness, Balestier Road, another one of my other stomping grounds, remains.

After graduating, I stayed with seven others on Balestier Road in a flat above the Rose Dispensary. Most of us were from 'upcountry' and working in the Civil Service.

We would indulge in the neighbourhood's eateries famous for dishes such as *char kway teow*, chicken rice and *satay*, which I believe are still there today.

Sometimes, we would drive to Johor for dinner. It was easy in those days as no travel documents were needed. We went in our own cars. If you had a car then, your prestige in the eyes of others would go up.

I had a two-tone Ford Prefect; Paul Wilson had a Morris Minor. Among my Civil Service friends were Francis d'Costa, who had a First Class honours degree in Mathematics, and who later became an important civil servant; another was TS Sinnathuray, a lawyer, who later became a High Court judge. Incidentally, it was Sinnathuray's brother who delivered my second son Ron in the University Hospital in Kuala Lumpur in 1968; soon after, we moved back to Singapore.

In our flat at Balestier Road, sometimes we played mind games, card games such as open and closed poker and canasta.

I became a bit of an expert in closed poker. Whoever won would pay for dinner. It was a bit tricky as you do not know your opponents' cards so you have to call their bluff and play along with it yourself. I was good at this and would thus often end up paying for dinner but I didn't mind.

As a result of my constantly winning, some of my friends decided I should play for them but as I found out, it is not easy playing for others. I ended up exceeding the limits imposed by my friends as to how much they would be willing to lose. In closed poker, if your opponents know your limits, that would be a liability. After that, I decided never to play poker for anyone. It also led to my unwillingness to invest money for others in later years, including for my relatives. However, I turned out to be a successful investor, and was in high demand to give advice or help out in management.

I too had the privilege of working with SR Nathan who was in charge of the welfare of Singapore's seamen. According to the protocol of that time, he would route his correspondence to the Permanent Secretary through me. I was learning in the process. Mr Nathan later became Singapore's very distinguished sixth President.

My role as peacekeeper

In our transition from colonial rule to self-government, the tide carried with it anti-British sentiment among parts of the population.

One day, as I was riding pillion on the scooter of a friend from Balestier Road on the way to Orchard Road, we saw a well-built drunken English man being beaten up by a group of about 10 people who were shouting "Pah! Pah!" (Beat, beat). The man fell to the floor. They stepped on him repeatedly.

It was frightening to witness this. Growing up in Malacca, my father had warned me against getting involved in such situations. But when I saw the beating, I instinctively got my friend to stop the scooter and I ran towards the crowd. Shouting confidently in Mandarin and Hokkien, I told them to stop immediately before I called for the police. Thank goodness, the crowd dispersed. I was glad I summed up enough courage to stop the continued beating. I was pleasantly surprised that the crowd heeded my warning. My friend marvelled at my courage, or was it foolhardiness, I wondered?

On another occasion, I was walking from my Empress Place office on my way to lunch. I witnessed a taxi driver accusing a Caucasian woman of refusing to pay her fare. She in turn said she could not because she had discovered that she did not have her wallet with her.

After finding out that the fare was $6, I paid the cab driver who grumbled about the woman being a cheat. The woman in turn asked for my name and address so that she could repay me the fare. I pointed out my office. Although I did not expect it, she turned up two days later with the money. She was English, probably a housewife.

I remember another incident that happened when my friends from Balestier Road and I were celebrating Chinese New Year at a seafood restaurant in Ponggol, which was a popular place for alfresco dining by the sea. The string of restaurants there has long gone.

Most of us did not return to the Federation to celebrate the festival back home then. Apart from wanting to avoid the long journey, we had started to take deeper roots in Singapore.

In those days, it was a tradition to light up firecrackers to create a festive mood. You would hold a firecracker in one hand and use the other hand to light it with a match. When it started sizzling, you would throw the firecracker at random and it would explode with a loud bang.

At dinner that night in Ponggol, I noticed a group of local soldiers at one table. At another table were some New Zealand soldiers who were stationed in Singapore then.

One of the local soldiers fired a cracker which landed in the soup bowl of a New Zealander. A noisy quarrel erupted. One of my friends suggested that we should move away but I went over perhaps out of indiscretion; how I got the courage or foolhardiness to interfere, I do not know. I was still a young and idealistic man then.

The New Zealand soldiers were cross that the local soldiers had ruined their night and the enjoyment of their meal for which they insisted that the latter should pay.

They were asking for $80, which was the price of the whole meal; the locals refused to pay the full amount, saying they were willing to pay only half of it.

I thought well, if it was just a matter of paying the bill and having everyone forget the whole affair, I told the New Zealanders that I would foot the other half of the bill. The matter got settled, just like that.

Among us was a local journalist called Paul Makinden who was impressed by what had unfolded. He said to me, "Chong Yah, you are a good Samaritan. Can I report this to The Straits Times?" I replied, "No, Paul," not wishing to be in the limelight. I had just started life as a civil servant.

After that incident, I somehow developed a little ability to settle some testy situations. I was not always successful though.

A lesson in monetary economics

Back at Balestier Road, my room-mate, Chong Kwee Hin, who was working in the Prudential Insurance Company as an insurance agent sold me an endowment policy. It cost $15,000, which was a large sum of money as my pay as a civil servant then was only $400 per month. I was told that I could pay in instalments and that this could be viewed as a savings plan. The CPF scheme was not well developed then so I decided to take up the policy. It would mature 30 years later when I would be 53. I was then 23. The retirement age was then 55.

Looking back, it was a gross error to have taken up the policy as it was not inflation-proof. All it needs to wipe out any savings made is inflation. The value of money does not remain the same as it deteriorates over time because of inflation.

On hindsight, I should have taken out a life insurance policy and not an endowment plan which was like a savings policy. As I was to discover later, money can deteriorate in value with persistent inflation. That, in fact, is one of the weaknesses of our CPF system; its annuities are not inflation-indexed.

I couldn't forgive myself for buying the endowment policy as I had studied economics; I should have known better. Truly, when I received back my money 30 years later, its value had eroded a great deal. Luckily, I did not have to depend on it for retirement.

My obsession from civil service times

As a civil servant, I began to develop a deep interest in macroeconomics. This was thanks to my postings in various parts of the Civil Service which gave me a bird's eye view of the economy and society.

One of the side-line assignments given to me as an administrative officer concerned the 1957 census of population. I was appointed assistant superintendent for the census.

My task was to train supervisors and enumerators who would go from house to house to fill up questionnaires. The enumerators were mostly schoolteachers while the supervisors were the principals of schools who were all much older than I was.

As some neighbourhoods were considered dangerous — Bukit Ho Swee and Sago Lane, for instance — I had to make sure that women enumerators were not sent there. What's more, to ensure safety for all census takers, we made sure that they went in pairs and that in dodgy neighbourhoods at least one of the enumerators had to be a male. No male chauvinism was implied. "Safety first" was the guide.

In those days, gangsterism was rife and thugs were a menace in certain neighbourhoods. Poverty was prevalent and slums ubiquitous.

When people suffer from poverty and deprivation, they do not display the welcome mat. Things have improved a great deal in Singapore since then as more people are now much better off and better educated.

Another side-line job that may come as a surprise was that I was appointed an election officer in the Tiong Bahru by-election in 1957. In those days, the number of Indian voters outnumbered Chinese voters as many among the Chinese population were not citizens. The Indians were British subjects and had automatic voting rights. I came from Malacca and had the right to vote as a British subject.

I was also asked to serve on various staff selection committees to interview recruits for all kinds of jobs in the Civil Service. At times I thought diminishing returns would set in for me with more of such assignments.

One exception I can remember well though. Years later when Professor Ruth Wong was tasked to upgrade the Teachers' Training College to a full-fledged degree-awarding institution, she got me to serve as a member of her three-person selection committee for academic staff. It was also time-consuming but I forgot about diminishing returns.

In later years, when I started work at the Nanyang Technological University (NTU), I was sometimes asked to be part of various selection boards. To the annoyance of some of my new colleagues I at times declined to do so. I felt that unless it was a selection board for deans or full professors, I would do it but not for positions as clerks, secretaries or lecturers. I had become too old to do things I had done decades ago in the Civil Service. A few newcomers were most unhappy with my behaviour. I understand their unhappiness. They were new and young foreign academics who did care about our individual working backgrounds.

While I was still a civil servant, I was working part-time as an examiner for A-level students. It was Professor Tom Silcock who got me onto this. He used to come to my house at Jalan Chengkek with papers for me to mark for A-level economics. He was a coordinator for Cambridge University on this. That was in 1958–59.

Professor Silcock also appointed me as a part-time tutor to supervise the theses written by the university's honour year undergraduates. At one time I was supervising the theses of 13 of them.

I can still remember distinctively a most outstanding thesis written by Ngiam Tong Dow who would later become one of Singapore's most prominent permanent secretaries.

First meeting with Goh Keng Swee

The People's Action Party (PAP) came into power in June 1959 and formed the next government headed by Mr Lee Kuan Yew. I was to leave the Civil Service three months later in September. Dr Goh Keng Swee was appointed the first Minister of Finance in a self-governing Singapore. The Ministry of Commerce and Industry was subsumed under the newly created Ministry of Finance.

One day soon after his appointment, I received a call from Dr Goh to go to his office to discuss some important matters. The direct call was rather unusual, as I was quite junior and the summons to see him should have gone through my permanent secretary or deputy secretary according to protocol. Dr Goh, however, was not someone who cared for procedures of this nature.

I did not think it discreet to report to my superiors either, so I made my way to Dr Goh's office. There was someone else there — Devan Nair, a trade unionist who had been jailed by the British and had just been released when the PAP came into power. He had just been appointed as Dr Goh's political secretary.

Dr Goh said that the purpose of the meeting was to brainstorm and explore other lines of action other than industrialisation to develop Singapore's economy. On industrialisation, his mind was already made up.

I remember mentioning the possibility of developing tourism. He laughed, "Do you know who would come here? Drunken sailors! We have instability, disorder, poverty, who would come?"

I mentioned I read a report by a Canadian consultant advocating the promotion of tourism. This consultant felt the potential for tourism was there especially among Americans who were keen to visit the exotic East.

Dr Goh was adamant against the idea so we went on to discuss other possibilities.

Several years later, when I was living in Kuala Lumpur and teaching at the University of Malaya at Pantai Valley, I was told by friends in the Civil Service that Dr Goh had changed his mind regarding tourism.

He saw the need to develop some attractions to bring in tourists. He was not sure of having a zoo as many animals like elephants have voracious appetites whereas an aviary would make more economic sense as birds do not eat that much. So it was not surprising that Jurong Bird Park was established two years earlier in 1971 before the Singapore Zoo was opened.

This anecdote illustrates Dr Goh's firm belief in championing causes. If he thought a cause was good and if he could find the right person to do it, he would go all out for it.

Lee Kuan Yew's personal touch

When he became prime minister, Mr Lee Kuan Yew took an unusual step.

He visited every ministry to get to grips with what it was doing. When he came to our ministry, we briefed him on our work. He spent time talking to us. I remember talking about the need to outlaw strikes, which were very rampant then, to make life less disruptive. He responded by saying it was difficult to outlaw strikes.

It was a shrewd move on the part of the prime minister then to visit the Civil Service as he wanted to direct the machinery that would be implementing government policy to ensure an effective government.

Joining academia in Kuala Lumpur

In 1959, the local newspapers gave full coverage of the moving of factories making items like soap, paint and joss sticks from Singapore to Petaling Jaya. The headline screamed: "They marched with their feet". Indeed, The Straits Times too moved to Kuala Lumpur. So did the other Singapore-based newspapers: Nanyang Siang Pau, Sin Chew Jit Poh, Utusan Malaysia and the Malay Mail.

As it so happened, I too moved to Kuala Lumpur.

I was asked by many if I had done so "because you did not like PAP rule?" I said no. I was not anti-PAP. On the contrary, I had great admiration for the stalwarts of the ruling political party: Lee Kuan Yew, Toh Chin Chye, Goh Keng Swee and S Rajaratnam. They might have been extreme sometimes in their actions but they were very able people. These were men of integrity. They were serving the country.

I left simply because I could not get a job in the University of Malaya in Singapore because I was not qualified, possessing only a BA honours degree. I did not have the required master's degree or PhD. Besides, I had no publications to my name. And I wanted to be an academic. Kuala Lumpur gave me this opportunity.

In Singapore, I had been accepted as a part-time teacher and tutor but was not considered part of the university establishment.

At the same time, the newly established University of Malaya at Pantai Valley was recruiting lecturers and it was casting its net among locals. That gave me the glimmer of hope that I could join the university as an assistant lecturer and work towards obtaining at least a master's degree once there.

I was encouraged by Professor Silcock who had been appointed acting head of its economics department to join. There were other locals working in Singapore who moved to Kuala Lumpur at about the same time as I did: Ungku Abdul Aziz, Yip Yat Hoon, Siew Nim Chee, and Hamzah Sendut, to name some familiar names to me. Wang Gungwu too moved to Kuala Lumpur. They all went to help set up the branch of the University of Malaya there.

That was the real reason for my resignation from the Civil Service and my move back to the Federation. I felt also at that time that the Civil Service in Singapore lacked meritocracy as it only recognised seniority when making promotions. I felt this made it uncompetitive and it held no challenge for me.

After my resignation from the Civil Service, I left for the newly formed University of Malaya at Pantai Valley. I was to be at the university till 1969 when I returned to Singapore. There was a job vacancy in Singapore in that year following the early and unexpected death of one of my professors, Professor Lim Tay Boh.

When I left both my jobs it was with much sadness but at the same time there was a good challenge ahead. I was still in the same old British Malaya, except that they were no longer one country.

CHAPTER 7

MY DAYS IN KUALA LUMPUR AND OXFORD

Joining new department of economics

With great reluctance, I resigned from the prestigious Singapore Administrative Service in 1959. I had been placed on the pensionable establishment a year earlier and so had to forego all pension benefits associated with the post.

Worse was the thought of whether I should let Dr Goh Keng Swee know. I feared that if I did, he would have stopped me from joining the University of Malaya despite the fact that this new campus just outside Kuala Lumpur was modelled after the University of Malaya in Singapore as a branch of the university.

The University of Malaya had grown rapidly since its inception and it was decided that a separate division be set up to cater to the burgeoning number of students from Peninsular Malaya. So on 15 January 1959, a new University of Malaya at Pantai Valley was set up to supplement the University of Malaya in Singapore.

Both campuses would have a common vice-chancellor, Sir Alexander Oppenheim, a well-known mathematician, although later, he based himself at Kuala Lumpur in the Pantai Valley campus.

Most of the teaching staff were drawn from the Singapore campus although each university would have its own principal. Heading the Pantai Valley campus was Professor Mason, who was the Dean of Education and Professor of Education at the University of Malaya in Singapore.

When the Department of Economics in Kuala Lumpur started in 1959, it was part of the Faculty of Arts. It only had 14 students and three full-time academic staff. I was one of them. But when I arrived to take up my appointment, I felt naked academically. I did not have a higher degree unlike most of the university staff from Singapore or those who had been appointed directly. Among them were very well-qualified academics from Ceylon (now Sri Lanka), most of whom were Tamils and were escaping political persecution in their country.

So my immediate preoccupations were to register to get a master's degree and to get some articles published, considered *de rigueur* as part of an academic's portfolio.

In 1961, legislation was passed to change the status of the two divisions into that of a national university each. So on 1 January 1962, the University of Malaya came into its own while the one at Bukit Timah was renamed the University of Singapore. At that time, I thought to myself: The child has taken over the mother's name.

The head of the Economics Department at the Kuala Lumpur campus was a local, the very capable Professor Ungku Aziz, who had clinched the post amid stiff competition from other candidates including Professor Tom Silcock, who was Ungku Aziz's boss in Singapore and the very person who had invited me to go to Kuala Lumpur.

However, most of the academic staff were not surprised that Professor Ungku Aziz got the appointment. For one thing, he was an outstanding candidate. For another, there was a lot of nationalism then and the authorities naturally had preference for a local. Under Professor Ungku Aziz, the department expanded to become a faculty in its own right when it was made the Faculty of Economics and Administration in 1966. The change in name was to reflect the faculty's focus on equipping its graduates to meet the demands of the rapidly growing business world. Today, the faculty is a flourishing academic community with over a thousand students and some 60 academic staff.

I put my shoulder to the wheel to get my MA (Master of Arts) degree as soon as possible doing this while handling a full load in teaching as an assistant lecturer. According to tradition, all masters' candidates had to have external examiners to examine their work and Professor Ungku Aziz showed his strong preference for Asian scholars when he appointed Dr KN Raj as one of my external examiners.

Dr Raj was one of India's foremost economists and a renowned agriculturist. I was not supposed to know about his report but in some social gatherings, of which there were many in our department, I was told that Dr Raj considered my thesis worthy of a doctorate but since I had submitted it for my master's degree, I was awarded accordingly. Sure, I may have missed out on the ultimate prize I had been gunning for but I was just happy then to have finally gotten my MA.

Threatened by thugs

As part of my research contributions in economics, I published several papers which were submitted to the Malayan Economic Review based in Singapore and edited by Professor You Poh Seng of the University of Singapore's Department of Economics. I had done this upon the advice of Professor Ungku Aziz to support local academic journals rather than submit the papers to overseas journals.

One of the articles that I wrote concerned the rubber replanting cess or rubber replanting tax. There were two funds: Fund A for owners of big rubber estates and Fund B for smallholders.

The Funds, introduced by the Rubber Industry (Replanting) Board from 1952 to 1972, were to encourage the replanting of rubber trees. Bigger grants were given to Fund B comprising smallholders while larger rubber estate owners were eligible for smaller grants under Fund A. However, I noticed that there were more applications for Fund B than for Fund A and that most of the Fund B applications actually came from the large rubber estate owners who subdivided their land into smaller plots to qualify for the more generous grants. I highlighted the need of the government to pay attention to this anomaly.

The Chinese newspapers in Malaya, which had always had a free hand in publishing matters on economics and politics, serialised my articles. As a result, a few days after that, I had four persons turning up in my office in the Department of Economics, unsolicited.

In those days, it was easy to gain access to an academic's room unlike today where security is fairly tight.

Luckily, I had the habit of getting visitors to jot down their names and addresses in a log book as soon as they entered.

I ushered my visitors into my room wondering what they wanted to see me about. It was not a social call. I soon realised that they were thugs sent by others to intimidate me. Speaking in Mandarin, they told me that if I were to continue publishing articles similar to the ones I wrote about rubber replanting, I had to watch out for my family's safety. They left as abruptly as they had come.

I was shaken, and for a week, my family and I did not venture out to watch movies as we were wont to do since that was our only form of entertainment in those days when there was no television or other forms of distraction.

But feeling very stifled confined to our home, I decided to see Raja Mohar, the permanent secretary of the Ministry of Commerce and Industry, a well-liked and well-respected civil servant. He was co-supervisor for my MA thesis. I told him what had happened. He was sympathetic and after I had given him a description of the four men and their names and addresses as recorded in my visitors' book, he advised me not to fret and encouraged me to resume my usual routine.

Two weeks later, I met one of the four thugs who said he had assured the CID (Criminal Investigation Department) man who had paid him a visit that I was no longer on their radar screen. He explained to me that he was simply delivering a message for which he and his comrades had been hired; who the person was he did not divulge. I did not care to find out who the culprit was. I was just grateful for Raja Mohar's timely intervention and thankful of living in a society where law and order was able to prevail.

Confrontation with department head

At the time of my thesis submission for a master's degree, our campus received a visit from Professor Leslie Wang of the University of British Columbia (UBC) in Canada who had arrived to investigate the possibility of establishing a business school in Malaya with a branch each in Kuala Lumpur and Singapore.

Professor Ungku Aziz assigned me to take care of Professor Wang including arranging meetings with likely stakeholders such as the Chinese, Malay and International Chambers of Commerce as well as the editors of the national newspapers.

At the conclusion of his visit, Professor Wang confided in me that he would recommend the setting up of a school for business administration in Kuala Lumpur. Graduates of this school could then go on to UBC to earn a master's degree. At his farewell dinner, Professor Wang invited me to go to UBC under this programme and on my return head the business school.

I declined his invitation explaining that I already had a master's degree and asked if he could instead arrange for me to go for a PhD course.

Professor Wang kept his word and I soon received an invitation with a scholarship to study business administration for a PhD degree at the University of Toronto. I approached Professor Ungku Aziz to seek his permission to take up the doctorate programme.

He told me I could not be spared as he needed me to continue teaching for another year, adding that perhaps I should go to England instead, to the University of Oxford which he could arrange as he knew people there. That sounded attractive so I accepted his offer despite the one-year delay.

However, I later found out that the Professor had sent someone else, a Ronald Mah to UBC in my place and that he would take over the business school upon his return. Mah was an expatriate lecturer from Hong Kong. I also found out that Professor Ungku Aziz had known Mah when Mah was teaching in the Singapore Polytechnic. Ungku had managed to entice Mah to Kuala Lumpur to teach with the promise that he would one day be sent overseas to do a Master's in Business Administration. Mah was an accountant.

I was upset and in my imprudence and impertinence I questioned Professor Ungku Aziz on his decision to send Mah, an expat, to UBC when, as I had pointed out to him, the agreement signed with Leslie Wang of UBC was that only locals would be sent.

The professor was taken aback that one of his mentees would dare question him while news of my "confrontation" soon spread through the campus. I regretted not only that I had too much nationalism in my blood but also the imprudence and impertinence of questioning the decision of my own boss.

Despite this episode, the good professor turned out to be truly magnanimous at one of the most important junctures of my life. The year was 1962 when I spotted a government advertisement for PhD scholarships under the British Commonwealth Scholarship programme to Britain and applied. I was already on the permanent staff of the University of Malaya, having served three years as an assistant lecturer.

I had to appear before the selection committee for an interview. The chairman was Hamdan bin Sheikh Tahir, who was then the Senior Assistant Secretary of the Department of Scholarships and Training in the Ministry of Education. He would later become the sixth governor of Penang in 1989. Professor Ungku Aziz was one of the committee members.

I had known Hamdan as a "mature student" during campus days. He had also stayed at the Dunearn Road Hostels and I remember him asking me for advice on how to cope with exams when he had first arrived.

After the interview, Hamdan came out of the room to speak with me briefly saying that he would make sure that I would be given the scholarship to go to Oxford as I had received the support of all the committee members. But he added, "Your department doesn't seem to be happy with you going." Apparently, what transpired was that if I had gotten the scholarship, I would be leaving the economics department in September and would not be around to mark my students' examination scripts at the end of the academic year.

Letting bygones be bygones

As it turned out, the department finally relented to let me take up the scholarship when Professor Ungku Aziz stepped in to say that he would mark the exam scripts on my behalf. It was a relief and I was grateful to Professor Ungku Aziz for his kindness. He had not let my outburst affect him.

It was soon time to take leave of friends and colleagues through the usual round of farewell parties.

One of the most unforgettable was a dinner hosted by Professor Ungku Aziz and Mrs Aziz at their home. My wife and I brought along Fern, our four-year-old daughter and our two-year-old son Wun, who would be accompanying us to Oxford. At the dinner was the Professor's daughter, Zeti, who was then in her early teens. She would later become the most outstanding Governor of the Central Bank of Malaysia. The Professor's wife gave our children toys to bring with them on the trip.

Another turning point

The British Commonwealth Scholarship was for an initial two years, renewable for another two years depending on the University of Oxford and my employer, the University of Malaya.

It provided an allowance for my wife and children and healthcare was free. So in September 1962, my family and I flew on BOAC (the forerunner of British Airways) to London and made our way from there by train to Oxford.

At the university, I was told not to expect too much regarding the choice of supervisor for my work so imagine my surprise when I found out that my supervisor would be none other than John Richard Hicks, a prominent economist who would become a Nobel Laureate in later years. His appointment as my supervisor was to spark off, for me, a deep and lifelong relationship with Professor Hicks and his very able wife, Lady Ursula Hicks, also an economist, an expert on public finance who also became my *de facto* mentor.

Although Professor Hicks' appointment as my supervisor turned out to be the second most important turning point in my life, there was nothing at our initial meeting that hinted of this.

It was a gloomy winter's day when I turned up to meet Professor Hicks for the first time. It was cold and although our appointment was at 4 pm, the sky was already pitch dark outside.

We were in the Wharton room at All Souls College. This residential college for senior professors was also an intellectual centre where some of Britain's top academics, including the likes of Sir Isaiah Berlin, the great philosopher, resided.

Professor Hicks' books were widely used throughout the British Empire and I had read some of them including those on social framework, theory of trade cycle and theory of wages. He seemed impressed by my knowledge.

The purpose of our meeting was to consider what I wanted to study.

I told Professor Hicks that I was interested in doing course work which would allow me to register for a B Phil degree that could be converted into a D Phil.

However, he disagreed; in his view, the B Phil was meant for youngsters fresh from university. Since I was a mature student, I would fare better to do a D Phil thesis and bypass B Phil.

"You study what others have written and sit for exams," he said of the B Phil course. The D Phil thesis would be more suitable as I had been teaching several courses as an assistant lecturer and was promoted to a full lectureship. Besides, I had had several academic articles to my credit.

He suggested that I should do my thesis on the economic development of Malaya as this would be of use when I returned home.

I was to submit to him a paper on the subject every two to three weeks for discussion. This went on for one-and-a-half years. At that time, it seemed like an endless slog.

One day, when my two-year scholarship was due to end, I approached him for help in extending it for another two years.

He was puzzled, asking, "Why do you need to extend your stay when you have more or less written your thesis?"

But they were only background papers, I reminded him.

"Put them all together in one volume and send it to the board of examiners. I am pretty sure they would award you with a D Phil."

That sounded easy enough and in a month's time I submitted my thesis to Professor Hicks who forwarded it to the examination board. In Oxford, the supervisor was and still is not an examiner. (Later, I introduced this practice to the University of Singapore.)

Later, I had to sit for the *viva voce* (oral examination). The three members of the examination board were present. The purpose of the oral exam was to allow the examiners to probe further into my written work. I must have done well as I was told I would be awarded a D Phil.

Fast forward to 20 years later. I was back at All Souls College when I was on sabbatical leave from the University of Singapore, where I was dean of the economics department.

Professor Hicks had retired by then. He had also been knighted and had won a Nobel Prize in economics — the first in Britain.

It was at a dinner function hosted by his successor, the first Asian to win a Nobel Prize — AK Sen — that I met Professor Hicks again. He had asked AK Sen to invite me to the dinner.

During a dinner discussion and after good wine, Professor Hicks said, nodding towards me, "This man, Lim, in my memory is the only person to be awarded a D Phil in two academic years."

Sen looked at Hicks and said, "John, you have forgotten me — I did my PhD in only six months!"

Professor Hicks was still at his best. Without missing a beat, he said, "I am talking about Oxford. He got his D Phil in Oxford, not Cambridge."

Sen was from Cambridge. There was a good laugh all round. Of course, we all in the academic world had so much respect and admiration for both Hicks and Sen.

Visit of Hicks to Asia

Years later, Professor and Lady Hicks would visit Singapore or Malaysia, depending on where I was based. In fact, it became quite a habit of theirs to escape the severe winter chill in Oxford for the warmer climes of Singapore and Malaysia.

When I was in a position to do so, I later instituted in the Nanyang Technological University, Singapore, a gold medal award for the best student in economics in their memory and in their honour.

Professor John Hicks and Lady Ursula Hicks were well-suited to each other. They both had brilliant minds but I noticed that Lady Hicks often got more attention than he did especially in the realm of public speaking. At seminars and in private, Professor Hicks was clear, lucid and even poetical. But when it came to public speaking, he would stutter. So it was difficult to get him to appear on television. Lady Ursula was the opposite; she shone in public speaking.

I remember on one occasion Lady Hicks' lecture on "Development from Below" focusing on India. She made such an impact on the audience that she was featured in the headlines of The Straits Times the next day rather than the coincidental visit of an important British minister.

You see, we have our strong points and weak points.

For their visits, I would usually arrange for their accommodation and come up with a programme of activities with some free time for themselves. On one occasion when I was head of the economics department at the University of Singapore, I got a call in the evening from one of her former students that Lady Hicks had a fall and sustained a thigh injury.

Lady Ursula was fond of meeting up with her former students; on this occasion, it was on a visit to the home of one of her former students that she had a bad fall.

The student was distraught as she refused to see a doctor. He asked if I could send a doctor to check up on her at the Garden Hotel where I had arranged for her to stay.

I rang up my personal physician who went along straightaway. He came back to say that she had fractured her thigh bone and so should immediately be checked into a hospital, adding that such a fracture was dangerous for people of her age — she was in her late 70s then. He arranged for an orthopaedic surgeon, Dr Pillay, to attend to her.

She was cheerful despite having her leg in a cast. "You want to see a strip tease?" she teased waving her leg, when my wife and I visited her.

But when the bill came, I had a shock. And I found out that the Hickses were trying to get money transferred from their bank in the United Kingdom to pay for it.

When I tried to find out why the bill was so huge, I was told that she was treated in a private hospital and in any case, since she had a title, it was presumed she would be able to pay it.

I was upset and rang our deputy vice-chancellor Reginald Quahe, impressing upon him that Lady Hicks was a guest of the university and whether he could help to get the bill reduced. He did after explaining to Dr Pillay that the Hickses were academics and not rich titled barons!

Dr Pillay decided to drop the bill altogether as a fellow academic. We did not expect this. We did not want the Hickses to pay the whole bill but we thought it would be fair to charge for something at least.

Eventually, the very capable Reggie negotiated a reasonable charge. Dr Pillay obliged. All was well that ended well.

She passed away first, several years after returning home to England. It was tough for John Hicks to be left alone, as he was so dependent on her. Later, a nurse or relative would take care of him.

The Hickses lived in Porch House. I used to visit them quite often in their old age. There, Lady Hicks whose father was a director of the Botanic Gardens in Northern Ireland, had many plants and she had gotten them from all over the world.

But even in his old age, Professor Hicks was still writing and his mind was still sharp. When I last visited him he told me about his intention to write another theory book. I remember that Monte Carlo was mentioned. He showed me the outline of his book. His spirit of endeavour and his spirit of scholarship were most impressive.

He passed away in 1989. I wrote an obituary on him in the *Singapore Economic Review.*

Back to Oxford days

Back to my student days at Oxford. They were some of the most memorable times of my life. However, initially, there were some hiccups. Because we were one month late in arriving, my wife missed the briefings held for the wives of newcomers to acquaint them with life at Oxford. The topics typically cover tips on handling the weather, coping with a different cultural environment and useful contacts with other wives.

We were given a flat to stay in on Museum Road. It belonged to St John's College and was located next to it. It was a roomy flat but it had a very old and archaic heating system. It would only work if coins were put in. Once, when my wife was bathing the children, the water turned cold as the radiator had run out of coins. So we soon learnt always to have extra coins ready. Still, it was too expensive to keep on feeding the heating system with coins. Maybe a smaller home which needed less heating might be a solution, we thought.

Move to Boars' Hill

So we got a house on Boars' Hill, 10 kilometres from Oxford. It was a two-storey terrace house, one of four. It was on Boars' Hill, I learned later, that Matthew Arnold, the 19th century poet used to roam.

Because of the distance to the university, I had to get a car, a small second-hand one. That winter was particularly cold at Boars' Hill upon which pitch darkness easily descended. Snow was everywhere, at times over a metre high.

On one occasion, all four of us in the family got sick with flu. Although our two-storey house was not very big, it was very draughty and the heating was not circulating effectively. The flu became very tough for my wife and me to handle.

As I was wont to say later, "The Lord was with us", in those days of darkness. I heard a knock on the door. It was Ying, wife of a fellow student Timothy Seow, who was studying architecture at Oxford. Ying was a nurse and she and Timothy would come to our house now and again for dinner.

She had dropped by serendipitously as she had not seen us for a while. But what providence! Seeing us in a state of stupor, she quickly telephoned a doctor to make a house call. We were given medicine. Ying dropped by the next few days to ensure we were on the mend, making tea for my wife and me and warm milk for the children. Before long, we were up and about. The world was bright and cheerful again, notwithstanding piles of snow and the immense cold outside. The white scenery became so beautiful again.

Britain was great

On another day, the electric supply went off and we had to get someone to fix it. My wife did get a workman to come who said the power failure was due to a short circuit but though he knew how to fix it, he was unable to do so because of trade union rules which specified that only electricians could fix it.

I realised then that though Britain was great, it had its rigidities. It was also reported that in some parts of England that as water was free some people would simply let their water run without any thought of the need for conservation.

I thus came to the conclusion that the state cannot give scarce things free as it would be subject to abuse. The demand curve might easily become a horizontal straight line.

On the brighter side, though, in Oxford and in much of England, an honour system that was in place was much respected. Newspapers would be left on a table in the street. If you wanted to buy the newspapers, you would simply take it and place your money there. At times, there would be quite a lot of money, mainly coins, accumulated there, unattended. But the honour system, I understand, is no longer practised. It could no longer be practised because of declining values.

In those days too, mothers could safely leave their children in prams outside the doors of supermarkets. My wife frequently did that whenever she went shopping for groceries at Marks and Spencer leaving our second daughter, who was only several months old, outside the store. Every mother did it. My wife followed suit.

The degree of social discipline since then seems to have deteriorated.

Old friends from home

While I was at Oxford, Ramdas, who was my colleague in the Civil Service, was in London reading law. He visited me in Oxford with SS Ratnam who later became a well-known gynaecologist in Singapore. He brought curry with him on every visit. Ramdas also once brought his younger brother, S Jayakumar, who was visiting him in London. Jayakumar then was reading Law as an undergraduate of the University of Malaya (in Singapore). He was then the honorary secretary-general of the University of Malaya Students' Union (UMSU).

On several occasions Ramdas brought a lady friend, Winnie, who later became his wife. She was a jovial young English woman and a livewire. At times, Winnie would take the opportunity to babysit our children. After our return to Singapore, Ramdas remained a good friend until he died. Winnie later migrated to Australia with their two children. Jayakumar later became Singapore's Minister for Foreign Affairs and Deputy Prime Minister.

Another visitor was Harry Chan Keng Howe, another of my Civil Service colleagues. The previous practice of the Civil Service was to send administrative officers to England for a year's training in Devonshire where Harry had been before. It was fortuitous that Harry came back to England during my time at Oxford. When he visited us, his first words were, "You must give me some crumpets." Of course, I made sure that he had crumpets. I drove to town to get some crumpets for him. He also asked to be taken to Stratford-upon-Avon, Shakespeare's birthplace, as he had studied English Literature at the University of Malaya. Harry had been the founding secretary of the students' economic society at the University of Malaya. He went on to have an illustrious career as a diplomat and as a permanent secretary. We still keep in touch.

First paid publication

Soon after my arrival in Oxford in late 1962, I had an unexpected visitor — Cranley Onslow, an Oxford graduate himself who was in the British Foreign Service and had a tour of duty in Burma (now Myanmar) before he returned to England to stand for elections as a Conservative Party candidate as member of parliament for Woking, a post he was to hold from 1964 to 1972.

Onslow wanted a number of Asian scholars to write on Asia's economic development for a book. He already had a publisher, Donald Moore, who was a well-known figure in Singapore.

He wanted me to write a chapter on Malaya and its economic development after World War II up to 1962.

He said he would pay me for the article. It was the first time that someone was offering to pay me to write. It was a princely sum then for a newly registered PhD student — 500 pounds sterling. I was thrilled. I felt greatly honoured. I needed the money very badly too, having four people in my family to look after as a PhD student.

But what made the prospect even more exciting was the fact that the other contributors to the book were established authors and well-known world economists. One of them was VKRV Rao, founder of the Delhi School of Economics. The other was Dr Gamani Corea, senior deputy governor of the Central Bank in Ceylon who had also been a student of John Hicks. Then there was Dr Puey Ungphakorn, governor of the Central Bank of Thailand and dean of Thammasat University's Faculty of Economics, Professor Nurul Islam, Director of the Pakistan Institute of Development Economics (later Bangladesh Institute of Development Studies) and U Tun Wai, one of Burma's most distinguished economists. I was in august company. The book was published under the title *Asian Economic Development.*

Return to Malaysia

It was 1964 when my family and I sailed home on board the *Orcades*, which is now in a museum in Melbourne.

By that time, the Federation of Malaya had become part of the Federation of Malaysia formed on 16 September 1963, together with Singapore, Sarawak and Sabah.

It was a happy homecoming for me as I had achieved what I had coveted for so long, a PhD in economics and in much less than half the required length of time, and with another new addition to the family to boot — our third child and second daughter, Suet Lynn. I was on top of the world.

I continued my appointment at the new University of Malaya as a lecturer and later senior lecturer and headed its newly created Division of Applied Economics. I was to stay for another four years.

It was a tumultuous time, personally and politically. It was a time of nation building in Malaysia and somehow, I was drawn into it.

Live debates were often telecast on Malaysian television and on many occasions, I was invited to participate in a programme called Opinion. The well-known, good-looking and capable presenter was Sulaiman Alias. The subject discussed at one of the fora was monetary policy and exchange rates. At that time, there was a riot in Penang because the Chancellor of the Exchequer had said in private that there would not be a devaluation of the sterling pound but soon after, he devalued it. The Malaysia ringgit was then directly linked to the pound sterling. The ringgit was thus also devalued. I was asked about the appropriateness of the ringgit devaluation. I gave my view.

Bank Negara at an emergency meeting discussed how to stop me from speaking at the Opinion programme as they said I did not exercise sufficient discretion in what I said. Yet there were other top civil servants who wanted me to continue appearing against the wishes of the central bank. They supported what I said. They said I had exercised a lot of discretion and diplomacy. I was not axed. Better judgement prevailed.

Upon my return, Oxford University Press in Kuala Lumpur contacted me to say that they wished to publish my thesis. I made a few changes and it was out in 1965 with the title *Economic Development of Modern Malaya*. I was proud of it as it was my first book, the forerunner of many to come.

I was invited to market the book on Malaysian television. The publicity worked well as the first edition sold very quickly and a second reprint had to be done.

I became a minor celebrity and was invited to many functions to talk on nation building and economic development in Malaysia.

At one such event — a heads of secondary schools conference nationwide in Kuala Lumpur where I was to give a keynote address — I met my former teacher and principal at the Anglo Chinese School in Malacca Goh Choon Lim, who had specially driven up from Malacca to hear me speak. I was truly touched.

I also received a letter from then Singapore's premier Lee Kuan Yew praising me for rationality. He wrote.... "If there are more people like you in Malaysia it speaks extremely well for the future of the country..."

Mahathir on me

Another of my articles published in Malaysia in 1968 later also drew the attention of former Malaysian Prime Minister Mahathir Mohammad. He devoted almost the entire blog on 27 July 2008 to my article on the Malaysian economy. He singled out my advocacy of industrialisation, on the importance of foreign investment in this process and the rapid replacement of the rubber-growing industry under the threat of synthetic rubber competition with the palm oil industry. I was greatly honoured that this most charismatic and influential former prime minister of Malaysia should single me out for attention in his blog in 2008 for an article written by me in 1968.

Delicate Malaysia-Singapore relations

Life in Kuala Lumpur was eventful. One evening, sometime in 1965 when Singapore had opted out of the Federation of Malaysia to become independent, I was invited by Tun Abdul Razak, then the prime minister to dinner at his official residence. I was surprised when he placed me on his right, which according to protocol, indicated that I was the guest of honour.

Also present, among others, were Abdullah Majid, his deputy who was a very popular student at the University of Malaya (in Singapore) and a roommate and close friend of SR Nathan, who later became Singapore's sixth president; political activists James Puthucheary and S Woodhull as well as Abdul Kadir Jasin, Tun's assistant principal secretary who later became the editor of The New Straits Times.

At the dinner, Tun Razak said he wanted to discuss with us a number of important matters facing the country. One of them was how to end corruption of which there were endless suggestions, but no controversy. The next question regarding how to handle Singapore as an independent nation was more problematic. He queried: "Must we adopt a new policy towards Singapore or must we preserve the status quo?"

Tensions ran high. Many of those present voiced the opinion that it was not right that "one third of our exports and one third of our imports have to go through a foreign country" saying it was simply not acceptable. Several felt that Malaysia should cut economic ties with Singapore as soon as possible and build up Port Swettenham to serve the southern part of Peninsular Malaysia.

I was listening intently but did not say a word. Tun Razak turned to me and asked, "Dr Lim, what do you think?" I paused before replying, "Port Swettenham can take care of the volume of goods going through central Malaysia but that does not take care of Negri Sembilan and Johor as they form the hinterland of Singapore. It has been so historically." I was thinking of Benham's paper which he shared with me years ago when I was in the Singapore Civil Service.

"If trade ties are cut off, Malaysia's exports and imports at the southern end would be blocked; it is tantamount to cutting off one's nose to spite one's face," I warned.

I also cautioned that Singapore would be in big trouble as well, and this would give a chance for the extreme left to emerge. "What would happen if Malaysia had to face a communist south?" I asked. The Communist Party of Malaya was still active in fighting in the jungles of Malaysia then.

I summed up that it was better on the whole to maintain the status quo. It would even be better to build better relations, treating Singapore as an independent country and maintaining good ties for the good of both countries. I said rationality must prevail — in hurting each other we would hurt ourselves as well.

Unfortunately, the prime minister and many others present did not take my analysis well.

I had come as guest of honour but at the end of the evening, I had the feeling that I had become an unwanted guest. Some had expected me to drown Singapore. I would prefer to be dead, if I were to contribute to the drowning of Singapore or Malaysia. To drown both, the most unthinkable, is madness.

But to the credit of Tun Abdul Razak, he took cognisance of my suggestion in Malaysia's relations with an independent Singapore. He allowed rationality to prevail. Good trade and economic ties today continue to prevail, despite occasional hiccups.

Years later, I met Abdul Kadir Jasin at a party to celebrate Professor Unkgu Aziz's 80th birthday in Kuala Lumpur. Mr SR Nathan was also there. He went incognito as he had already become Singapore's president.

Jasin asked me, "Do you recall when we last met?" Nodding, I replied that fortunately things have turned out well between the two countries. He seemed to share my joy.

In 1969, when I decided to return to Singapore, Tun Razak through Tun Tan Siew Sin summoned me with the offer of a ministerial post in his Cabinet. More of this later in the book.

The national language

Ungku Aziz formed a committee to coin appropriate new words in Malay in economics primarily for the benefit of A-level students who would sit for A-level examinations in the Malay medium. The committee was called Jawatan Kuasa Istilah Ekonomi. I soon found that I was the only non-Malay member of the committee. Each week we would meet for three hours finding suitable Malay equivalents to economic terms in English. There were many Indonesian terms that were already available by then, but at that time, the Indonesian Confrontation against Malaysia was on. We tried to avoid as far as possible just using their words. We also tried to avoid using Arabic scripts, calling, for example, economy, "iktisad", and politics, "siasat". Eventually we ended up with "ekonomi" for economics. Tougher still were to get Malay terms for words like marginal propensity to save, income elasticity of demand, commodity terms of trade, liquidity preference curve and balance of payments on current account. We tried. We made it. We published a book, a glossary on the subject. Not many years later, I found out that most of us on the committee had forgotten the words that we had coined. The students, however, would use them, and use them well. Looking back, the term I proposed and accepted for vested interests were "kepertingan tertentu". I also learned much later in life that all three of my older children have learned the language, a very beautiful one, quite well in Singapore. At least two won elocution contests in school in Bahasa Kebangsaan (the National Language).

National debate in Malay

Two teachers' unions could not see eye-to-eye with each other over the Federal Government's offer of pay increases for the teaching profession. The Malay-speaking union was keen to accept the offer. The English-speaking union wanted a better deal. Both, however, wanted to have a common front. The end result was to settle for a public debate on the controversy. Malay, the newly affirmed national language, was to be used in the debate. I was approached to be the chairman. I presumed they could not get Professor Ungku Aziz, who would be the ideal person. They had to settle for me, their second-choice chairman.

For the first time in the history of Malaya/Malaysia the Malaysian National Language was utilised to settle a public controversy over a public wage dispute. The hall was packed to capacity with teachers. I had to brush up on my Malay. I brought with me two dictionaries, one from Malay-to-English and the other from English-to-Malay. Of course I took the liberty to use English words when I fumbled for Malay words. That too was the accepted style then.

When the two-and-a-half hour public debate was over, a show of hands was taken for or against the motion. I have now (50 years later) forgotten the outcome. All I can remember was that the debate ended amiably, very amiably. The teachers were polite and full of humour. They too wanted to set an example of good behaviour. As the Malay saying goes, "Bahasa melambangkan jiwa", meaning, the language one uses is a reflection of one's soul.

Three other inerasable memories

It was on a bright and sunny Saturday afternoon that Mustafa (not his real name), one of the office boys in the Faculty of Economics and Administration (FEA) dropped in at my house at Petaling Jaya. He came, as an office friend, on a scooter. I was pleasantly surprised. Mustafa too came from Singapore. Mustafa told me that he was collecting money — instalment payments — from his borrowers. He was shrewed, intelligent, hard-working and enterprising, but I was surprised that he had accumulated enough money to lend to borrowers. More surprising and disturbing indeed was that the borrowers were the very much better paid academics in the precinct where I lived. My fellow academics and I, through co-operative arrangement, had built for ourselves each a bungalow in the very modern "kampong" (village) close to the university. More disturbing and completely unbelievable was when he showed me the list of his debtors, with instalment payments due and their addresses. They were some of my dear academic colleagues and friends. Up to today, nearly five decades later, I still remember the list of Mustafa's debtors with complete disbelief.

On a different topic but also on money was that I always knew when the end of the month came. A man would sit and wait discreetly in front of my house. He wanted to collect money from my maid, knowing that she would just have been paid by my wife. I asked my wife, "Why is that pitiful-looking man waiting outside our house?" She replied, "It is Asiah's ex-husband. He was asking for money from Asiah." I also learned that the man had divorced Asiah for another woman, but left her with two small children to take care. That was why she had to leave her village to work for us as a maid. My wife did frequently counsel her to keep some money for herself and her two young children. I heard her reply, "Kesian lah" (pitiful). She pitied her ex-husband and still helped him as much as she could.

My wife and I had a "complaint" against Asiah though: She worked too hard. I heard my wife said, "You do not need to wipe and clean the doors and windows every day, you know. You also do not need to sweep the floor every day you know. Give yourself a rest from time to time."

My family and I went to Port Dickson for a short break. In part, I wanted to pay a courtesy visit to Ungku Aziz, who had been absent from the office for about a month, trying to write up a research paper. I had only three children then with Lynn as our youngest. She was 3 to 4 years old and spoke perfect unaccented

Malay. She went to a nursery school in front of our house, run by the wife of one of my colleagues from Perlis. Lynn went with me to buy some breakfast for the family. We bought two packets of *nasi lemak* (coconut rice with chillied fish). She did the ordering. The two adult female sellers refused to take any money from her. I gently protested and said, "Please accept payment. You need the money to continue your trade." They replied, "No, no. Your daughter speaks perfect Malay. And she is so cute, so loveable. The food is just a present from us, and on a good and lovely morning." More persuasion followed without success on my part.

7.1. White Rock, Boars Hill, Oxford. It was my son Wun's 4th birthday party. My daughter, Fern, is in the second row. It was a very friendly and international neighbourhood with most of the families connected to Oxford University. Lynn was born here.

7.2. Our three older children at our house at Petaling Jaya, Kuala Lumpur. We designed and built the house ourselves. My youngest son, Ron, was born here.

7.3. Back in Singapore in very early 1969, now with all four children.

CHAPTER 8

RETURN TO MY ALMA MATER

Only one professor as head

In 1968, Professor Lim Tay Boh, who was one of my mentors when I was a student at the University of Malaya in Singapore before it was re-named University of Singapore in 1962, suddenly passed away. He was head of the department of economics and the university's vice-chancellor.

Singapore was then already an independent republic having separated from Malaysia in 1965.

Months later, the vacancy for the chair in economics was advertised. After weighing the pros and the cons, I decided to apply for it. Dr Toh Chin Chye was then the new vice-chancellor. Two candidates were shortlisted for an interview with Dr Toh. I was one of them. When I appeared before Dr Toh, he was most encouraging and indicated that he would welcome me back to the university.

However, there was a problem. The other shortlisted candidate was Professor You Poh Seng, my former professor in statistics at the Bukit Timah campus. I was grateful to Dr Toh's frankness when he said, "Since there is only one vacancy and because of seniority, I would have to appoint Prof You. But I will try to create a position for you should you decide to come back."

The university then was following the old British model where departments could only have one professor as head.

Dr Toh kept his word.

After my return to Kuala Lumpur, he continued to keep in touch with me. One day, he asked if I would consider coming back to Singapore to take up an initial position of readership at the department of economics. He assured me that I would be paid at the highest point of the salary scale. However, on balance, that would still be a big pay cut for me as the Malaysian ringgit and Singapore dollar were then at parity. What's more, I had several consultancy arrangements in Kuala Lumpur that gave me additional income. One of them was as the economic consultant of the First National City Bank in New York, based in Kuala Lumpur; the other was as economic consultant to the UNESCO-IAU (International Association of Universities) project — which focused on higher education and economic development in Southeast Asia. I was also economic consultant to the World Bank on aid and global economic development.

It would be difficult to give up these jobs with extra remuneration, I felt, but finally emotions held sway and I decided to take up Dr Toh's offer. I was fortunate that the World Bank assured me that I could continue as a consultant even if I were based in Singapore.

Difficult farewell to Kuala Lumpur

Although I was determined to go back to Singapore for good, leaving Kuala Lumpur was more difficult than I had thought. Malaysian friends and colleagues to the last man discouraged me from returning.

At the many farewell parties they held in my honour in their homes, my hosts would voice their concern. I remember two well-established academics whose views I valued tut-tutting loudly. They had been academics in the University of Malaya in Singapore before moving to Kuala Lumpur when the university opened its Pantai Valley branch.

One of them said, "Chong Yah, do reconsider your decision. I must remind you that Singapore is now an independent country and it is no longer the old world order when the Federation of Malaya and Singapore were considered as one."

"Singapore is very small. Do you think Singapore can succeed? It has no hinterland."

The other equally distinguished colleague said, "Singapore is a marketplace and not a place for scholarship but you are an academician and you are interested in scholarship so please weigh your options carefully."

As they were my hosts I politely listened to what they said. But my mind was already made up. It was not just Dr Toh's assurance that I could look forward to being considered for a higher position beyond that of being a reader; I would be returning to my alma mater.

I had worked in Singapore for four years before becoming an academic. I had met my wife in Singapore, married there and my two older children were born there. What's more, I had also studied there and I had fond memories of my time spent in the Dunearn Road Hostels and at the Bukit Timah campus.

My critics did not know that it was precisely that Singapore had become independent that I wanted to go back. If Singapore were still part of Malaysia, why would I want to simply move from one university to another?

I was also impressed that Singapore had started to introduce national service, which would compulsorily require all male citizens and permanent residents on reaching 18 to serve for two years in the armed forces.

The fact that the mostly ethnic Chinese population there were prepared to defend their position as a separate independent entity was an encouragement to me. In Kuala Lumpur, the professional class I knew of held the view that ethnic Chinese in Malaysia should not join the army or police. I held the opposite view; I thought they should contribute to the security and defence of the nation and that young ethnic Chinese men there should be encouraged to move in this direction.

According to some, quoting a Chinese proverb, "Good people do not join the army just like good iron should not be made into nails (好男不当兵, 好铁不打钉).

In Singapore, this was the view also advocated by those in the then powerful opposition Barisan Sosialis political party.

So mine was a voice in the wilderness that the ethnic Chinese in Malaysia should join the police and army and be part of its national defence and security.

In fact, years ago, just before the British left, then British High Commissioner Gerald Templer, who had been despatched to Malaya to deal with the Malayan Emergency had wanted to set up two regiments which would be made up of 50 per cent ethnic Chinese to fight the Communists in the jungle. People then were divided on this issue as they felt that the conscripted Chinese would not want to kill or fight with the Chinese in the jungles. However, history proved Templer right when he was credited with ending the Malayan Emergency.

Just as important was that socially and emotionally, I felt that I would still be in the same country that was called Malaya of which Singapore was an integral part. Going to Singapore would not be a real migration as it was not too far away from Malacca where my siblings and all my other relatives were still living.

An all important factor favouring the move was that every time I was in Singapore, I was treated as a local and not as an outsider.

Re-rooting problems

There were some inconveniences, of course, in upping sticks and re-locating. My wife had to resign as a school teacher in Kuala Lumpur and she had to find a new job in Singapore. She had been away for 10 years. Fortunately, she was accepted as a teacher in Geylang Methodist Girls' School.

We also had to find schools for the children. There was no vacancy for Fern, the eldest daughter in Methodist Girls' School, so we enrolled her in St. Margaret's Primary School instead. Our second son, Suet Wun managed to get into the Anglo-Chinese School, a Methodist school. The other two children were not of school-going age yet. Lynn went to a nursery school. Ron, our youngest son, was just a four-month-old baby.

During our stay in Kuala Lumpur, we took up dog breeding as a hobby and became quite good at it. We had our own pedigree Alsatian which we did not want to leave behind, so we brought it with us when we travelled to Singapore by train together with some furniture. When we arrived at the Tanjong Pagar Railway Station in Singapore, while the rest of the family travelled in a taxi, I accompanied our pet dog in a lorry with the furniture to our temporary house.

At that time, the university found a house for us to stay temporarily at Dalvey Road, near the Bukit Timah campus.

Later, more permanent accommodation was provided for us in a two-storey house on Eng Neo Avenue which was a wooded place with lots of space for the children to play.

Our neighbour was the University of Singapore's registrar, one Mr Lewis. He would visit us sometimes. One day as we were having dinner, he said in dismay, "Do you know that I am about to retire yet all my savings will not be enough to buy a house — the two-storey bungalow that I have long aspired for, because prices have shot up?"

Suddenly, it dawned on me that if my family and I continued to live in the house provided for by the university, the same thing would happen to me — I would not be able to afford a place of my own.

So we should move out as quickly as possible, I thought. After some house hunting, my wife and I found a single-storey bungalow with a small garden that was within our means. It was on Jalan Berjaya in the Thomson area. The house cost $80,000 but we were able to secure a university loan for half the sum. The interest rate was nominal as the university was happy to have locals buy their own property as this would free university-provided lodging for the use of expatriates.

Years later, with the children growing up and needing more individual space and with property prices appreciating we traded the Jalan Berjaya house for a $220,000 two-storey bungalow with a bigger garden and still in the Thomson district which we had grown familiar with. That was in 1972. We have been living in this house in Caldecott Hill ever since. If we had waited longer, the price tag would have gone up and with my meagre professor's salary, the house would have been beyond my means.

One of our most frequent visitors to our home was Chua Sian Chin. He was a childhood friend from Malacca and we had been lodgers at Dunearn Road Hostels when we were studying at the University of Malaya in Singapore.

He was a dear friend and even though he had been appointed Minister of Health then, he was still the same humble unassuming person that I had always known. He would drop in for dinner alone, always dressed casually and in slippers. He was happy to see us back in Singapore.

Once, I complained to him about the frequency of mosquitoes in the neighbourhood. I don't know if what I said prompted it, but sometime later, he launched an anti-mosquito campaign.

Pipe smoking at the Istana

When I was teaching at the University of Malaya at Pantai Valley, I took up pipe smoking. I was probably under the influence of Professor Syed Hussein Alatas and his brother who was also an academic colleague. When I returned to Singapore I continued with the habit. When I found it difficult to recall a particular date or a particular name, I would scratch my tobacco or light my pipe. The seconds doing so would help in my recollection.

One day I was having dinner at the Istana in Singapore with my Vice-Chancellor Dr Toh Chin Chye playing host. I noticed that he had a running nose, quite a bad one at that. When dinner was over, I asked the Deputy Vice-Chancellor Reginald Quahe about Dr Toh's running nose. Only two of us were there in a corner. He said, "You, you are the cause." I could not understand him, and said "Reggie, please explain."

Dr Toh's deputy continued, "He is allergic to smoking, particularly pipe smoking."

"Oh, I did not know that. Dr Toh or you should have told me that. I would immediately have stopped smoking," I said.

He replied, "Dr Toh, being the host, was too polite to tell you. We just wanted to accommodate you, being a new member of staff."

I apologised profusely. I stopped smoking since then in the presence of Dr Toh or in his absence. My two lovely and unusual looking pipes, one given as a present by Hussein and the other by his brother Naquib, have remained with me for display only at home. Each had bought the pipe separately, from Amsterdam.

Kuala Lumpur comes a-calling

When I resettled, I was not given much of a chance to re-adapt to living in Singapore. No sooner than I got back, I would receive frequent calls from the Malaysian capital. There were two that I remember clearly. One of them came from Professor Hamzah Sendut, who had just been appointed the vice-chancellor of Malaysia's second university set up in Penang in April 1969. First known as the University of Penang, it was re-named Universiti Sains Malaysia in October 1971.

I had known Hamzah when he was studying at the University of Malaya in Singapore and we had been hostel-mates. He was my senior by a year or two; he was studying geography. After graduation, he was appointed a lecturer in the Geography Department. When the University of Malaya established its Kuala Lumpur branch, he decided to return to Malaysia; he was appointed the university's head of geography.

Administrative duties were part of his role as vice-chancellor and that included the hiring of academics. He was keen to get me back to Malaysia and in particular to help him establish the new university in Penang.

He said, "You come first as dean of arts and social sciences; my plan is to appoint you later as deputy vice-chancellor."

I thanked him profusely and told him that I was honoured that he had trust in me but I could not accept his kind offer as it would be difficult to uproot myself and my family again. Professor Hamzah asked me to reconsider and to get a few referees in the meantime.

I wrote to Professor John Hicks revealing Professor Hamzah's approach and I asked if he could be one of my referees.

He was aghast. "I thought you had just re-located to Singapore," he wrote back.

"Why find another job in Penang when, in my view, it's better for you to remain in Singapore? You can participate not only in the economic development of Singapore but that of Southeast Asia too.

"The whole region is finding its own identity," he emphasised. He added, "Besides, Singapore can provide you with a more stable environment. But if you still need me as a referee again, I will gladly do it for you."

I pondered over Hicks' advice. Then I called Professor Hamzah and told him I had to decline his kind invitation to join the university in Penang as the difficulty in re-rooting my family all over again would be too much to bear.

Another call was from Dr KC Tai, who had worked as an engineer in Singapore's City Hall. When the new university branch in Kuala Lumpur was set up, he moved north to Pantai Valley to become a lecturer in the engineering department. We became good friends in Kuala Lumpur where he became active in politics; in fact, he had often discussed politics with me when we were colleagues at Pantai Valley.

He had become the chief editor of the MCA journal and was one of the right-hand men of Tun Tan Siew Sin, then Minister of Finance. The MCA is the Malaysian

Chinese Association, one of the main political parties for ethnic Chinese in mainland Malaysia.

He called me to say that Tun Tan Siew Sin was keen to invite me back to Kuala Lumpur as a minister for land, resettlement and local government. Many among the ethnic Chinese community were being resettled and he needed a Malaysian of Chinese extraction to head the ministry. The incumbent then was Mr Khaw Kai Boh, who was also the deputy president of MCA.

Mr Khaw was the head of the Special Branch in Singapore before he went to Malaysia in 1963 when he was appointed a senator and later Minister without Portfolio. He was the Minister of Housing and Local Government but was being moved to a new portfolio as Minister for Special Functions. At the time, the May 13 riots of 1969 had already erupted and there was a widespread feeling of instability among Malaysians especially in race relations.

According to KC Tai, it was felt that an academic, rather than a politician, would help greatly in pacifying people. I thanked Tai for thinking of me and asked him to also convey my thanks to Tun Tan Siew Sin. But I could not take up the offer, I said. I could not function well as a politician.

My wife was curious about the many calls I kept on receiving from Kuala Lumpur and queried me about it one day. Overhearing my explanation, Suet Fern, my 12-year-old daughter who has always been precocious from a young age, piped up, "Please, don't go back to Malaysia as a politician. I don't want a dad to be much older than his age and be a premature old man before his time."

Apart from personal reluctance coupled with family disapproval to move back to Malaysia, I had also agreed to be the PhD supervisor to a younger colleague and it seemed unfair to back out from this commitment.

The colleague was VV Bhanoji Rao, who later became an expert on poverty and income inequalities. Rao's intended thesis was on the national income of Malaysia. We managed to obtain a grant from Yale University to do a study on this; the US was very interested in Southeast Asia then, so getting the grant was quite easy. With this, Rao decided he should go to Kuala Lumpur to gather first-hand statistics.

As his supervisor, I went along. I had to connect him with my friends in the Statistics Department. We stayed at the Majestic. He noticed that I was receiving many calls at the hotel during the time we were there.

One was from the leader of the opposition party, Dr Tan Chee Khoon who had studied in the King Edward VII College of Medicine in Singapore. He was the leader of the Opposition in Malaysia from 1964 to 1978 and was fondly nicknamed Mr Opposition. A strong advocate against race-based politics, he was one of the co-founders of Parti Gerakan Rakyat Malaysia (Gerakan). When I was living in

Kuala Lumpur, Dr Tan would consult me every time the budget was announced in Parliament.

When he called, he went straight to the point, "Are you here (in Kuala Lumpur) to have dinner with Tan Siew Sin?"

I said yes, he did invite me for dinner at his house, though I had not decided yet on going. Dr Tan went on, "Don't be too associated with him and the MCA. Temperamentally and in other ways you are so different from all of them."

Another call came from Dr Lim Chong Eu, who was the President of MCA before he broke away to co-found Gerakan with Tan Chee Khoon. He later became the chief minister of Penang.

He told me not to be made use of by the Perikatan Alliance, saying, "Birds of a feather flock together. However, you are of a different plumage and I don't think you can flock together with them."

The Parti Perikatan or Alliance Party comprised the United Malays National Organisation (UMNO), MCA and the Malaysian Indian Congress (MIC). Formed in October 1957, it was the ruling coalition until it became the Barisan National in 1973.

I surmised from all these calls that news of my sojourn in Kuala Lumpur must have been circulated to politically-minded Malaysians.

I eventually did meet Tun Tan Siew Sin but my mind was 99% made up, as it was when I was in Eng Neo Avenue discussing the Malaysian overture with my family.

Tun Tan was not aware of the calls I had from Dr Tan Chee Khoon and Dr Lim Chong Eu. We spoke at length. Tun Tan said that after the May 13 riots, the Malaysian government was finding it difficult to re-establish race relations which had been cordial before. "A lot of confidence has been broken," he sighed.

He continued, "The prime minister and I have tried to fill the vacancy and this is with some urgency because of the number of Chinese being resettled in new villages.

"We needed someone of Chinese extraction who can speak Chinese. I have discussed it with the PM and he has supported my approaching you."

I learnt later they had other people in mind as well. Among them were Professor Wang Gungwu and Professor Ho Peng Yock. I told Tun Tan Siew Sin that I was not Chinese-educated although I had picked up the Chinese language as a boy in Malacca. I reminded him that I was not a true-blue *baba* either, although I spoke the Malay language.

I added, "You know how things are like coming from the same state (of Malacca)."

He said, "Yes, yes, I know you. We know your background. If you were a real *baba* you would not have the same zeal and determination that you have, and you would not be able to communicate in Chinese."

"I cannot speak Chinese," he confessed, "so you would be a tremendous complement to me."

Like me, he belonged to the same generation that viewed the Federation of Malaya and Singapore as one common country with the same Malayan identity and communality that we had taken for granted before the independence of the Malayan Federation and later of Singapore.

But I protested that I had just re-rooted my entire family back to Singapore and that I was unable to accept his offer, however tempting that might be. Besides, I said. "I could turn out to be a burden to you and to the prime minister. I think I could not survive as a politician."

I did not tell him then, but one of the reasons that I could not accept his invitation to become a minister was that I believed in a "Malaysia for Malaysians" concept similar to the view held by Singapore's leaders, which was contrary to the view in Kuala Lumpur that only the Malays should hold a very special position in Malaysia.

Tun Tan was disappointed when I could not accept his offer and it showed in his attitude when I left him; he suddenly was a bit brusque. I guess he considered it a failure not to have been able to convince me to take up the ministerial post; to me, he had viewed himself too harshly.

Like the prime minister Tun Abdul Razak when he invited me to his house — at first he welcomed me warmly — when I left his attitude had changed.

When I went back to the Majestic Hotel, Rao already guessed at what had happened. Brushing it aside, he reminded me of an invitation from the University of Malaya Economics Society to address the great economic debate started by me some time ago. Each year, the society would host, in the university's great hall, a big debate on economic issues facing the country.

I was quite popular with students of all ethnic groups perhaps because of my neutrality and firm commitment to my country and now that I was back on a visit, they were keen for me to participate again.

It was a talking forum and I was not sure whether it would interest him. Besides, talking has its limits, I said.

"Talking suits me fine, get them to invite me too," he urged, saying that coming from a village in India where there were no games or hobbies, people would just gather to talk.

He joked, "If you fall asleep while talking you lose. I always won."

I rejoined, "With your ability to talk and discuss you will surely do well in your thesis."

Sure enough, several years later, Rao got his PhD without any problem. He subsequently returned to India where he is an eminent economist. He has kept in touch with my writings and last reviewed my book on the National Wages Council. He has contributed greatly in teaching and research as a professor at the National University of Singapore.

Permanent establishment

My stay in Singapore was perhaps sealed for good when I was placed on the permanent establishment at the University of Singapore and was offered a full professorship in 1971. I was also elected dean of the Faculty of Arts and Social Sciences in 1972.

I was interviewed for a full professorship by Dr Toh Chin Chye and the deans of the university. Dr Toh told me later when the offer was made that the interview was "just a formality" and carried out according to rules.

Most people think of Dr Toh as tough and a disciplinarian, but I also saw a softer and kinder side of the man. In fact, I noticed he always displayed a tremendous amount of courtesy and kindness towards me.

I was the interviewee and he was the interviewer but here he was apologising for the inconvenience of having had to interview me.

At the interview one of the deans asked, "You have been back in Singapore for three years. How have you found our job in the university and the Singapore environment? Has it been conducive to do research and teaching?"

Dr Toh was quick to rebuke the dean. He said, "This is a private and personal question. Our job is to find if he is suitable and if so, confirm him."

Looking back, my work at the university has been made easier because of Dr Toh's magnanimous attitude.

In fact, a mutual friend once remarked, "It appears that you are the only gem he has managed to gather for the university." He probably did not like Dr Toh.

I recalled an earlier incident that occurred when Dr Toh was hosting a dinner reception for new appointees at the university.

This was after the May 13 race riots had erupted in Kuala Lumpur. I had moved to Singapore a few months before, on 1 March not because I had foreseen the riots breaking out as some people had thought but because the University of Malaya (in Kuala Lumpur) was able to release me earlier.

I was supposed to leave Kuala Lumpur in June after serving six months' notice when I resigned but as I no longer had any duties to keep me at the university I asked for permission to leave earlier and this was granted.

Dr Toh's reception was a week or two after the riots had occurred. I was having a slight cold and asked the university registrar if I could be excused. He said, "There are a lot of guests, and people will not notice your absence."

On the day of the reception, I felt better but told the registrar that although I could attend, I would be late.

I was 40 minutes late, and when I arrived, I noticed that dinner had not yet started; Dr Toh had been waiting for me!

He also seated me to his right, making me the "guest of honour".

I was honoured by his action bearing in mind he was also a minister and chairman of the ruling People's Action Party, not just the university vice-chancellor. He was treating me as if I was his most precious professor.

His action encouraged me to think that perhaps I could find myself a decent, permanent place in the new independent Singapore, but I must add one more instance to say why I was thinking that way.

On my first day of work in the university, I had to attend a faculty meeting of the amalgamated arts and social sciences departments which had been separate before.

There would be an election of the head of the new faculty and all the teaching staff were expected to vote. I was in a dilemma. There were two eligible candidates and I knew both of them. There was Dr You Poh Seng, the head of the economics department and my former professor. The other was Professor Wong Lin Ken; he was two years my senior when we were students in the university. He had just returned as our founder ambassador in the United States.

Their supporters asked us to vote for the candidate of their choice. A secret ballot was conducted and Professor You had the most votes. I can never forget this maiden return to the university: Professor You had won by secret ballot, not a show of hands.

Professor You had many hats to wear. He was the head of department, head of the Economic Research Centre, financed by the Ford Foundation, and dean of a newly created business school. He was also elected to be dean of the new arts and social sciences faculty. I was asked to be the acting head of the Department of Economics when the incumbent resigned to return to Hong Kong.

As a reader, I was not expected to do administrative work but due to circumstances, I was persuaded to take up administrative duties.

Prior to coming back to Singapore, one American professor warned me that the university would load me with very heavy teaching work. But I was prepared to take this on. As it turned out it was true — I found out I had been given treble the teaching load of others.

Taking on the role of acting head would add to an already heavy workload but it meant that I would have more flexibility to change work schedules. Besides, I had the feeling that a few among the younger staff for professional or whatever reasons did not welcome my coming home. Some of them were already established figures in the department but they were ambivalent in accepting my return. I was 10 years their senior and we had a tenuous connection.

So I tried to make myself acceptable as an acting head; I don't know if I won any hearts but after a tough year of work juggling and my efforts in building up a relationship, there seemed to be less hostility. When I was made the head of department later in 1977, I knew that I had been fully accepted.

Appointment as dean

By my third year, I gained more confidence and found it easier to cope. Then I became a full professor in 1972. At that time, as luck would have it, the vacancy of deanship also arose.

Dr You had problems with his retina and decided, after consulting with Dr Toh that he should step down as dean of the Faculty of Arts and Social Sciences. That was to reduce his very heavy work load.

Dr Toh asked me if I was prepared to stand for election as dean if Professor You stepped down. The vote would be carried out by staff members of the faculty.

I was just 40 years old then and full of energy. So I took on the challenge and became the dean.

I was elected dean for two three-year terms. I was particularly proud to be dean as the heads of the departments under the arts and social sciences faculty were very prominent local people. Professor Syed Hussein Alatas, for instance, was head of Malay Studies, Professor Wong Lin Ken was head of the history department, Professor Ooi Jin Bee was head of the department of geography, Professor Maurice Baker was professor of English and Professor Wu Teh Yao was professor of political science. The professor of sociology was Hans Evers.

These were all well-known academics with first rate credentials and I was very humbled that they agreed to have me serve as their dean even though I was relatively new.

Election of vice-deans

As dean, I had to appoint two vice-deans who would also have to stand for election. Being from the social sciences department, I thought it prudent to choose candidates from the arts and humanities for a more even representation.

I had two local scholars in mind — Dr Shahron Ahmed from the history department and Dr Edwin Thumboo, who was teaching English.

I knew Edwin from campus days. I had ragged him together with SR Nathan, our future president when they were 'freshies' and I was a second-year student. I might add that the ragging was rather mild unlike other forms of ragging practised by others. All I got them to do was to sing some songs and crack some jokes.

Later, Edwin would become dean after I declined to serve again after a second term as dean but continued to serve as head of the economics department.

Regrettably Shahron, who was born in Singapore, later resigned when his Perlis-born wife could not obtain citizenship. They left for Malaysia.

I approached Ernest Chew, also of the history department to take Shahron's place. Ernest also became dean later and it was he who was the university's public orator when years later, the university conferred on me an emeritus professorship.

As dean I could also appoint sub-deans to help carry out some special tasks. They were not elected posts. I appointed a young lecturer from the political science department, Dr Chan Heng Chee, who was instrumental in organising annual dinners for the Faculty. Years later, in 1996, when I had stepped down as dean but was still head of the economics department she told me she would be resigning as she was being appointed ambassador to the US. I organised a farewell lunch for her and wished her the very best.

1972, another turning point

1972 was a watershed year for me in other ways. Other than having been promoted to a full professorship in the university, barely a year before having been elected as Dean, the government appointed me as chairman of the newly established National Wages Council (NWC), which would put me in the spotlight — and limelight! — for almost 30 years to come.

Soon after my appointment, there was hyperinflation in Singapore in 1973 and I was given the task to combat it in 1974. My colleagues and I in the NWC did so successfully. That made the NWC useful to the government and in the eyes of employers and employees in Singapore. I will dwell more on this in a later chapter.

So, after my return, contrary to my earlier doubts, in just three to four years later, I became fully re-entrenched in Singapore and in the new Singapore society, of which I became very much a part.

I began to sing with conviction *Majulah Singapura* without forgetting how to sing *Negara-ku*. I love the two countries dearly.

8.1. ***Elements of Economic Theory*** **and** ***Economic Structure and Organisation*** **were two A-level textbooks popularly used all over Singapore and Malaysia. They went into third editions with many impressions. They were also made available in Malay and Chinese.**

CHAPTER 9

LIFE AS DEAN

Memorable episodes

As dean, I was head of the arts and social sciences faculty. Its role is mainly administrative, although one is expected to get the approval of the University Senate on polices. One is also expected to continue with the usual teaching load and research duties, so I had a heavy load when I served for six years as dean (1971–1977). That was the tradition and practice at that time.

My door was always open to staff and students who needed a listening ear and some guidance. At the time, after the May 13 riots, there was a big shift in ethnic policies in Malaysia in favour of Malays; for Malaysians of Chinese and Indian ethnic origins that meant their opportunities for advancement in the public sector were being stripped away.

I had several high-performing graduates in economics of the University of Malaya in Kuala Lumpur approaching me in Singapore for advice about going abroad.

Among them were two good second upper honours graduates and one with a first class honours who were all not able to find jobs in Malaysia. They thought perhaps it was best to study for a PhD. They had heard that the Ford Foundation in Singapore was giving scholarships for local students to study abroad and were wondering if they were eligible as Malaysians now that Singapore had become independent.

The Foundation said that as long as the Malaysians could gain entry to a good university in the US that would be the deciding factor. At that time, Malaysians were often treated as locals in Singapore and vice versa.

I had found out that nobody had ever been sent by the university's economics department to do a PhD abroad, so I saw an opportunity to do this with this batch of graduates. The only requirement was that they should return to Singapore to work. They assured me that they would do so.

I had to see Dr Toh, the vice chancellor, to get his approval.

When I was head of the division of applied economics in Kuala Lumpur, I made sure there were opportunities for academically gifted students to do their PhD at Oxford or Cambridge University.

Among those who benefitted from this development strategy of mine was Abdul Halim, who came from a family of farmers in Kedah. He later successfully completed his doctorate at Oxford. There was also Eddie Lee who was fond of claiming that he completed his doctorate in the same amount of time as I did, his professor. He is now based in Switzerland. There was also Naidu Govindasamy, who is now an academic in the University of Malaya.

It was against this background that the Malaysian graduates then came to see me in Singapore. When I spoke to Dr Toh, he said, "Why not? No one is utilising the money anyway; Ford Foundation still regards them as locals."

So Rex Toh went to Minnesota where he obtained first his MA in 1972 and in 1975, his PhD in logistics and marketing. Kau Ah Keng also got his PhD from the University of London in 1981. Kau who has retired is now doing part-time teaching at the National University of Singapore (NUS) as a Professorial Fellow.

Rex Toh returned to Singapore to serve his bond, teaching at the department of business administration. Tall, about six feet, he emigrated to the United States to teach at Seattle University after completing his bond when his American-born wife, a doctor, could not get a job as Singapore then did not recognise US medical degrees although they accepted medical degrees from Manila. What a shame to lose someone as gifted as Rex Toh, and his wife as well.

I still keep in touch with him. Years later, when I retired from Nanyang Technological University (NTU) as emeritus professor in June 2012, he told me he was also conferred the same title on the same day by his university. So we congratulated each other.

One of the roles I gave to myself as dean was to establish ties with other universities in the region. One form this took was to confer doctorates on outstanding personalities. One of those I had successfully proposed to the university was Dr Puey Ungphakorn from Thammasat University in Bangkok.

We had adopted the British style in university administration whereby full professors were heads of departments. We also had a Senate that had to formally approve students who got first, second or other degrees. It would also decide on the public orator for those being conferred honorary doctorates. I was asked to be the public orator by the University Senate on six separate occasions. Later, the Senate changed their rules to appoint the dean of school concerned to be the orator. When Lim Kim San was being conferred an honorary degree of Doctor of Laws in 1982 I was asked to be the public orator, although I was no longer the dean. The Senate felt that since Lim Kim San was the Minister for Finance, it was appropriate for an economics professor to be the public orator.

There were also two famous artists on whom the university conferred honorary doctorate degrees. One was the renowned Indonesian artist Affandi from Jogjakarta; the other was Chen Wen Hsi of Singapore. I was asked by the University Senate to be the public orator for both.

However, it was difficult to get in touch with Affandi despite sending him several letters.

The university finally sent Professor Syed Hussein Alatas, the head of the Malay Studies Department, to Jogjakarta to personally deliver the invitation.

When Affandi came to Singapore for his conferment, he was moved at the conferment ceremony by my citation of him.

He wondered how come I knew so much of him. I told him I had help from the Singapore embassy in Jakarta and was myself impressed when I did research on how he had spent time in prison and did much to depict the poor and needy in his paintings.

Later, when he had a solo exhibition of his paintings in Singapore, he urged me to turn up at the exhibition to pick a painting that I liked as a gift. I had thought it was *ajak ajak ayam* — a mere courtesy. I did not turn up. He wrote to me again, so I went to pick one. It was a painting of fighting crabs. I also picked one for my friend Syed Hussein Alatas.

I had to declare it to the university as was required under the rules and was told that I could keep it if I paid $2,000 to the university. It was a big sum for me then, but I had no choice but to pay up. I still have the painting; it is one of my favourites and has become a family heirloom.

A troublesome colleague

One day, I received a letter from the students' union addressed to me as the Dean of the Faculty of Arts and Social Sciences claiming that the sociology department had meddled with the marks of a resigning American professor attached to the department. The professor in question had met the students' union representatives to say that all the marks he had given to students' papers had been tampered with by the department. The students' union sent a copy of the letter to the vice-chancellor, Dr Toh.

Dr Toh asked me to see him about the letter. I asked if he would allow me to handle the matter. I knew he would as such matters were better handled by an academic.

So I called the head of department, Professor Hans Evers, a well-known sociologist of German extraction, who could speak eight languages. The charge against him was made by an American of Chinese origin; he accused Evers of having tampered with the marks. I had a meeting with the whole department.

According to Evers, the American had given every student an A+. That was not possible, he said, it just showed that he did not mark the papers at all. Evers decided to distribute the papers among the rest of the teaching staff for re-marking. The papers came back with some students getting a C, others a B and the top ones scoring an A. I was happy that the marks had been moderated, and in a manner that the department did, openly among themselves.

As far as I was concerned Hans Evers and the department did not tamper with the marks. It was the department's duty, anyway, to deal with any aberration. Among members of the department, there was Dr Aline Wong who also supported the action of their head.

I asked the students' union representative to meet me. I told them that I was puzzled as to why the American professor had made a complaint to them rather than to me as dean. Their answer was that the American believed that deans tended to support their academic colleagues. It was the time of the Watergate in the US. I said this is the academic world, not politics.

I explained to the students what had happened and said that prior to this, I had complaints from my helper Professor Shahron Ahmed who was my vice-dean and who had warned me to pay attention to this American professor who was indulging in most inappropriate racial remarks to students.

So when this episode happened, I was not at all surprised.

The students' union accepted my explanation and dropped the case.

I went one step further. I took punitive action with the departing professor. I found out in the Central Provident Fund (CPF) rules that CPF pay-outs could be held back to determine if there were debts not paid so they could be deducted. I gave instructions to hold it up for a little while and briefed the US ambassador on this.

In those days, some embassies wanted to keep in touch to make sure their nationals were treated properly. The ambassador was sympathetic to the university and said he would leave it to me to handle the case. But the person was so frightened that he left Singapore without withdrawing his CPF. He knew he was not right in trying to run down an entire department and ruin the university's reputation.

So as a result of solving this case, whenever Dr Toh had academic problems of this type, he would turn to me.

New York Times

One day, Dr Toh showed me a letter from The New York Times seeking an interview with him on political control over the university. Since he was in politics, he felt it would not be appropriate for him to be interviewed.

I told him that I would like to handle the matter. He readily agreed.

I wrote to the reporter that we would give him a full scale interview. He promised an objective report.

Our meeting was fixed at 4 pm which was fine with him he said as he was arriving in the morning and this would give him time to tend to other matters first. Time passed and at 5 pm, the official clock-out time for the university, the journalist still had not showed up. I had two secretarial staff members waiting with me and although I encouraged them to knock off for the day, they refused saying that they wanted to be with me to ensure that nothing untoward happened.

It was only at 6.30 pm that the journalist turned up. He was very apologetic saying how he had absentmindedly left his briefcase with his passport and contact numbers in the taxi when he arrived at his hotel from the airport. He made a police report and for two hours did not know what to do, when at last the police came a-calling with his briefcase. He thus could telephone me, saying he would be very late.

Pleased to have his briefcase returned, intact, the journalist was clearly in a happy mood.

"That made my day," he declared, "and I have found that you have even waited for me and with a welcoming cup of tea." I replied, "We just want to be sure that nothing harmful had happened to you. I am so glad to meet you." We chatted about the university.

He replied, "Everything here seems to be fine. I would report very favourably of Singapore and the university."

From initially hoping to find fault with Singapore's university system, he ended up with a glowing report of how well run the university was.

When I reported the events to Dr Toh, he was surprised though pleased with the outcome. That was how he thought his confidence in me was not misplaced.

John Kenneth Galbraith

Another memorable episode was the visit of John Kenneth Galbraith, a world famous American economist from Harvard and a prolific author, best known for his book, *The Affluent Society*. He was invited by the National Productivity Board to Singapore by its chairman, Dr Augustine Tan, himself an economist, to study productivity.

He was to give a talk which I would chair. Before the talk, however, he paid a courtesy call on me. I showed him all his books on the table in my room. He was surprised and suitably impressed.

The talk, "How to achieve affluence," went down well with the students. After it was over, then Prime Minister Lee Kuan Yew and his wife hosted Galbraith to dinner. I was invited as well. That was when I saw Mrs Lee at her best.

She discussed with him various speeches made by the then US President Nixon between 1972 and 1976 which Galbraith said were mostly written by him. It was the first time I heard Mrs Lee in action. She was brilliant. Galbraith was very impressed by her.

As if to prove his point, he wrote in another of his books on Asia that Singapore was the greatest intellectual centre outside Japan. At that time Japan was viewed with the highest favour because of its highly affluent democratic society. Outside Japan, Singapore was number 1 in Asia in Galbraith's opinion. At that time, there was no international ranking of universities yet.

Gunnar Myrdal

Another prominent visiting professor was the famous Swedish economist Gunnar Myrdal who later won a Nobel Prize. He wrote a highly acclaimed book entitled *Asian Drama: An Inquiry into the Poverty of Nations* in 1968.

On his visit to Singapore he gave a talk which I chaired. Later I discussed with him on television about his work *Asian Drama*.

I remember Myrdal had quoted me in the footnotes of this book on some GDP figures.

To Myrdal the nations in Asia were "soft states" meaning they tended to make statements on policies but not implement them — with the exception of Singapore.

To him, Singapore was a country that was efficient and non-corrupt, so unlike other countries. He was confident even then that Singapore would develop well. He sent me 60 copies of his book *Asian Drama*.

I sent a circular to my academic colleagues in the Faculty that if they wanted a free copy, they could get it from me.

All copies were taken up and I ended up having to buy a copy for my own use!

Medals for top students

During my deanship, I instituted a move to have prizes and awards for the most outstanding scholars as a form of recognition. So a system of gold, silver and bronze medals was set up. At the time, I was chairman of the National Wages Council (NWC) which put me in touch with the trade union leadership and employers' federations.

That enabled me to raise funds to launch medals such as the NTUC (National Trades Union Congress) gold medal, SNEF (Singapore National Employers Federation) gold medal and the SIA (Singapore Airlines) gold medal. The scheme was new but it caught on and today our universities have many benevolent donors awarding scholarships and medals to deserving students. In my days as a student, no medals were given out at all!

Advice to new students

As dean, as the tradition then required, I had to give a talk each year to welcome a new batch of students, known to the student community as "freshies".

I was fond of incorporating in my welcoming talk the following points:

(1) Be very free to disagree with your lecturers and professors, but try not to be disagreeable. Similarly, be very free to argue with your lecturers and professors, but try not to be argumentative.

(2) Dress appropriately when attending lectures, seminars and tutorials; try not to expose too much of your anatomy in the process of keeping cool.

(3) Marks and grades are awarded purely on the basis of merit, and no presents are expected or required from students.

I found these suggestions were particularly appreciated by students from outside Singapore.

Endowed chair professorship

One day in 1975, to my most pleasant surprise, I was invited by Tan Sri Tan Chin Tuan, the managing director and chairman of the Oversea-Chinese Banking Corporation (OCBC) to Raffles Hotel for lunch. At that time I was told I would be the only guest and that he wanted to have a private lunch meeting. When I turned up, I met two very important lunch companions in Professor Tommy Koh who was then dean of the Law faculty and Dr Tony Tan who had just resigned as a mathematics lecturer from the university and had joined the bank of OCBC as general manager. Tan Sri Tan was his uncle.

Throughout the lunch Dr Tony Tan was reticent. Professor Tommy Koh was chatty. Tan Sri Tan expressed admiration for my work as NWC chairman. He said he used to spend a lot of time on union matters before NWC. Now he could run the bank and have the union cooperating with him; instead of being a problem the union had become an asset, thanks to the NWC.

Tan Sri, who was a well-known philanthropist, said he wanted to do something for the university. I suggested that he set up an endowment chair in his name in the Department of Economics. He was not receptive to have his name there but I said it would add credence and fame and also would mark the first time that a local person was founding an endowed chair, leading to more chairs to follow. It turned out I was right.

When he retired, the bank set up a chair in his honour at the university and donated money for it. The Chair Professorship in Economics in the Department of Economics kicked off the start of many subsequent public donations to NUS for Visiting Professorships and Professorial Chairs.

Ong Teng Cheong

When I was dean, there was the fear that the university would be an ivory tower, so I suggested to my fellow deans some of whom were non-locals that every month we should invite a luminary outside the university to have lunch with us. They agreed. One of the luminaries was Ong Teng Cheong, then a well-known architect with the Housing and Development Board. Later, he became the secretary-general of NTUC and was a useful ally during my time as NWC chairman. He later became Singapore's fourth president. Another luminary we invited for lunch was Tan Sri Tan Chin Tuan.

Lee Hsien Loong

When the Prime Minister of Singapore Lee Hsien Loong was a young man making preparations to go to the University of Cambridge for higher studies, I was given the honour, at the request of his mother, Mrs Lee Kuan Yew, of coaching him in Economics for his A-level examination. He passed with flying colours, topping the list among the candidates from Singapore.

He was hard-working and brilliant. He completed all his essay assignments in good time reading all the materials given to him. His mother later wrote me a personal note thanking me very much for the help in coaching her son.

Devan Nair

Sometime in 1973, the well-known NTUC's Secretary-General Devan Nair (who later became Singapore's third president) dropped in to see me in my office at the

Bukit Timah campus. It was a completely private visit. Several days prior to this, he had telephoned me about his personal problem. He said, "I would like to seek your advice for placing in a US university my second son Janamitra. He has got a place in Rhode Island, USA. May I see you to discuss about the matter?"

When I saw him, I said, "The degree of the higher institution which your son has got a place in is not only unrecognised in the USA, but also in Rhode Island itself."

He was shocked and said, "What should we do? Janamitra has already paid all the fees required."

"Still, I think, you must put your son in a better university, such as the Indiana University. I have seen his grades, he should have no problem in getting a place there," I continued.

He asked, "Does it mean you can and you know the procedures of finding him a place there?" "Yes, I will try to help" was my reply.

When he left, I quickly got in touch with Professor Howard Schaller of Indiana University to seek his help. I knew Professor Schaller when he was the Ford Foundation representative in Singapore. He had been instrumental in seeking the funding of the then Economic Research Centre (SRC) of the University of Singapore. Soon, I received a reply from Schaller that his university would be glad to accept Janamitra Devan as a first year undergraduate in its School of Business.

Years later, I heard that Janamitra not only graduated with an honours degree in business administration, but also, subsequently, a PhD degree. When Mr Devan Nair was forced to relinquish his Presidency in Singapore, he moved his family to the Bloomington campus of Indiana University, where his son Janamitra was so successful in his academic pursuit. He had also maintained very good ties with our mutual friend Professor Schaller and others at Bloomington.

The music department

At that time too, the arts and social sciences faculty did not have disciplines such as music. With Dr Toh's support, we started a music department. It did not turn out to be as successful as we wanted it to be, as it was difficult to find a suitable academic who was also an eminent musician and a local too which was the requirement. It was only decades later that the music department turned out to be viable.

Stepping down as dean

Six years later in 1977, just when I was ready to step down I was asked to stand again for re-election as dean.

The vice-chancellor then was Kwang Sai Kheong, formerly the brilliant director of education at the Ministry of Education. Although he had a life-long connection with education — mainly primary and secondary education — albeit at the highest administrative level, he had no real life experience with the university academic world.

He was unfamiliar with university procedures, its culture and norms and thus had to rely on some old academic hands such as me. I had to exercise my utmost discretion in making constructive suggestions to him.

But when he asked me to continue as dean, I had already made up my mind not to do so as it was almost completely an administrative job which by then I had found taxing. So with his agreement I returned to the economics department as substantive head of department. He let me go with great reluctance and accepted my recommendation of Professor Ooi Jin Bee of the geography department when he asked me to name a replacement. Professor Ooi was an eminent scholar and had been dean before. He too had a D Phil from Oxford.

CHAPTER 10

LIFE IN THE OLD ECONOMICS DEPARTMENT

Economics' popularity

After the deanship, when I returned to head the Department of Economics in 1977, I had become a fully accepted head among the other teaching staff in the department. This was unlike eight years ago when I had come back to Singapore to work as a Reader in Economics at the university and was appointed acting head amid some resentment.

Economics, in the late 1970s, had become a very popular discipline. The demand for a university education in economics was high on the agenda of most of the students in the Faculty of Arts and Social Sciences for its practical value and the career opportunities it would offer. Since statistics taught by our department was also popular the department was renamed the Department of Economics and Statistics.

In part, statistics was offered because my immediate predecessor Professor You Poh Seng was in fact a statistician. I learned much of my statistics from him as an undergraduate.

Both subjects in combination were in such great demand that to cope with the high number of students in the department and to allow a spread of disciplines, I instituted some benchmarks that a student had to get in their A-levels: a B grade in Economics or Mathematics and a good pass in the General Paper as pre-requisites. Those otherwise well-qualified students without these specific grades could then get a place in the other departments, which should also have some of our best students.

But the academic barriers for entry constituted a problem when ambassadors serving in Singapore complained that they could not send their children to study economics in our department even though they could be accepted in other globally well-known institutions such as the London School of Economics. We were the only university that had introduced these prerequisites.

At that time, students graduating from the university would obtain a Bachelor of Arts (BA) or Bachelor of Social Science (BSoc Sci) ordinary degree in three years. If they wished to, they could study for another year to obtain an honours degree. I decided it was necessary to place restrictions on students proceeding to do honours in Economics too, because if there were none, our department would be completely flooded with students compared to the other departments.

For me, the idea for setting restrictions was to ensure a distribution of talents. So we initiated yet another barrier — graduates had to achieve at least a B grade in Economics in their third year exams to do honours in Economics. It might have seemed a tall order then but we did have enough students with B and A grades. With this barrier, other students with high marks in other disciplines as well, though not in Economics or Statistics could go to do their honours in other departments thus ensuring a spread of good students all round.

In those days, most students would do two subjects as a major and a third as a minor so when it came to awarding graduates with a BA or BSoc Sci degree, there was a problem of how to give weightage to the subjects. To solve the problem, I decided that the board of examiners for the faculty would have to meet to discuss the weightage. Indeed, we handled marks more carefully than we handled money — that's meritocracy.

When students sat for their exams too, they were given numbers which they would write on their papers and not their names so that we would have no inkling who they were. This was to ensure that there would be no discrimination on grounds of race, religion, gender, family or other connections.

When it came to awarding prizes as well to top students, I played an important role in deciding who would get the first, second and third prizes.

I always had a clear mandate from my department in Faculty meetings. In those days, department meetings must be held to finalise departmental grades before submission to Faculty for Faculty grades.

Would you believe it, most of the prize winners were females? If any time a male student won, I would say to myself, "Hallelujah!"

Not only were the prize winners mostly females, they also dominated in the honours year class!

In the department's third year, we decided that each lecturer in the department would be a supervisor to a student doing a thesis as we had enough staff. We were very student-centric then. The training of students was topmost on our priority list, not our own individual research as academics; we only pursued that necessity when we fulfilled our student obligations first.

It was decided by the department that as head of the department and as the most senior academician, I would be given the option of supervising the two best students. As a result of our non-identifiable meritocratic process using student numbers instead of names, all the students were invariably females. I thus did not have the chance to supervise male students. But one of my female colleagues one day was brave enough to pipe up, "Professor Lim, do not associate yourself as a male chauvinistic pig!"

However, I also discovered to my delight, that most of my female students were bright and elegant. A few were keen to show me off and would invite me to student functions. I normally turned them down. I also noticed on the downside though that many of them did not have a strong career drive; they had in particular no desire to go on to do a PhD in economics. Besides, our elite Administrative Service then gave more preference to male graduates and I would have liked some of our students to enter its realm.

So I decided to break a sacred rule — I would continue to pick the best two students each year to be supervised but I decided to pick only the best male students to the horror of most of my female colleagues who said I would come down in esteem among them.

I chose Ravi Menon and Niam Chiang Meng both of whom later became permanent secretaries in the Civil Service. I noted then that they were the only permanent secretaries who had received their first honours degree from our local university, the National University of Singapore (NUS). Ravi is now the managing director of the Monetary Authority of Singapore while Niam is the permanent secretary in the Prime Minister's office. I had, of course, also picked some other top male students to supervise in the later years of my career in NUS.

Department produced luminaries

Later on, when I was long enough in the department, I noticed that it was unique with well-known Singaporean and Malaysian personalities who had studied at the time when the department was part of Raffles College. Among the illustrious students in the pre-World War II years were the former Prime Minister Lee Kuan Yew and Mrs Lee Kuan Yew, Dr Goh Keng Swee, Mr Lim Kim San, who later became finance minister, Ungku Abdul Aziz, Tun Abdul Razak, who went on to become Malaysia's second prime minister and Tun Tan Siew Sin who was Malaysia's first trade and industry minister and later finance minister.

Years later, Professor Tom Silcock was invited by me as head of the economics department to write a book on its history. I still have a copy of this invaluable now out-of-print book. Professor Silcock must be regarded as the *de facto* founding head of the department.

Professor Silcock told me years later that he considered Goh Keng Swee as the most brilliant of his students. Kwa Geok Choo, the future Mrs Lee Kuan Yew, also topped the list in economics, clinching the Queen's scholarship to study law in Cambridge. Then, in later years, other luminaries from the department included none other than Goh Chok Tong who became our prime minister and S Dhanabalan who went on to become foreign minister and chairman of Temasek Holdings.

Among some of Singapore's top civil servants who received an honours degree in economics and went on to become permanent secretaries were Sim Kee Boon, Ngiam Tong Dow and Tan Chok Kian.

Other luminaries from the department were Tan See Peng, who was staying in the same G block as I was at Bukit Timah Hostels. He was originally from Batu Pahat, Johor and was the first local person to become auditor-general of Singapore. Wong Lee Hoon, my classmate in the economics department, became the second local postmaster-general of Singapore. Yet another prominent economics graduate was Leong Chee Seng who was for a time comptroller of income tax. They were among the top pioneer civil servants of Singapore after self-government and later independence.

The department's unique role in producing such a long list of distinguished persons who have contributed greatly to the growth of Singapore and Malaysia was in part because at that time we did not have other faculties such as law, engineering, accountancy and business competing for these students.

The department of economics also has had the unmatched distinction of having been awarded by the university with three emeritus professorships: Professor Silcock in 1960, Professor You Poh Seng in 1978 and myself in 1992. Professor Lim Tay Boh, another head, went on to become the vice-chancellor of the university. He passed away in London whilst in office.

Tapping on the department's expertise

From time to time the economics department would receive calls from Goh Keng Swee when he was finance minister. Not only was he brilliant but he had a lot of foresight.

He would now and again invite me to lunch with nothing on the agenda though he would often bring in an outsider as well. On one occasion, his guest was the general manager of an American bank. The American banker spoke of how a US dollar account should be created in Singapore as it had been successfully done in London. Dr Goh replied that if the American banker was that confident, he would grant him a licence. Its success soon led to all the other banks then, including local ones, clamouring to have licences too.

That was the beginning of Singapore as the financial centre of Southeast Asia. The University of Singapore gave the American banker an honorary doctorate of letters for this innovative measure of instituting a dollar account system in Singapore.

Yet another call from Dr Goh concerned a request for me to write a short paper on the hog cycle. He wanted to relate it to the property cycle, which Singapore was also facing then.

I sent him a note that the hog cycle in mediaevel Europe was used to explain the prices of pigs. When prices went up, more farmers would produce pigs and when prices went down, the number of pigs being produced would go down.

It was in many ways very similar to the property cycle in which prices would go up if the market had a housing shortage encouraging developers to build more. But if there was a property glut, prices would go down and developers would cut down on building.

He was happy with my explanation.

Dr Goh also asked me on another occasion how I would view a family quota system for cars. I spoke against it, preferring the use of money incentives.

Ong Pang Boon

In academia, our normal visitors to our office are fellow academics and our students. When the Minister for Labour Ong Pang Boon said that he would like to see me in my office, I regarded that as a great honour. The National Wages Council (NWC) was new then. The recommendations on wage increases and changes to the wage system were also new. Minister Ong would drop in on Saturdays and we discussed about NWC matters. And as Mr Ong and I were students together at the University of Malaya (then in Singapore), we also talked about old times and old friends.

Minister Ong's visits were soon to be followed by the visits of his Permanent Secretary Kwa Soon Chuan and the Deputy Secretary Wong Heng Khim. Mr Kwa and Mr Wong were as devoted and conscientious as their minister. They were committed to one goal: The success of NWC and the success of Singapore. This was the tie that bound all four of us together.

Yong Pung How

Mr Yong, a very distinguished lawyer and banker, had just been appointed as the CEO of the Monetary Authority of Singapore (MAS). He came to see me in my office at the Bukit Timah campus. He wanted me to recommend to him my top students in Economics for MAS. By top students, he meant only those with a first class honours degree.

I said, "My university is parsimonious in awarding first class honours degrees. My department has been trapped in this tradition as well. Perhaps, you may wish to consider getting our good second class upper degrees as well?"

He was most reluctant to open the employment door a bit wider. I tried to be diplomatically persistent. I think finally he gave way, taking with him a respectable first class and second class honours list of graduates from the department. I did not follow up with his success or otherwise with graduates from the department. I was thankful to him, nonetheless, for putting the department on his top priority recruitment list.

As an aside, Mr Yong later became the Chief Justice of Singapore, and in a later part of this book, I sought his advice on my newly-discovered prostrate problem.

Mr Yong saw me in 1982. It is by coincidence that today's (2016) Managing Director of MAS is a very distinguished graduate of the Department of Economics of NUS, Mr Ravi Menon, whom I had the privilege of supervising his BSocSci honours degree thesis.

Dr Goh Keng Swee and economic forecasting

One day, there was another call from the Finance Ministry. It was Dr Goh's permanent secretary Ngiam Tong Dow on the other line. He told me that Dr Goh wanted our department to pay attention to macro-economic forecasting as was done successfully in the West.

In those days, Singapore did not have anyone who could do forecasting so I suggested that we should send several people from the economics department to study at the Pennsylvania Wharton School, which had a good name for forecasting. These days, most banks and other financial institutions have forecasters.

However, we did not have available funds to send people to the US for training until a benefactor, the owner of Goodwood Park Hotel, Mr Khoo Teck Puat, stepped in with a generous donation to the university. Later, I learned that it was Dr Goh who persuaded him to help in this area. With the funds, I sent a handful of academics to Wharton with the intention of building up a small pool of forecasters.

When they came back, they produced a model for economic forecasting. We then started a committee to meet regularly to do forecasting. I would chair the meetings. My able colleagues would make a forecast of GDP (Gross Domestic Product) using parameters such as employment rate, inflation rate and exchange rate. I was told that their model was found to be useful to MAS.

The committee did wonderful forecasting work and often with almost perfect accuracy. It was this forecasting that got me and the then president of Nanyang Technological University (NTU) Su Guaning into deep trouble at a later time.

On one occasion in 2003 my two colleagues in the forecasting committee mentioned that for all the new jobs created in Singapore, 80 per cent would be taken up by cheap foreign labour. At this rate, they said, there might be too many low-income earning foreigners in our population and this would have negative impact on our low-income groups. This soon became public news and created a furore with the government saying that their assessment was unacceptable. We did not know that we had stepped on a very sensitive topic — in effect, a political minefield.

The two committee members, Professor Cheng Kang and Professor Tan Khee Giap were not anti-government; they were simply stating a fact, based on their research.

One very able and charismatic minister even told me that I should not have chaired the meeting when the two academics made this forecast as I was lending my name to them.

I pointed out that I had been chairing these meetings every year for nearly two decades since I was at NUS and that the two forecasters were unbiased academics; they had no intention of revealing the government's Achilles' heel when it came to its manpower policy. I told him, "My learned colleagues were just making a statement as part of their forecasting work that of every 10 new jobs created, eight would go to foreigners in Singapore."

That, by the way, turned out to be the case. But the minister at the time was very upset. All of us in the department and including Professor Su, our university president, prayed for some tolerance on the part of the government to our research findings.

Years after this episode, an important member of the establishment confided in me that if the government had taken heed of these unpleasant research findings, the need for the current purposeful economic restructuring might not have been necessary. Since 2010, the government has been tightening foreign labour intake, particularly that of cheap foreign labour, with emphasis on qualitative growth.

Setting up PECC Singapore chapter

One day, I received a visit from a group of distinguished Australian academics led by an economist who was also the vice-chancellor of the Australian National University (ANU).

He had met Dr Goh who had tasked him to see me about leading a delegation from Singapore to attend an inaugural meeting at ANU in Canberra with a view to form the Pacific Economic Cooperation Conference (PECC), later renamed the Pacific Economic Cooperation Council. The setting up of the Council was at the initiative of Mr Masayoshi Ohira and Mr Malcolm Fraser, then prime ministers of Japan and Australia respectively.

The idea was to create a tripartite platform for leading individuals and decision makers from government, business and academia to discuss freely on policy issues affecting the Asia-Pacific and to develop regional initiatives to help towards the stable and sustainable economic development of the region.

Comprising initially of the five developed nations of the US, Japan, Australia, Canada and New Zealand, the intention was to bring on board the countries of ASEAN (Association of Southeast Asian Nations) then comprising Brunei Darussalam, Indonesia, Malaysia, the Philippines, Singapore, and Thailand. I accepted the invitation to attend the inaugural meeting of the PECC in Canberra.

As the PECC developed, it became very popular among non-founding members of the region. I pushed for the institution to adopt the principle that future membership in the group would be based on the unanimity of support from all existing members. Small nations had expressed the view that they would not want to be free riders or mere followers. This principle was accepted.

On this principle, we managed to bring in China, Hong Kong and Taiwan as members at the same time. The original intention was to invite China only but I did not subscribe to this divisive political view. At that time, the PECC was a pure economic institution; it had little to do with politics. And Taiwan and Hong Kong then had more economic ties with the world than China.

Yet, we needed to get China out of the bear hug of Russia. We did not want them to hug each other too closely.

I too managed to get the PECC to have its secretariat in Singapore.

Exposure to outside world

Among other things, Dr Goh was very concerned with the lack of exposure of Singaporeans to the outside world. He wanted the intelligentsia of Singapore to be in tune with what was going on in the world, particularly in the Asia-Pacific region.

He tried to bring eminent professors to come in to give us, as it were, a window to the world so that we would not be so isolated or dare I say, ignorant.

The first visitor was Professor Peter Bauer who later became Lord Peter Bauer. I never asked him if he was the doctoral supervisor of Dr Goh at the London School of Economics (LSE); my guess is that he was. Dr Goh showed him a lot of respect and vice versa. Bauer was professor of development economics at LSE. He was invited to Singapore to give the inaugural public lecture at the NTUC Conference Hall at Shenton Way. When it was time for him to speak, he could not be found in the VIP holding room. I quickly eased everyone's anxiety by interjecting that he would soon come out of his quite habitual prayer in another room prior to the lecture. I knew this, as I was assigned to look after Professor Bauer.

Fund for public lectures

Professor Bauer's successful visit reinforced in Dr Goh's mind that more could be done in this sector — getting in overseas experts to speak. That was rare then.

So he suggested to then finance minister Hon Sui Sen that some money be put aside for this. MAS would provide the funds. Its managing director then was Wong Pakshong who envisaged that the audience would be huge so he asked Professor Sandhu, Director of the Institute of Southeast Asian Studies to help out in dealing with the logistics in organising the talks.

But Dr Goh insisted that I should be the third member of this group. Our task was simple: Get people in regularly to give public lectures and provide us more links with the outside world. Dr Goh was truly afraid that we in Singapore would live in isolation.

Our first job when the three of us met was to draw up a list of prominent names that we could invite to Singapore to give a talk. But first, we needed to give a name to the talks itself.

Wong Pakshong proposed The Raffles Lecture while Sandhu suggested The Southeast Asian Lecture. I came up with The Singapore Lecture.

None of us could come to an agreement. So it was felt that we would leave it to Mr Hon or Dr Goh himself to decide. They both concurred that the talks would be known as The Singapore Lecture series. It is gratifying to note that up to now the Singapore Lectures are still being conducted.

Singapore Lecture's distinguished speakers

After the series of public talks were decided, I proposed inviting Professor Milton Friedman to be our first distinguished speaker. The world famous American economist and writer had taught at the University of Chicago, where I had first met him years ago. In 1976, he won the Nobel Prize in Economic Sciences. I was particularly familiar with the book which he had written with his wife Rose under the title *Free to Choose*.

He was a strong advocate of using market forces to develop a country and not to have excessive government intervention which he believed would slow down the entire economy. I supported this theory, though with some qualifications.

I also proposed Henry Kissinger who was then the National Security Advisor and Secretary of State in the two administrations of President Richard Nixon and President Gerald Ford.

Other names were put forward but to my delight my proposal to have Friedman and Kissinger be the first two speakers was accepted by the government.

Milton Friedman was the first guest. The NTUC Conference Hall where he spoke was full. The enterprising Professor Sandhu arranged for television coverage and I even got to interview him on television which meant there was maximum publicity for him and his ideas.

One year later, Kissinger came. Because of his political stature, our political leaders were very involved in meeting and welcoming him.

But since Kissinger's visit, The Singapore Lecture series was no longer decided by Wong Pakshong, Sandhu and me. The Ministry of Foreign Affairs had taken over; it decided that only top political figures would be invited since then.

Professor Peter Bauer and rubber replanting dilemma

I had known Professor Peter Bauer long before he gave the first public lecture initiated by Dr Goh. I had just returned from Oxford University and was in Kuala Lumpur then at the University of Malaya.

He came to see me in 1965 and I took him out to lunch. I had thought that he wanted to see my department and meet its eminent head Professor Ungku Aziz. No, he said, undiplomatically. "I came here to see you."

I was surprised. "You came all the way from Britain to see me?" I blurted out. "Surely there must be something you want to see me about?"

He went straight to the point. "I don't agree with your suggestion about the replanting of rubber trees in the same areas where they once were. New rubber trees should be replanted in new areas to help in the opening up of the country."

I protested, arguing that one needed infrastructure such as hospitals, schools, water supplies and so forth which would take time to build if rubber trees were replanted in completely new areas. On the other hand, replanting trees in the old areas where they once were made more sense since there were already roads, schools, hospitals and public services, police stations, security and other facilities.

It took some time but he later came around to my way of thinking. I had wondered about his interest when I found out that his PhD thesis was on the rubber industry in Southeast Asia and the British colonies. He was right, however, about what he had said. When the replanting of old trees had been completed or replaced with oil palms new areas had to be found for further expansion. At that time, the world did not talk about deforestation.

Dr Mahathir Mohammed's visit

The head of the Economics Department was expected to be the president of the Economic Society of Singapore and be the editor of the *Singapore Economic Review* as well.

When I was president we used to have annual dinners at which we would invite guests-of-honour. One of them was Dr Mahathir Mohammed who at that time was not the prime minister but the trade and industry minister of Malaysia. It was obvious to me, however, that he was on his way to become the prime minister of Malaysia.

Serving as secretary to the Economic Society and assistant secretary were Dr Basant Kapur and Dr Amina Tyabji respectively. Both helped to coordinate the visit.

They received a letter from the Ministry of Foreign Affairs that we should get in touch with them concerning Minister Mahathir Mohammed's impending visit. The letter said: "Please tell your professor that certain protocol requirements have to be complied with."

One of the requirements was that we had to go to the airport in two cars to welcome Minister Mahathir and his entourage and go in a car with a driver and that the car had to be big and dignified enough — a Mercedes no less. We also had to arrange for him to arrive at the VIP airport lounge.

In reply, we indicated that our department did not possess such a car nor did the professor; what's more, I had no driver either.

However, Amina did have a Mercedes and driver, so we asked Foreign Affairs if we could be provided with another suitable car as we were told to go in two cars.

They replied that since Minister Mahathir was coming in as a private guest of the Economic Society, a government car could not be used since a flag would have to be flown making it official.

I then turned to the EDB (Economic Development Board) for help. We got it. They would lend us a suitable car with a driver.

Basant, the Society's secretary, had presented Dr and Mrs Mahathir with a first class return ticket each. But Mahathir was oh-so-polite; he said nothing. He had actually flown in on his official jet so the return tickets were of no avail!

My wife and I had also gone to the airport to receive our guests. It was the first time that I was personally receiving dignitaries. And what an experience that was!

At that time, I whisked from the airport through the streets of Singapore without a single traffic light holding me up. The government had switched off all the traffic lights along the route to facilitate Dr Mahathir's visit. What an experience it was to be part of it, I told my wife later. Yes, she was with me too, as was the requirement.

During his visit, on the way to the hotel, Dr Mahathir told me he wanted to pay a courtesy call to see then Prime Minister Lee Kuan Yew. It was so courteous of Dr Mahathir to want to call on PM Lee first. Probably that was the proper protocol too.

Minister Mahathir struck me as a polite and elegant figure. Leaving aside his communal politics, he has many compensating factors, such as his charming personality and his great command of the English language.

I must also add a note about his humility. At the Shangri-La Hotel, before delivering his keynote speech, he told me, "Chong Yah, I am a bit uncomfortable, must you have as many as eight people to guard me? That means I cannot talk to you freely. Can you ask your bodyguards to stay a distance away from us?"

What he said came as a surprise as I didn't know there were bodyguards in the hotel; later I learnt that they had been dispatched from our Foreign Office for the protection of VVIPs like Dr Mahathir from Malaysia.

Dr Mahathir was overall impressed with his visit to Singapore calling it "an efficient country." His visit became a talking point among the academics for a long time to come.

Dr Sumitro Djojohadikusumo and Professor Sinichi Ichimura

Apart from Mahathir Mohammed, the Economic Society was honoured to have been able to welcome two other distinguished guests.

One of them was Dr Sumitro Djojohadikusumo, father of Prabowo Subianto, who had stood for the presidential elections of Indonesia in 2014.

Dr Sumitro was a wonderful and impressive figure. He spoke English beautifully and was conversant in Dutch as well as French. An economics expert, he held important government positions. Years later, I successfully proposed for him to be the first and founding President of the East Asian Economic Association (EAEA).

The other was Professor Sinichi Ichimura, an old and dear friend, the founder of the EAEA in 1987. He had invited me to be the visiting professor at Kyoto University in response to my invitation to him to be a visiting professor at the University of Singapore. He stayed for a year and forged valuable friendships with the university academia, student body and my family.

Despite being the founder, Ichimura declined to head the organisation as president. I gathered it was because of Japan's World War II history in most of the member countries although he did not give any reason. It was agreed that members should elect a Southeast Asian to be president. I suggested Dr Sumitro Djojohadikusumo who carried out the duties well.

I would meet Dr Sumitro again and again at EAEA annual international conventions held in various cities of member countries. One day, after 10 years of being president he said he wished to resign. At a convention held in Seoul which he was unable to attend, he left word with the large Indonesian delegation that he wanted me to serve as the next president.

However, I noticed Ichimura was getting old and so I approached him and asked if he wanted to be president since, after a decade, political sensitivity would not likely pose an issue. Ichimura indicated that he was ready to succeed to the presidency. My next task was to convince the huge Indonesian delegation to have Ichimura and not me as president as they were under instructions from Sumitro to choose me. Thank goodness, I managed to persuade the Indonesian delegates and it was befitting that as soon as Ichimura was made president in 1998, he could preside over the 11th EAEA convention being held in Kitayushu, Japan in the same year. I was glad to have been able to step aside for him.

Muhyiddin Yassin

Nearer to home, another one of the Economics Society's guests was the Menteri Besar, or chief minister, of Johor, Tan Sri Dato Haji Muhyiddin Yassin. I considered the relationship with Johor to be of the utmost importance and because of its proximity, the value of our friendship could not be overrated.

I hosted a dinner for the Menteri Besar at Hotel Equatorial, one of Singapore's best hotels then; it also happened to be close to our university campus. After my salutations and welcome, Muhyiddin made a speech eliciting laughter when he said, "Ladies and gentlemen, I must have been a very average undergraduate when I was studying economics at the University of Malaya at Pantai Valley because the

President of the Economic Society of Singapore, Professor Lim Chong Yah, does not seem to remember me."

He went on, "If I had been a top student, I am sure he would remember me as his student; similarly, he would remember me if I was the lousiest. It so happened that I did not give him trouble at all. I was just average or above average, but not top or last.

"I was among his first batch of students studying applied economics; he was head of the Applied Economics department then."

The audience cheered.

It was friendships like these that made my tenure at the university so memorable.

Rafidah Aziz

I remember another occasion in 1990. It was the year when it was Singapore's turn to host a plenary conference of the PECC. It would be presided over by Chandra Das, an eminent Member of Parliament, who had succeeded me as chairman of the Singapore chapter of the PECC.

The keynote speaker at the conference held in Shangri-La Hotel was the Malaysian Minister of Trade and Industry Rafidah Aziz. She was a good speaker and she played a good-natured game of golf with the delegates, breezily refusing to accept the ladies' handicap and teeing off at the same tee as the men.

But things were a little less cordial during the plenary proceedings when a controversy broke out. I recall it was about Malaysia's controversial capital control imposition. The lady minister replied, "You know in this controversy my professor, Professor Lim Chong Yah, is on record supporting Malaysia's position." The audience cheered.

We used the Economic Society of Singapore to help build good relationships, particularly in Southeast Asia. One of the results of this was a book I wrote in 2000 based on Southeast Asia. I called it *Southeast Asia — The Long Road Ahead*. It has since run into three editions.

Abdullah Badawi

Speaking of friendships and encounters, there was another incident that I found uplifting. This was in 1989, when I had just had my quintuple heart bypass. I was recovering but felt somewhat discouraged and at times despondent. I found solace walking in MacRitchie Reservoir, which was close to my home. It was the place where I could relax while admiring the beauty of nature in the quiet reservoir grounds.

I lacked the inclination of attending conferences. I seemed to have lost all exuberance.

One day, I received a call from Professor Sandhu about the visit of the then Malaysian Foreign Minister Abdullah Badawi who he had invited to speak to the Institute of Southeast Asian Studies.

He cajoled me, saying, "Chong Yah, you should come out; why not come to the talk?"

A little reluctantly, I went. At the talk, Badawi said, "Do you know, in Malaysia they like to criticise me saying that I only know about the Islamic religion because I specialised in the Malay Studies Department but they forgot we had to do three subjects. One of them was economics and Professor Lim Chong Yah was my professor and he passed me," pointing at me after he had searched me out among the audience. I was a bit taken aback but felt honoured, nonetheless.

All present cheered. After that, Badawi came over to shake my hand. It seemed that the image of the future prime minister of Malaysia shaking his former professor's hand was beamed nationwide in Singapore.

Badawi may not have realised it but that night he helped to dispel my gloom. I snapped out of my inertia after his visit and went back to work.

Paul Chan

Another uplifting episode involved being an examiner not once, but three times, to one of my outstanding students. I had first met Paul TH Chan when I was at the University of Malaya in Pantai Valley. He was a student in my economics class. After obtaining his honours degree, then MEc, (Master of Economics), Paul left Malaysia to go to Canada to further his studies. During the thick of winter during his stay at Hamilton, he wrote me a letter to say that he was feeling cold and lonely especially since his wife Kam Yoke, who was also one of my economics students at Pantai Valley, was still unable to join him because of her work commitments.

He wrote, "The only friend I have is your book, *Economic Development of Modern Malaya*. I go to the library to turn the pages and remember old times when we were in the Pantai Valley in Kuala Lumpur." Actually, I had supervised his BA Hons thesis as well as his MEc thesis.

A year later, Paul moved to a less harsh place in Canberra, Australia to complete his PhD at the Australian National University (ANU), after obtaining his MA from

McMaster University at Hamilton. Three examiners were required for his doctorate of which two would be provided by the university while Paul was allowed to make his own choice for the third examiner.

I was flattered when I was informed by ANU that I was selected to be the chief examiner for Paul. The reason? His thesis was on export taxes, which was also my speciality. In fact, long ago I had written about it for my master's degree. So Paul flew from Canberra to Singapore where I examined him orally, with the help of a well-known visiting expert in agricultural economics from the US who was then in Singapore.

So, Paul did his honours degree and master's degree under my watch and was later examined by me for his PhD.

Decades later, when I visited Kuala Lumpur, Paul called to update me on his life. He was able to found a private university (the first in Malaysia) and his wife Kam Yoke too had great success in equity investments.

As it came to pass, Kam Yoke too came from a humble economic background. I gave a great deal of my typing duties to her to help her with some income, in her undergraduate days.

It was good to know that Paul and his wife were doing very well. Teasing him on their new found affluence, I joked, "If I have to borrow money, I now know where to go!"

What a privilege it was to have had people like Paul Chan, Kam Yoke, Rafidah Aziz, Muhyiddin Yassin, and last but not least, Abdullah Badawi, as my students.

Academic life in Kuala Lumpur and then in Singapore to me was but a continuity in the world of higher learning and research. As we approach the end of this chapter, I will round off with a saying from Malcolm Forbes, "The biggest mistake people make in life is not trying to make a living at doing what they most enjoy."

Premier Zhao and my EGOIN theory

It was in May 1989. I was invited to a dinner function in Beijing together with more than a hundred conference participants from Third World countries. The international conference was held in Shanghai. As a post-conference event, we were all invited to Beijing for a banquet presumably to celebrate the success of the conference and for the delegates to look at the rapid, impressive growth of Beijing, the capital of China.

Premier Zhao Ziyang said that he had sent the blueprint of China's further development for the next ten years to Mr Lee Kuan Yew. He was glad to announce that

Prime Minister Lee had given him his strong support and blessing on the direction of China's further economic development. Both Mr Wong Meng Quang, Singapore's trade representative in China (both countries had yet to establish diplomatic ties) and I were pleasantly surprised by the high esteem Premier Zhao gave to Mr Lee Kuan Yew. We felt that Singapore was singularly honoured by the Chinese Premier.

There was another pleasant surprise. Premier Zhao continued, "I have gone through many of the conference papers. I would like to recommend to you to read the one from Singapore as the most relevant and the most enlightening for the rapid development of Third World countries." He did not mention me by name, but the delegates present knew that he was referring to my paper.

On my table sitting next to me was an editor-in-chief of a mass-circulation daily from India. He turned to me and remarked, "Beware of the Trojan Horse. The Chinese Premier is taking the first step to incorporate Singapore as a part of China."

My paper was published together with other conference papers by the Chinese Association for International Understanding in a book with the title "Development Strategies for Third World Countries," March 1990. My article was entitled, "THE EGOIN THEORY OF DEVELOPMENT AND UNDERDEVELOPMENT," pages 13–42.

10.1. Book launch of essays in my honour. This was the very generous initiative of Professor Euston Quah (seated fourth from left). The book was launched by Professor Tommy Koh, a long-time academic colleague at the National University of Singapore (second from left). February 1996.

NUS convocation ■ Reports by Sandra Davie and Joan Bungar

S'pore 'can reach top of rich nations' league'

New Professor Emeritus Lim Chong Yah gives formula for growth

Top honour ... Mrs Lim Chong Yah helping her husband, a noted local economist, dress for the presentation ceremony.

10.2. The Straits Times newspaper clipping showing my wife, Nah Nah, helping me with the mortarboard. This was on the occasion of the conferment of Emeritus Professorship on me by the National University of Singapore, September 1992.

Source: The Straits Times © Singapore Press Holdings Limited. Permission required for reproduction.

10.3. Visit to my office by Nobel Laureate Professor Milton Friedman and his wife, Mrs Rose Friedman, in 1980. He gave the inaugural lecture, "The Invisible Hand in Economics and Politics", in the Singapore Lecture series.

10.4. Nobel Laureate Professor Sir John Hicks was my D Phil supervisor in Oxford and he and his wife, Lady Ursula Hicks, also a distinguished economist, made frequent visits to Singapore and the Department of Economics. They both gave lectures at the department in 1982.

10.5. As President of the Economic Society of Singapore, I invited Nobel Laureate Professor Wassily Leontief to give a public lecture at the National University of Singapore in 1982. Mrs Leontief was so impressed with the visit that she subsequently wrote a flattering article on Singapore for The New York Times.

10.6. National Wages Council at work, trying to solve the 1973/74 economic crisis.

CHAPTER 11

OVERSEAS SABBATICALS

Sabbaticals, the best perk

My academic career in the University of Singapore, later renamed National University of Singapore (NUS) when it merged with Nanyang University in 1980, spanned 23 years from 1969 to 1992.

One of the greatest benefits of this career package was its liberal sabbatical leave granted every three years to full professors for a period of six months each. I was made a full professor in 1972, so I was able to enjoy this generous perk. The package also saw me provided with a car when I was appointed Senior Professor in 1983.

The granting of sabbatical leave was seen as a means of retaining good teaching staff and to help the university attract new capable staff. To be honest, the pay for lecturers and professors then was far from being globally competitive, unlike in the last 10 years or so. Getting world class professors was always a problem. So, the introduction of sabbatical leave was seen as an added fillip to an academic career. The scheme, widely practised in western universities, allowed professors to go on leave on full pay with air-passage paid. Host institutions could — and often did — add their own perks, such as subsidised housing and in rare cases, an honorarium.

Thanks to this programme, I was able to visit various universities in different countries and the time spent in each of them was very dear to me, building up a cache of memories which have stayed with me till this day.

Sabbaticals offer a break from work allowing those who go on them to return refreshed and invigorated. It is a time when you can visit universities globally to deliver lectures, do research, pick up a new skill or simply meet with fellow academics to get an insight into the work they do and how universities elsewhere are run. They are truly eye-openers often giving new perspectives to participants. And without exception, all my lengthier overseas trips were in this category.

However, because of my National Wages Council (NWC) commitments, I was not able to take the full period of six months; I was able to spare up to four months at a time only. Still, the extended leave provided a precious break from work, and allowed me to build up useful relationships with host institutions. I would also sometimes split the four months to cover two different countries.

The sabbatical programme gave me the opportunity to visit many countries. I will dwell on some of the more significant ones which also offered me a glimpse into another culture, another world. These sabbatical visits included the Australian National University (ANU) in Canberra, Australia, Kyoto University in Japan, National Taiwan University (NTU) in Taipei, Ohio University in the United States and my alma mater, Oxford University, in the United Kingdom.

Australian National University

I had been to Australia several times to attend international conferences. I had, however, never been attached to any of its well-known universities, although the idea of being a visiting professor someday was uppermost in my mind every time I made a conference trip Down Under.

Professor Heinz Arndt

So, I was pleasantly surprised when Professor Heinz Arndt of ANU invited me in 1976 to be a Visiting Fellow, which was akin to a visiting professorship, one of many to come in the next two decades. Unlike in Singapore where we would let academics deliver a lecture or two whenever they wrote to us of their desire to do so, the system in ANU is different. One has to be invited.

Professor Arndt was one of Australia's most prominent economists, and one of the first to recognise the importance of the Asia-Pacific region to Australia. He had been professor of economics for more than 30 years, and was appointed emeritus professor in 1981.

Professor Arndt and I had many mutual friends. His parents fled from Germany in the 1930s to England where he studied and gained two degrees in economics at Oxford University. He taught at Manchester University thanks to Sir John Hicks who was the professor of economics there. He moved to Sydney in 1946 when he was offered a teaching position and stayed on in Australia ever since. Prior to my arrival at ANU, Professor Arndt was an external examiner for the University of Singapore and I had the opportunity to get to know him and his wife Ruth. He also knew Dr Goh Keng Swee, who was then minister of defence.

Apart from ANU where I gave several talks, Professor Arndt also arranged for me to visit other institutions of higher learning in Australia and deliver lectures. They included Monash University in Melbourne, the University of Adelaide and the University of New South Wales in Sydney.

Lunch appointments sans lunch

My most worthy successor in the economics department of Nanyang Technological University (NTU) when I retired, Professor Ng Yew Kuang, who was a distinguished professor at Monash University during my visit there and was tasked as my minder, has on several occasions told me that my talk there on entrepreneurship and economic development was considered an important event in the university's calendar.

During my stay in Canberra, Professor Arndt and I got together often for lunch and a game of chess.

However, I made a *faux pas* on the first occasion. When he ushered me to his room, he said, "You forgot to bring your lunch box." I was surprised and said I had no idea I was expected to do so. "Well," he explained, "it is customary here among academicians to bring their own lunch box at get-togethers."

I replied, "In Singapore, we bring them out to lunch!"

I brought my own lunch thereafter. Professor Arndt was a consummate chess player. I never beat him in all our lunch matches.

There were other occasions at ANU when I was invited to deliver lunch-time talks to various groups at 12 noon, after which I assumed we would all go out for lunch somewhere. But at each of these talks, all would bring their own lunch boxes except me! However, there was always someone who would make a run to a restaurant to get a sandwich and coffee for me.

As I was to find out time and time again on all my sabbaticals, there are different practices in different countries, some of which are so different even in places where a visitor may speak the same language.

Throughout my sojourn, I found the Australians to be very polite and friendly. On one occasion, my wife, who accompanied me on all my sabbaticals, was driving a hired Beetle which unfortunately stalled in the middle of a busy road. A long line of cars was behind her, yet none of the motorists hooted at her to get out of the way. They waited patiently while she managed to coax the car back to life again.

The only disagreeable thing during our visit was the huge cow flies that stubbornly stuck to our clothes wherever we went. We found out they were abundant in summer and made a mental note to avoid visiting Australia in summer in future.

What was also unforgettable was the rate of the Australian dollar to our currency, equivalent to S$3.30 then. So, my daily dose of coffee was very costly indeed. In fact, I found everything to be expensive except wine, which was cheaper than water. I was thus often offered wine instead of water. Even in posh restaurants when I asked for water I would be told, "Why not have wine, which is cheaper than water?" The Singapore dollar has since appreciated and is now more or less on par with the Australian dollar.

Professor Max Corden

During my time in ANU, I also met W Max Corden, the future successor of Heinz Arndt. Professor Corden was, coincidentally, also born in Germany, in Breslau (now Wroclaw in Poland) as was Arndt. He had been attached to Nuffield College in Oxford for nearly 10 years and had just returned to Australia. He confessed to me that he had difficulty adjusting to Australia. He said he had more affinity with European/ British culture and found Australia to be different. I guess I had adapted more than he did, as I found little difference between the two.

Years later, after my return from Canberra, Professor Corden who later became one of Australia's best-known academics spent his sabbatical leave attached to our economics department at the University of Singapore for several months in 1981. He became one of the treasured members of our teaching staff and was even part of the university's delegation to present fiscal issues to our Ministry of Finance.

Professor Hal Hill

Professor Hal Hill, until recently the head of the department at ANU, renamed Arndt-Corden department in honour of the two pioneering heads, told me when he was a distinguished visitor at Nanyang Technological University (NTU) where I moved to in 1992 that he was a PhD student at ANU during my sabbatical visit.

In Australia, I noticed that all academic staff was expected to turn up to listen to invited outside lecturers; if they could not attend, they would call and render their apologies. Back here, because we have many such outside lectures taking place, there was no expectation of attendance from the teaching staff at all. We only want our students to attend.

Putting out a fire

ANU did not have many visitors then. My wife and I were often invited to fellow academics' homes. In one of them, home to a professor, a fire broke out suddenly in the kitchen. I rushed to put it out by pouring water on the flames which I later was told was a dangerous deed as there could have been oil and there could have been an explosion. But all ended well. Years later, I was glad to learn that the wife of this professor was appointed high commissioner to Malaysia.

Professor and Mrs Wang Gungwu

Among the homes that we visited was that of Professor and Mrs Wang Gungwu. Professor Wang was then the Director of the School of Pacific and Asian Studies. He was world famous by then for his research on China and the Chinese diaspora.

During our four-month stay, my wife and I were given a choice of staying in an apartment or house. We were advised to select the apartment, as it was more expensive and more exclusive. But coming from Singapore where landed property is scarce, we opted for the house. This was located on Campbell Street near Lake Burrie Griffin which provided us with many pleasurable moments walking around it beneath shady trees, an experience enhanced by cool weather. Houses in Canberra had no fences.

Completing a chapter on Schumpeter

It was in ANU that I wrote my chapter on Schumpeterian entrepreneurship which later became a chapter in my book *Development and Underdevelopment* published in 1991.

That was my first sabbatical in a foreign country for which I felt greatly privileged.

Ohio University

Immediately after Canberra, I continued with another sabbatical in the United States, at Ohio University in Athens where I spent another four months. Our university had allowed us to accumulate our sabbaticals, so I decided to use the unspent ones in the USA. This time, my wife and I brought all our four children with us.

When we went to Canberra, we only brought our two younger children, as they were still very small while we left our two older ones with my wife's parents. We felt they were big enough to manage without us. In fact, the oldest, Fern, was just starting her first year in National Junior College.

After we came back to prepare for our move to Ohio, the second leg of my first sabbatical leave, we took all our four children along. It would be our family's first-ever visit and sojourn in the US.

We arrived at midnight in Cincinatti, Ohio where we were picked up and driven to Ohio University in Athens.

I had been invited to Ohio on the Fulbright Scholar-in-Residence Program, a prestigious scheme that brings foreign scholars to lecture and/or conduct post-doctoral research for up to a year at American colleges and universities.

Technically, I was expected to stay for at least a year, although I was appointed a Fulbright professor for two years. However, because of my NWC work, I hinted that I might have to cut my visit short but would strive to stay as long as I could. There was also a clause in the programme that in unforeseen circumstances I could shorten my stay and return home.

Teaching at Ohio University

I was given a class to teach Southeast Asian economy to students on the master's programme. I found out that the class was using a textbook written by Gunnar Myrdal, which was a revamped version of his original book. *Asian Drama*.

The teaching was structured and every week, there would be a fixed topic to teach.

We had arrived in early winter in 1977 and were given a flat to stay at a place called Carriage Hill, which to our delight, had an excellent heating system, far superior to the one we had in Oxford.

I also observed during my stay that the American standard of living was much higher than in Britain and noticed that the US too as a whole was more technologically advanced.

I bought a second-hand Buick to ferry the family around. It was a huge car that needed at least two equivalent Singapore car park lots for parking. It was a gas guzzler too but petrol was still very cheap in the US despite the OPEC oil crisis then.

I wanted to buy a comprehensive motor insurance policy. I was told by the insurance company I approached in Athens not to bother. Apparently, motor insurance was not compulsory, and in a town like Athens (which had a smaller population than Toa Payoh Town) where cars were not so numerous, the danger of accidents was minimal. I was told to just drive carefully; besides, cars were so cheap they could easily be replaced. I was unhappy, being used to compulsory car insurance in Singapore. I felt happier if I could buy at least a third party insurance policy. I finally got one to the bemusement of the insurance company.

The weather in Athens was cold, with winter temperatures often minus 20 degrees Celsius. It was so cold that the huge Ohio River stayed frozen for most of the winter season. But it was so beautiful to see it covered with ice and all of Athens in snow many feet deep.

It was the first time that my family had been to a place that was so cold. With so much snow we spent a lot of time on weekends, enjoying tobogganing.

My youngest son, Ron, who was then five years old liked it the most and would cry if I did not join him in sliding down the snowy slopes on a wooden sledge for a thrilling descent.

Fast forward 30 years later — we still do the same thing in Switzerland but the roles are reversed with him accompanying me to make sure that *I* would be safe! Apart from tobogganing in Switzerland, the children and grandchildren learnt to ski as well.

On Sunday mornings, we would go to the Methodist Church near Ohio University to worship. We were the only Asians present. The pastor was kind and friendly. "You have a beautiful family," he said on a few occasions. The congregation was intrigued by us and some invited us to their homes now and again, as in Australia.

One thing I will never forget though was the chime of church bells at noon, especially during the thick of winter when we would be teaching. This brought back memories of the church bells ringing out the same tune when I was a child in Malacca. Here at Ohio University, it was a signal for professors to call a break for lunch.

To our surprise, the cost of living in Ohio was reasonable with food, wine and just about everything else inexpensively priced. Even with four children we could afford decent food and did not have to forego favourite items. We had mostly home-cooked meals though as my wife had developed her cooking skills and there was no necessity to go for fast-food, though this was the children's favourite.

Helping a Filipino pastor

One day, while I was driving from our Carriage Hill home to Ohio University, a two-kilometre drive away, I saw a man walking about aimlessly. He looked lost. He did not strike me as a homeless person though, as he was elegantly dressed.

I parked my car and got out to speak with him, asking him if he was lost and needed help.

He said yes, asking me for help, suggesting perhaps that I could buy him breakfast as it was a while since he had eaten. I noticed he was Asian and thought he was perhaps a visiting scholar from Thailand. He told me he was a Methodist pastor from the Philippines and had been sent to Ohio to study with donations from his parishioners. But he had mistakenly flown to Athens in the state of Georgia instead which was a long way off from Athens, Ohio. By the time he realised his mistake and with the need to buy a new ticket to Ohio, he had run out of donation money.

He had arrived on a red-eye flight and told the taxi driver to bring him to a church — after several attempts, the driver managed to locate a Methodist church. It was just past midnight. The church was shut. He was left in the cold.

He said he felt abandoned and perhaps it was a sign that God wanted him to return home to the Philippines. He added, "But now you appeared and perhaps

God has sent you as an angel and now I feel less desperate to go back." This was said after breakfast and hot coffee.

After breakfast, I brought him to the registrar's office to register for his course. I also gave him my telephone number to call if he needed any help. He then declared that he would now only go home after he had completed his master's degree as intended.

In Ohio, I noticed that American universities were rather collegial, keen to establish links with its teaching staff, which included a requirement for all to attend faculty meetings to keep in touch.

I also observed one of their rules which I had not encountered in other universities before. As soon as examinations were over, all teaching staff was not allowed to leave the campus for at least two weeks during which all examination scripts had to be marked and handed over.

Student wanted higher grades

One day, after completing my marking, I had a delegation of eight burly young men barging into my room. They were all students hailing from Thailand, and they were petitioning me to pass a fellow Thai student who had received very poor grades from me. I said that I could not give him a passing mark, as he could not write even a proper paragraph without incurring grammatical errors. Yes, I told them I noticed that the failed student had already a BA degree to his name from a completely unknown US college but I knew that many American colleges had differing standards.

I told them in reply, "In the interest of ASEAN pride and dignity, we cannot please everyone by purposely giving a student passing marks for him to get a master's degree just because he is from ASEAN." The student delegation had pleaded to me to pass the failed student because he hailed from ASEAN.

I stood firm on this principle even though I thought the burly Thai students might threaten me. But they were polite over the whole matter and left my office. They agreed that the failed student could not be granted his MA without further studies.

Apart from the Thais, Ohio University had a diverse student population coming from Asia. It received regularly various Asian newspapers including Singapore's The Straits Times, Malaysia's The New Straits Times and even Nanyang Siang Pau. It had a substantial number of Malaysians among the student population but few Singaporeans.

I was not in contact with many Asian students, as I was teaching the master's programme which had mostly Americans. I found out that the Malaysian students in the university were nearly all Malays and had been sent on government scholarships. One of them, from Johor, took particular care of me and my family.

Prior to my going to America, I had the impression that most American students were impolite, aggressive and rowdy, culled from watching Hollywood movies. Nothing could be further from the truth. In fact, the students were similar to those back home; they did not always ask questions nor were they argumentative. Sometimes I wished they were not as reticent as our students. I had to provoke them to ask questions and I had to urge them to read. In many ways the American students were as likeable as our own students back home. This was one aspect of the American society that I was exposed to even though I was aware that Athens might not be representative of the entire country.

One day, I received a message from Singapore that my presence was urgently needed to convene an emergency meeting of the NWC. I informed my hosts who thought it was a pity that I should leave after only four months. Prior to this, they had even suggested that I could spend some time with other universities in the US as well. I decided to take up on their offer and arrangements were made for me to give lectures in the beautiful mountain state of nearby West Virginia at two universities, one of which was Marshall University, which made a deep impression on me with its highly regarded economics department and research programme.

University of Kyoto

I think I might have been the first Singapore academic to have gone to Japan on sabbatical leave when I was a visiting professor there from June to December 1983.

Many of my colleagues and friends in Singapore were curious about my choice of a non-English speaking country. Their first pick was invariably the US or Britain.

But I wanted to have first-hand knowledge of the miraculous economic transformation of Japan. A book written by Ezra Vogel — *Japan as Number One: Lessons for America* (1979) — then an emeritus professor at Harvard University, had already propounded Japan as one of the most developed economies in the world.

Prior to setting foot in Kyoto, I had visited Japan on several occasions participating in regional forums on economic development in Southeast Asia and Japan, but not on a long-term basis.

Before World War II, Japanese universities virtually shut out foreigners, who were not allowed to teach. I had always considered knowledge and universities as a conduit of knowledge to be universal and felt that an interchange of scholars would benefit the host and guest country alike.

At the time of my visit, Singapore and Japan had instituted a taxation agreement under which visiting scholars would not be subject to the host country's taxes. This was to encourage Japanese and Singapore academics to go on mutual exchange programmes. Prior to this agreement, there were hardly any such exchanges.

It was against this background that I was invited to the University of Kyoto. The person responsible for the invitation was Professor Sinichi Ichimura, who was then director of the university's Institute of Southeast Asian Studies. He also provided me with a research assistant.

I was appointed with the understanding that I would be there for a minimum of a year and up to two years in order to allow time for friendly ties to take root for the mutual benefit of both countries.

Again, I had to caution my hosts that I might have to stay only for four to six months, because of my work with the NWC that I valued so much. As it turned out, I was in Kyoto for seven months, the longest time I had spent on any sabbatical.

It turned out to be a very fruitful sojourn and an eye-opener.

My wife and I were housed in an elegant Japanese-style bungalow built of wood, which was essential as Japan was prone to earthquakes and wood structures were considered safer. The double-storey house was located in the midst of rice fields. It was well-structured and well-located, and we enjoyed the beauty of the place, taking walks and observing frogs hopping about in the rice fields. I did not see fighting fish though.

The house actually belonged to a sociology professor at the university. In Japan, most well-established academics would have two homes. The house was newly built and the professor had not even used it at all but Ichimura was able to persuade him, Professor Chibouchi, to let us stay there.

However, it was some distance away from the university (about 10 kilometres), so I had to travel to work each day by bus. I had to memorise the name of the place to alight, known as Nagatani Wakare, so that I could get back without getting lost.

Although it was a lovely house, there was a bit of a problem whenever we hosted visitors. For instance, whenever one used the bathroom, it was possible to make out one's silhouette as there was basically just a glass screen in front of it. Of course, if there was just myself and my wife, there would be no problem, but for our first visitors, a good friend Hank Lim, his wife Celeste and their two boys, Mark and Matthew, we had to think of a solution of preserving one's privacy. We finally settled on putting up a poster in front of the screen to block out the silhouette.

That was my first introduction to the Japanese concept of privacy. In fact, the Japanese were some of the most uninhibited people I knew, for whom being naked when taking a public bath was considered normal such as when bathing together in an *onsen* (hot spring).

The Japanese *onsen*

Ah, the *onsen!* It is quite an institution in Japan and it may have taken a bit of time, but we soon learnt how to go to the *onsen* regularly and partake in the ritual of soaping the body and washing thoroughly before stepping into a pool of naturally hot water that is piped in from geothermally heated springs. And to do this completely naked in front of others, which took a while to get used to, I must admit!

In the old days, the *onsen* was the only place to take a bath. So, perhaps the tradition of having to strip completely before taking a bath started with this. In any case, the Japanese seemed to be very comfortable with the idea of nudity. I was told, "There is nothing to hide. That's how we become friends." Indeed, I noticed that colleagues would often go to the *onsen* together.

In the past, there was mixed bathing but now the *onsens* have developed separate facilities for men and women. Although mixed bathing no longer functions as public bathing in most places, going to the *onsen* is still a tradition among the Japanese, as the *onsen* water, which contains various minerals, is believed to have healing powers.

Years later, when a group of church friends and I travelled on holiday to Hokkaido, I arranged for a stay in a *ryokan* (traditional Japanese inn) with an *onsen.* At first, they all refused to use the *onsen*, saying that they would try it only if I took the lead, meaning going naked first. Next day, however, when I went there, I found the men were already soaking in the *onsen* bath! The sulphuric waters were relaxing and helped to shed their inhibitions. They were serenading their wives who were in an *onsen* next door, separated by a screen. No more lead or prompting from me was called for.

After the trip, whenever my wife and I planned to go to Japan, they would ask if they could come along!

Orderly Japan

My stay in Kyoto gave me other insights into Japanese culture. The Japanese have a strong sense of hygiene and like to have their own private space as well. In my office room, for instance, there was a basin with a mirror provided, so you could wash up without the need to go to the common restroom.

They are also mindful of the need to think of the needs of their subordinates. The institute had a common room for supporting staff such as secretaries and clerks. The spacious and comfortable room with tatami mats was for them to catch up on rest or even sleep, if necessary.

The university also had a lunch system whereby you order your food in advance for delivery at lunchtime. And you lunch in the privacy of your own room. Tea is always part of the menu.

Once a month, however, we were required to eat with others in a common room, when the president of the university would also participate. Japanese society is quite hierarchical so the visit of the president is well regarded. In fact, when I first arrived at the university, I was given an impressive invitation certificate signed by the university president himself so that I could be granted courtesies throughout the campus.

Japanese society is also extremely orderly; I don't think I ever saw a vagabond in the streets. To me, it was a great place and I felt that other countries could learn from Japan to achieve the kind of wealth and high quality of life and social discipline that its people enjoyed.

They also loved pedigree dogs and I would often see the Japanese walking their dogs in the streets and parks, carefully cleaning up their droppings after them.

During my stay, I spent a lot of time reading, and wrote a chapter on Karl Marx and Asian Development in my book *Development and Underdevelopment*, partly because the Marxist influence in Kyoto then was very strong.

After our stay in the house in the rural area and before returning home, we moved to a flat located on the grounds of the university. It was in a lodge specially built for visitors. That gave me the idea to propose to NUS to build similar lodgings for foreign visitors to our campus. Thus was born the Visitors' Lodge in NUS, and much later, the Nanyang Executive Centre (NEC) in NTU.

National Taiwan University

In 1987, I went to Taiwan for another of my sabbaticals. Again, like Japan, it was an unusual choice as it was not considered fashionable for Western-educated academics to go on sabbaticals in Taiwan. I was, however, interested in the miraculous economic metamorphosis in Taiwan. I wanted first-hand knowledge of it.

When I was appointed a visiting professor at the National Taiwan University, I was given a research assistant as well. I was pleasantly surprised because even as head of the economics department at NUS with 130 teaching staff to look after, I did not have the luxury of a research assistant, nor a department manager. Thank goodness, I had the good fortune to have a very able secretary, Mrs Annie Koh, to help out.

Looking back, years later, when I was recovering from a quintuple heart bypass operation, I wondered if the heavy administrative workload of the economics department, my NWC work and other community commitments had contributed to my life-threatening heart problem.

I was treated as a VVIP in Taiwan. I guess this stemmed from my time as a member of the Pacific Economic Cooperation Conference (PECC) steering committee when I moved to have Taiwan — and Hong Kong — also accepted as full members — when the international grouping suggested inviting China to the fold.

The Taiwanese were aware of this, and were immensely grateful for my efforts to get China to co-exist with them on the regional stage thus allowing them not to be so cut off from the rest of the world. During my stay at the National Taiwan University, I wrote a chapter on Taiwan's economic transformation for my book on *Development and Underdevelopment*.

As was my habit, after a prolonged stay in a country, I would give a public talk on the country's economy, providing an analysis as seen through the eyes of an outsider.

Honoured by Dr Shirley Kuo

At my first talk held in a host institute in town, I noticed the presence of the Governor of the National Bank of Taiwan, Dr Shirley Kuo Wang-jung, who was appointed a year later as the Minister of Finance. Her name in Chinese is 郭婉容 which was interesting to the mainland Chinese as this was also the name of the wife of Puyi, the last emperor of China. As Minister of Finance, she represented Taiwan at one of the PECC meetings in Beijing without any objections from China.

After my lecture, the chairman of the organising committee announced that I would be giving a similar lecture at the National Taiwan University a week later. The town lecture was very well attended, so was the university repeat lecture.

At this second lecture, I recognised a familiar face from the first talk among the audience. Governor Shirley Kuo turned up again. I remarked how honoured I was for her repeated presence and support.

The pretty lady stood up and remarked, "The lecture might be similar, but let me tell the audience that his jokes are totally different." Laughter followed.

My wife and I invited her to come to Singapore for the next PECC forum. She did come, much to the delight of the Singapore PECC delegation.

Honoured by Dr Koo Chen-fu

When I was in Taiwan, I was also able to meet with the chairman of the Taiwan PECC Koo Chen-fu, a very wealthy individual and a very well-known personality. He was not part of the government, but the most respected man with the government.

He often invited me to lunch at his home, declaring proudly that all the vegetables were grown in his own garden. That reminded me of our own Tan Sri Dr Tan Chin Tuan, who would serve his personal guests food and vegetables specially flown in from his gardens in New Zealand and Australia.

Years later, Dr Koo represented Taiwan to discuss with China on cross-straits relationship at a well-publicised meeting organised in Singapore. One Singapore host to both the cross-straits delegates was Mr Wee Cho Yaw, a renowned Singaporean banker. Mr Wee invited me to attend the dinner function as well.

Oxford University

I returned to the University of Oxford on sabbatical leave from December 1980 to February 1981. I went because Lady Ursula Hicks insisted that I should re-visit my alma mater, as it was 20 years since I had left. I was appointed a Visiting Senior Member of Linacre College, Oxford. Till this day, I am thankful that the College still keeps me posted on its activities.

By then, both Professor and Lady Hicks had already retired, but still maintained connections with Oxford, such as with Linacre College by Lady Hicks and All Souls by Professor Hicks.

Meeting Professor AK Sen at All Souls

Professor AK Sen who succeeded Hicks as Drummond Professor of Economics at Oxford would hold a monthly seminar with dinner at All Souls College, where Sir John had been associated. I attended all of the seminars in the three months that I was there. Not all the papers addressed the issues and problems of the British economy or world economy. Most were too abstract to me.

Revisiting the Hickses at Cotswold

My stay in Oxford was full of nostalgia. I was back again in familiar places that were so dear to me. It was a pleasure to find myself back at Porch House, the weekend residence of Professor Sir John and Lady Ursula Hicks in the lovely

Cotswold village of Blockley. This historic building was once a country residence of the bishops of Gloucester. I was familiar with Porch House which I had visited before during my student days.

My wife and I stayed in staff quarters for visiting professors at Little Clarendon Street, next to the famous Somerville College but would travel to Porch House now and then to visit the Hickses.

During my time in Oxford and on my other sabbaticals, I found the inspiration and had also the leisure to write my book *Development and Underdevelopment*, and in particular, to develop my EGOIN Theory of development and underdevelopment.

11.1. On sabbatical in Oxford in 1981. The bench is named after Lady Ursula Hicks, a dear friend and the wife of my supervisor, Professor Sir John Hicks.

CHAPTER 12

SURPRISES IN ACADEMIA

Convocation strike

When I returned to the University of Malaya in Pantai Valley in 1965 after completing my D Phil in Oxford, I noticed a general level of unhappiness among the younger academic staff. For some, there was an air of uncertainty because they had not been confirmed yet but even among those who were confirmed there was distrust with the university administration. I sensed some serious disconnect between the two.

At that time, the university had an academic staff association that was registered as a trade union. I served as vice-president, and when the then president Professor Syed Hussein Alatas left to work in the University of Singapore, I succeeded him as president.

Two unexpected events took place in the Kuala Lumpur campus that galvanised me against the university authority.

A lecturer in one department complained to me that he had to pay a bribe of RM3,000, then a big sum, in his second year of work so that the head (who was an Asian foreign national) would recommend him for confirmation. The following year, the head demanded more money to the tune of RM5,000. After assessing that the complaint was authentic, I took up the case and brought it to the attention of the university authorities. They were not keen to look into it, as they had other priorities. Later, I was told that the university actually did remove the head of department.

The university at that time was expanding very rapidly. They were recruiting many new overseas lecturers but were putting them in a hotel in a red-light district. There were complaints over this. I too considered that it was not right as the position of the university itself was being compromised. One reply by a powerful university authority really bothered me. He told me that should the overseas academicians misbehave themselves, they could later be "blackmailed by us", meaning by the administration.

To top things off, there were other problems over terms and conditions of work. There was also much resentment among the junior and not-so-junior teaching staff that they were not being paid justly.

I brought up these issues with the university administration as the president of the academic staff association. But our complaints fell on deaf ears; the authorities saw us as trouble makers.

I saw an opportunity to wake up the university administration when its annual convocation was due to take place. A month before this event, I met the authorities and told them that if nothing was done to improve the dignity and image of the university and improve the terms and conditions of work of the academic staff, the association would have no choice but to tell our members not to attend the convocation.

The authorities were not sure if this threat would be carried out. When they asked around and found out that the association members would be supporting the president's call if needed, they capitulated.

I was told, "Call off the threat to strike, we will look into the grievances."

So happily, the convocation strike never took place.

Standing up against injustices

Fast forward to the National University of Singapore (NUS) in 1980. It had just been formed with the amalgamation of the two universities — Nanyang University and the University of Singapore. We moved from Bukit Timah to the new campus on Kent Ridge. I remember joining the then vice-chancellor Dr Toh Chin Chye to plant some sapling trees to mark the beginning of campus establishment and campus life at Kent Ridge.

Some years later, I went on leave for a few days. When I returned to our Department of Economics and Statistics, then an eminent professor of statistics, Professor Saw Swee Hock, who is now a well-known philanthropist, spoke to me concerning a colleague, Dr SY Lee. He said, "I am to tell you that when his contract comes up, do not renew it."

I asked, "Who gave this instruction to us?" He replied, "It came from authorities above us." He would not tell me who they were.

I tried to get to the bottom of the story. One authority in the university told me that he had received a call from the Monetary Authority of Singapore (MAS) that SY Lee was a "lousy economist" and so his yearly contract should not be renewed. This was corroborated by another authority.

But I said to him, "I am the head of the department and an economist and it should be up to me to advise whether SY Lee is a good or lousy economist." I was truly not happy that an outside authority should give instructions to terminate the contract of one of my staff based on its own judgement.

I needed to find out more. I asked, "Who rang and must we follow their directive?"

I learned later that Dr SY Lee had proposed that the Singapore dollar be internationalised. That was considered offensive.

I said, "It may not be the prevailing view of MAS but that does not mean he is a lousy economist." He was entitled to his view.

I wanted to know the person who called our university. I was prepared to ring up then MAS chairman Dr Goh Keng Swee whom I had known from my earlier days in the Civil Service. I could also speak to my friends, chief economist and deputy managing director Dr Teh Kok Peng or then permanent secretary of the Finance Ministry Ngiam Tong Dow, to get MAS to tolerate or ignore Dr SY Lee's view.

Even if it had come from the lower rungs of the organisation, I was convinced that I could get this directive squashed. I just wanted to know the truth, but alas, I failed to know the source of the instructions.

Days passed; nothing happened until someone from the university called to say that Dr SY Lee's contract was due and could I consider writing an adverse report? I was quite upset and was tempted to tell the caller to go climb a coconut tree. But I managed to control myself. I did not have the inclination to antagonise the university administration, for whom I had the highest respect and admiration at any rate.

However, when it comes to inequities and unjust behaviour, I try to be tough. I replied that I would not write an adverse report because he did not deserve such a report. Instead, I wrote a fair and commendable report on SY Lee, with some praises in between.

I remember when I was visiting the US, eminent scholars such as Milton Friedman, had asked after him. I had supervised his doctoral thesis and he had written books and articles on monetary economics. He was by no means a "lousy economist" on one view alone.

But I must have upset the university administration; despite my intervention, his yearly contract was not extended. I was left to lick my wounds. Would I have to pay a price for my disobedience, I wondered?

Years later, another injustice concerning the university administration was to crop up.

It involved one of my teaching staff, Dr Xanadu (not his real name), who I was told was asked to leave the university immediately to return with his family to his home country. I got the news after I had come back from leave. I thought it was a bit sudden and since I had not been privy to his arranged departure, I tried to find out the truth.

Dr Xanadu had come to the Department of Economics and Statistics looking for a job after he had finished his doctoral studies in economics at the Australian National University. His supervisor was Professor Max Corden, one of Australia's most accomplished economists who had succeeded a friend of mine, Professor Heinz Arndt, an equally distinguished economist as head of the Economics Department there. Besides, Max had spent six months of his sabbatical leave with us and was a dear friend of the department.

In his report on Xanadu, Max confirmed that at he would be given his PhD in about three months' time once formalities were completed. In the meantime, he joined in with other referees to strongly recommend our department to take him, so I recommended to the university to appoint him subject to his obtaining his doctorate degree. This was the practice then.

In the interim, Xanadu had successfully applied to the Institute of Southeast Asian Studies for an appointment, probably a temporary appointment, instead of being unemployed whilst waiting for the formal confirmation of a PhD.

After three months at the institute, when Xanadu was conferred with his PhD, he told the Institute that he would be leaving to join the Department of Economics and Statistics at NUS. The Institute was upset. His service was terminated, and so he had to leave Singapore.

I explained to the Institute that he had earlier been offered a job at NUS subject to his getting his PhD and I said since he wanted to be in the company of economists, our department would be more suitable for him.

But to the Institute, a contract had been broken and Xanadu should leave Singapore. The institute even got in touch with the Immigration Department to have the latter's work visa revoked as was the standard practice.

I found out that the Institute had discussed the matter with the university authorities which were of the same opinion that there was no point in retaining Xanadu at the university. In those days, job hopping was frowned upon and what Xanadu did was perceived to be akin to job hopping.

Faced with this, I discussed with the acting head of the economics and statistics department during my absence, Professor Augustine Tan. He told me he had discussed and assigned Dr Xanadu his teaching schedule and also his room. So Dr Xanadu had been expected to come in.

In the circumstances, I considered the action to ask Xanadu to leave Singapore as too drastic. I did not like this kind of sledge hammer reaction to a fellow academician.

I instinctively thought that what we were doing was wrong. I asked the human resources department if we could consult our lawyer on the legality of the issue. After all, our department had already agreed to appoint him and he was even given a room and a teaching assignment, plus a letter of appointment by the university. This is what our lawyer more or less said, "Should this man take you to court, you would have no legs to stand on. Your contract with him cannot be terminated thus." The university wisely followed our lawyer's advice.

And so it is that Dr Xanadu has been working since 1995 with NUS. He is now an associate professor in a department at NUS.

I am glad things turned out well.

As an adjunct to this episode, when the university was told that Xanadu had to leave the country within two weeks (unless the situation was resolved), I approached Professor Ow Chin Hock, a member of our staff and also a Member of Parliament to ask if he could help prolong his period of stay a little longer, until his case was resolved.

We had intended to send Dr Xanadu and his family to Johor Bahru to wait it out while we sorted out his case. Chin Hock was very helpful. He managed to get the Immigration Department to extend his stay with his wife and school-going children in Singapore for one more week. That saved him and his family from deportation.

I must add that the Dr SY Lee and Dr Xanadu episodes came as a complete surprise to me, as I considered the university to be a very well-run institution, worthy of the highest praise and in many aspects, emulation. I surmised that we must not look out for perfection in others, as we would not want others to look out for perfection in us.

History of the Economics Department

One day in 1977, when I was in Canberra I chanced upon meeting my former mentor, Professor Tom Silcock, who had retired there.

I asked him if he would like to return to Singapore to write a book about the economics department. Much to my delight, he agreed.

He spent several months here interviewing people and doing research. The result was the book entitled *A History of Economics Teaching and Graduates: Raffles*

College and the University of Malaya in Singapore 1934–1960. It covered the days of the economics department from Raffles College and the University of Malaya to the University of Singapore from 1934 to 1960. It was commissioned by the Department of Economics and Statistics and published in 1985.

The book is a definitive work on the history of the department and has become the department's important resource.

It is a brilliant piece of work. He wrote of the department's important role in training people to run the administration in Malaya, then including Singapore.

I remember quite a number of luminaries that at one time were top administrators in Malaysia. They include Tong Yow Hong, ST Sundram, Rama Ayer, Abdul Wahab bin Abdullah, Cheroot (whose real name is Nasaruddin), Lin See Yen, Raymond Navaratnam, Jamaludin and Augus Salim.

There was also special mention of Goh Keng Swee and Lim Kim San who would go on to serve Singapore, *inter alia*, as finance minister.

He wrote: "Of the group who graduated in 1939, two are of outstanding importance. They are probably the most important graduates of the Economics Department from the point of view of Singapore's history and its influence in the world outside. These two are Goh Keng Swee and Lim Kim San."

He described how Goh "had the early mark of a leader while the young Lim had the temperament to be a generalist of distinction."

The book had some poignant pictures of Tom Silcock when he was head of the Economics Department at Raffles College with Tan Siew Sin, who later became finance minister in the Federation of Malaya and also, most importantly, future prime minister Lee Kuan Yew and Tun Abdul Razak, who was one of the most important founders of the Federation of Malaya and also the Federation of Malaysia.

Although his memory was sharp in his recollections of his days in Singapore, he seemed at a loss at times in the 1980s as he realised that Singapore had changed tremendously. He said it had completely metamorphosed from the time he knew it but he said it was for the better. The only landmark which he seemed to remember was the Padang — as we were driving past, he made me stop so he could have a long look at it — and Anderson Bridge.

My missed role as a PhD supervisor

When I rejoined the Economics Department at the University Singapore in 1969, I found there was a strong desire of many among the teaching staff to upgrade themselves. The department on its part tried to help them wherever possible by awarding scholarships, where these were available, to do their PhD abroad.

There was the option of also pursuing their doctorate locally. I was made the supervisor for those who chose this path.

Among the staff members who signed up were SY Lee, Bhanoji Rao, Amina Tyabji and Euston Quah, who incidentally now occupies the office next to mine as head of the Economics Division at Nanyang Technological University.

There were others outside the university who considered doing their PhD with us. One of them was Goh Chok Tong. It was 1960 when I first met him at the Goodwood Park Hotel where he had been presenting a paper on Singapore to the Lester Pearson Commission that had been appointed by the World Bank to deal with aid and global development. I was economic consultant to this commission on the recommendation of Silcock who was the previous senior consultant.

I was impressed with Goh's presentation. He was a young civil servant then who had returned to work in the Administrative Service after obtaining his master's degree in economics with flying colours at the famous Williams College in the US. His first degree, a first class honours degree, was from the University of Singapore. Goh confided in me when we met in the hotel car park that he wished to continue with doctoral studies with the view of becoming an academic. He even had a topic which he discussed with me. I can't remember what it was but I did not think it was suitable and asked him to come up with an alternative topic and to let me know when this was ready.

I did not hear from him again. I learnt later that he was seconded to the Neptune Orient Lines. His meteoric rise in this government-linked corporation caught the eye of the then finance minister Hon Sui Sen who invited him to enter politics, which he did in 1976 when he first stood for elections. As we all know, he went on to become the prime minister of Singapore for 14 years from 1990 to 2004. If he had done his PhD, Goh could have suffered the fate of all academics and be confined to a less than exciting academic lifestyle compared to being on the political stage. The economics department's great loss was Singapore's great gain. He could also have ended up as the vice-chancellor of the university; who knows?

Then there is Tharman Shanmugaratnam. It was in the 1980s when he first came to see me in my office. He said, "My father told me to do so." He had just returned from the University of Cambridge where he was awarded a master's degree in economics. His father, an eminent pathologist in the Singapore General Hospital, thought that a research and teaching career would suit his son.

I talked to Tharman about the senior tutorship scheme which had just been instituted. I looked at his results and said, "I see you are a brilliant scholar but my first duty is to send you to an Ivy League university in the US to get your PhD. You will be able to go under the senior tutorship scheme on full pay and on a scholarship but it will take four to five years to complete a PhD programme."

The thought of having to spend another four to five years to obtain a doctorate just to come under the tutorship scheme came as a shock to him. He said he would think about the proposal but he did not pursue it.

If he had, Singapore would have lost a brilliant finance minister and deputy prime minister.

Another potential PhD candidate that I missed out being a supervisor to was Mari Elka Pangestu, the daughter of Jusuf Pang Lay Kim, who was at one time the dean of the business administration faculty at Nanyang University, where I first got to know him.

Mari had studied in Singapore's St Margaret's Secondary School on Farrer Road and later went on to the Australian National University (ANU) to obtain a bachelor's and master's degree in economics.

Her father who was back in Indonesia as a banker after his stint in Singapore and was also with the Centre for Strategic and International Studies wrote me a letter to ask if his daughter could do a PhD in Singapore under my supervision after her return from ANU.

I replied that at that time we did not have the facility to do course work and mentioned that we would usually send our young students abroad for this, suggesting that he should do the same for his daughter. He followed my advice and it was from the University of California that Mari later graduated with a PhD in economics.

She would later on become a prominent member of the Indonesian Cabinet, serving as Minister of Trade from 2004 to 2011 and as Minister of Tourism and Creative Económics from 2004 to 2014.

Whenever I go to Indonesia to give a public lecture, I sometimes see her among the audience listening to my talk. It is such an honour.

Appointing other professors

The university might have been less exciting than being on the political stage but for me — and I suspect other academics as well — it was rewarding in other ways.

One was when the university appointed us to sit on various committees not only in the arts and social sciences faculty but in other faculties as well. One of the committees was the promotions committee where I interviewed various potential full professors such as Tommy Koh, Koh Kheng Lian and Tan Lee Meng. They formed the pioneer generation of professors in the Law Faculty and went on to serve Singapore most admirably. Professor Tan Lee Meng is now Senior Judge of the Supreme Court.

At that time though, we were plagued by uncertainties. We would appoint as full professors those we felt were capable of carrying out their duties. Where we were not convinced of the candidates' abilities, we would rather let the vacancies remain and allow associate professors to run the show.

This resulted in some departments not having full professors. I guess at that time we were quite nationalistic and preferred appointing locals to the posts; even if we could find none available, we preferred to let the posts remain vacant rather than appoint expatriates.

But we were thought of as being unnecessarily tough. NUS changed its policy later to cast the field wide open with a view to upgrade the institution to a world-class university. This the university did with great success, particularly under the vice-chancellorship of Professor Lim Pin, Professor Shih Choon Fong, and Professor Tan Chorh Chuan.

In two instances, my colleagues and I were overruled by a vice-chancellor who appointed two people to be full professors despite our reservations. He said that unless we wanted to get foreigners to fill the posts, which we did not, we would have to appoint the two locals to full professors. Most unfortunately, they did not turn out to be brilliant professors unlike the rest who went through the proper mill.

My 52 weekly articles

Thirty six years ago, whilst still discharging the responsibilities of Head of the huge Department of Economics and Statistics of the National University of Singapore, Chairman of the National Wages Council and Chairman of the Skills Development Fund Advisory Council, I voluntarily accepted the surprising but most welcome invitation of the editor-in-chief of Sin Chew Jit Poh Frank Wong to write a weekly article for its then most widely circulated Chinese daily in Singapore. Rather unexpectedly, the articles would appear prominently on the front page of the newspaper every Sunday.

The subjects I wrote on covered a wide range of topics that I thought would be of interest to the Chinese-educated intelligentsia of Singapore. The articles included Singapore's bilingualism policy, the de-population problem, the age of retirement, adult illiteracy in Singapore, and my advocacy of developing Singapore as a financial centre, an educational centre, and as a healthcare centre. I also wrote on topics like the China-Singapore diplomatic relationship and the then prevailing China-Vietnam War.

Faithfully, I wrote the weekly articles, 52 in all without fail, spanning from mid-1979 to mid-1980. I wrote them first in English, sent them to the press for translation into Chinese, and with some editorial changes by me, they were published. Sin Chew said that I received good feedback for my publications. I thoroughly enjoyed writing them.

As an aside, Sin Chew Jit Poh was later merged with Nanyang Siang Pau to form today's Lian He Zao Bao. In Malaysia, however, the daily Sin Chew Jit Poh still exists with its original name changed to Sin Chew Daily. My 52 weekly articles were later compiled and published, both in Chinese and in English by Federal Publications, Singapore.

Betting with MIT Dean

The year was early 1986. I was then still with NUS as Head of the Department of Economics and Statistics. The great and most widely circulated daily in Japan, Yomiuri Shinbun, continued to invite me to participate in its yearly Asia-Pacific economic forum. At the huge forum, I noticed that I was the only non-Japanese and non-American participant. To me, it was a singular honour. Among the very distinguished American participants was Professor Lester Thurow, who was then Dean of the world-famous MIT Business School. We discussed various matters on the future growth of the US and Japanese economies after the Plaza Accord of September 1985 at which the Americans managed to persuade or pressure Japan to significantly appreciate its currency.

At the lunch break, I sat in Dean Lester Thurow's table with the other distinguished American participants. Dean Thurow said, "Professor Lim, do you really believe that the Japanese economy would continue to grow at a higher rate than that of the USA?" He added, "Did you say it just to placate the Japanese participants?" I replied, "Yes, I believe in my forecast for the next few years."

"In that case," he interjected, "can you have a bet with me on your prognostication?" I jokingly replied, "Oh no, I am a Methodist, and as all of you know, Methodists don't bet." He would not give up. "Just for US$5 per year, what do you say? If the Japanese economy exceeds the US, I would pay you $5. If it is the other way, you will give me $5. The bet is to last for four years only, starting from 1986."

I must have taken too much *sake* that afternoon to agree to the bet. After the lunch, to my surprise, he announced the bet to the huge participating audience. It appeared prominently in the Yomiuri the next day, following my prognostication the day before.

The international conference ended fruitfully. We all returned home. Time passed rather quickly. In year one, I won the bet. I too won the bet in year 2, year 3, and year 4. I wrote a letter to Dean Thurow to remind him to give me a cheque for $20, after which the bet would be off.

The world-famous American economist did send me a $20 cheque when he came to Singapore to sign a MIT-NTU agreement for NTU's Nanyang Fellows'

Programme. Thank goodness, the bet was discontinued. After the fourth year and the years that followed, the GDP statistics showed that he was right, and I was wrong. I was thankful that the bet had been discontinued on time!

Forced retirement for me at 60

I was at the University of Singapore, later renamed National University of Singapore (NUS), for 23 years from 1969 to 1992.

One day in 1989, my vice-chancellor asked me to see him. He went straight to the point: "Everybody has to retire one day. When your contract is up, you will have to retire at the age of 60."

I said, "Yes, we all have to retire one day, but I am your Senior Professor and the retirement age for a Senior Professor is 65, not 60." In Medicine, there were four or five such Senior Professors, in Engineering, one, and I was the only Senior Professor in the campus of the humanities, social sciences, law and business schools.

"Other Senior Professors have retired at 65. Why do I have to retire at 60?" I continued.

He kept quiet for a minute then said, "Do you know when one retires one can still be associated with the university by being a senior fellow?"

I said, "Yes, except that senior fellows have half the pay. There is also a problem of nomenclature, as they will not be called a professor but a doctor like all my colleagues who have retired at 60 because they are not Senior Professors."

I saw my life as an academician in NUS fading away. This retirement announcement was a blow too as it came not long after my heart surgery.

Retirement has always been a nightmare for Singaporeans, as we do not have a pension scheme. Retirement means zero income.

At that time, many of my friends thought that the decision to retire me was because I had antagonised a lot of people in the corridors of power. They were certain that if I had been less troublesome and toed the line my tenure would have been extended to the age of 65, as they had done to all the Senior Professors.

I was still *corpore sano* (of sound body) and *compos mentis* (of sound mind), I told myself. I had to seek a new life elsewhere outside of my own beloved alma mater.

Little did I know that NUS had in mind conferring upon me an emeritus professorship on my retirement. Indeed, every cloud has a silver lining.

Unexpected professorship in my name

After I had left the university, I was informed by the vice-chancellor that I would be conferred with an emeritus professorship. This came as a surprise, considering my unhappiness over leaving as I thought I should have had another five years to serve at NUS. At the same time, I felt very honoured that the university was recognising the work I had put in over the last 23 years, as a researcher, educator and administrator; in short, as a long-standing senior academic.

I was even more surprised to be invited one evening to have dinner with a member of the University Council, Mr Lim Jit Poh, who also asked my wife and my eldest daughter, Suet Fern, and my elder son, Suet Wun, to come along.

He told me, "You know, Chong Yah, the purpose of this dinner is to get your agreement and your family's agreement to start a fund called the Lim Chong Yah Professorship Fund in your honour."

I was taken aback and asked, "Thank you for the honour but how are you going to raise the money?"

The reply was interesting and has to be put on record. He said, "When we heard you were retiring, I had the chance to speak with (then prime minister) Goh Chok Tong. I told him that we could not let you retire and fade away and that we should start a fund to honour your life-long work in the university. After all, NTUC and NWC have given you awards and it would be amiss if NUS did not do something similar."

He continued, "We will just solicit for money from the employers' associations."

I was told that Goh Chok Tong had replied to Jit Poh, "Of course, you can use my name as PM to raise the money."

Lim Jit Poh had been one of the very bright pupils at Raffles Institution (RI) and had won many scholarships; he knew the Prime Minister well as they were both classmates at RI.

I came to know Jit Poh as a senior representative of the Ministry of Education on the Skills Development Fund Advisory Council that Mr Goh Chok Tong had asked me to chair.

The Prime Minister said, however, that the creation of the fund hinged on two conditions: the support of myself and my family and that of the vice-chancellor. Professor Lim Pin, the vice-chancellor, supported the idea but said he would seek the support of his successor, Professor Shih Choon Fong, as he would be retiring soon and could not see to its successful implementation. Professor Shih kindly agreed to come to the rescue.

When there was agreement all around, a dinner was held in 1999 to launch the fund. Then President SR Nathan was the speaker at the event. At that time there was a recession but donations came in from many sources. I was worried that there would not be sufficient contributions. My daughter Fern was worried as well and she made a significant donation without telling me how much it was. All in, S$1.6 million was raised from companies, unions and individuals. The Government, following the practice at that time, would support the fund with a similar amount, matching it dollar for dollar.

The fund was meant originally for the Economics Department but it already had two funds — the Tan Chin Tuan Chair and Goh Keng Swee Chair in Economics — so it was decided to open the fund for use by other departments. The Economics Department was well endowed while other departments in the Faculty of Arts and Social Sciences were less so. The Economics Department by nature of its subject matter, dealing with finance, seemed to be able to raise money while other departments were less adept.

Thus, the fund was eventually used to launch the Lim Chong Yah Professorship in Arts and Social Sciences in February 2001, which was appropriate as I was a former dean of the Faculty of Arts and Social Sciences. The prime minister's name was never used throughout the fund-raising campaign: neither was there a minister or permanent secretary on the fund-raising committee. Mr Lim Jit Poh and Dr Arthur Lim, a prominent eye surgeon, did much of the spade work. I am grateful to them and to other members of the fund-raising committee for their invaluable help.

Whoever is invited to be a visiting professor under the Lim Chong Yah Professorship Fund would have to stay for no less than three months. They are to give public lectures, do research and interact with faculty staff. The professorship has attracted many outstanding visitors over the years, including a Nobel Laureate in Economics, Professor Edward Prescott. The world-famous development sociologist, Ezra Vogel from Harvard, was the first visiting professor under this programme. The search and find engine of the programme then, I was told, was under the leadership of Professor Liu Hong, who in subsequent years, became the Chair of the School of Humanities and Social Sciences of NTU, of which I occupy an office as emeritus professor. The fund now has been kept very much alive under the very able deanship of the Faculty, Professor Brenda Yeoh.

CHAPTER 13

NEW LEASE OF LIFE IN NTU

Looking for a job

In June 1989, I underwent a quintuple heart bypass operation. Although it was successful and I was given a clean bill of health by the doctors, the experience left me moody, vulnerable and wary. It took me months before I bounced back to life as it was before the surgery, teaching at the National University of Singapore (NUS), meeting up with friends again, attending events and resuming my co-curricular activities. So it was quite a blow when just two and a half years later, I was told by NUS that I would have to retire when I reached 60.

That would be in March 1992. The news came as a rude shock because I was a Senior Professor at the university and Senior Professors at NUS traditionally then retired at the age of 65. I was told this applied only to Senior Professors in other departments but not in my case, a department in the Faculty of Arts and Social Sciences.

I had no choice but to look for another job. I still felt young at 60 and had a family to look after. I also felt I could still contribute to academia and to society in general.

NTU, the open sesame

I rang up Professor Cham Tao Soon, then president of the newly formed Nanyang Technological University (NTU) upgraded from the former Nanyang Technological Institute. I told him I was retiring from NUS soon and that I was looking for a job. He agreed to see me in his office.

He listened to me with sympathy, then I said: "When I was told I had to retire, I felt like 出师未捷身先死, 长使英雄泪满襟."

I was quoting from a famous poem "蜀相" by Tang Dynasty poet 杜甫 (Du Fu). "蜀相" means "Prime Minister of Shu", and the poem describes the story of 诸葛亮, a great strategist during the Three Kingdoms period. The two lines can be loosely translated as "One was dead before one could complete one's work; this frequently made one weep with tears all over one's sleeves". In my case, my academic life was terminated three-quarters of the way in my life's journey.

President Cham was visibly moved when he heard that, and he said, "It would be an honour to have you join Nanyang Technological University. I welcome you most heartily."

However, he added, "The university will not be able to give you the pay or status of a Senior Professor, as there is no Senior Professor position in NTU. If you wish, I will have to submit a paper to the Cabinet to allow NTU to have a special position of senior professorship instituted."

I said, "No, please don't do that. Kindly compensate me in whatever way you feel suitable within the existing regulations and limitations of the university."

I thanked him for giving me a new job, though it would be on a year-to-year basis, and left, impressed by his decisiveness in taking a decision like that.

The next day, I had a call from his then Dean of the School of Accountancy and Business, Professor Tan Teck Meng. He asked me to have lunch with him. When we met, he told me that I could concentrate on research and writing if I did not wish to take on any teaching duties.

He also told me that since there was no Senior Professorship position at NTU, my pay would be cut by $4,000 a month, a big sum of money even by present day standards for an academic.

But I was just so thankful that I could get a job and so quickly that I was not too concerned with the pay cut. But he said that in lieu of the pay cut, President Cham and he had agreed that they would give me secretarial support. Both kept to their word.

When I arrived at NTU on my first day at work, Dean Tan told me that no qualified secretary was immediately available but they would give me a clerical officer instead, Christina Seet. Since that day, Christina has been helping me most faithfully and brilliantly in the last 22 years of my career in NTU, even after my retirement as emeritus professor in 2012.

I also noticed then that neither the dean nor the president had asked me to fill an application form as was the normal practice. In later years, I brought this up to Professor Cham saying, "You know, you forgot to ask me to fill in an application form." He replied, "We know you, we had your CV and that was good enough for us." I did, however, fill up the form with the names of three referees for the university.

Professor Cham did not seem to be the bureaucratic type. I guess he must have asked his secretary to fill up the form from my published CV. I was happy to have gotten a job and be functioning as a full professor again. I was embarking on my second life as a full-time academic in Singapore, my third if I were to include my stint at Pantai Valley in Malaya.

Every cloud has a silver lining

It's worth repeating that every cloud has a silver lining.

The moment the chairman of UOB Wee Cho Yaw heard that I was retiring from NUS, he called me to ask if I would like to be a director on the board of his bank, UOB.

I replied, "*Kam siah*," ("Thank you" in Hokkien, his dialect), "I would love to." When you lose a job, your mood is so different and when you get a personal call to be a director of such a well-known bank from the chairman himself, no less, I wanted to shout "Hallelujah!" as I was fond of saying in private when things turn out unexpectedly well.

More surprises were in store for me. When I joined the board, I was told by the company secretary, "Mr Wee's intention is that you be appointed first as a member of the audit committee and later as its chairman." This was another boost to my very deflated ego at that time.

Director, SABRE Centre

The dean, Professor Tan, said he would like me to take on the job of director of a newly set up SABRE Centre at NTU. I was in a jocund mood and asked jokingly, "What does it mean? Do you make special swords?"

He said, "No, it's for the School of Accountancy and Business Research Centre."

When I asked what would be the nature of my job, his reply was "The whole school is new. There are no books, journals or articles as we have to order everything from scratch. We will have to order new books and journal articles each year for the next 10 years and we will get whatever the academics need. We must also do research and have research materials for teaching on Singapore."

I had a clean slate to work with. I discovered that many staff members then, later called faculty members, did not have PhD degrees and quite a lot did not have publications to their name. However, they had work experience that was excellent and impressive as accountants or in the business world as managers of business organisations.

Promoting research and publications thus became my top priority. Towards this end, I launched a communitarian book writing programme. This involved every staff member contributing a chapter in a series of volumes to be launched at the same time. This resulted in 14 books which took a total of 18 to 24 months to complete, covering a wide range of topics from accounting to economics and business. The project had the participation of 150 people from the School and 30 guest writers from industry and other universities.

We were able to get the then minister of education Lee Yock Suan to launch the books in January 1996 but unfortunately there was no publicity due to a misunderstanding between the school and the university's public relations department. Still, some of the editors of the volumes won prizes. One of the chapters, "Exploiting IT for Business Competitiveness", edited by Professor Neo Boon Siong and similarly published by Addison-Wesley clinched the Highly Commended Award in the 1996 Singapore Book Awards.

The purpose in putting out the books was to demonstrate our commitment to research and publication and Professor Tan Teck Meng played a big part in spurring all the faculty members to work on them, each writing on his area of specialisation. In my view, the process reflected very much his ability as an academic leader. He could somehow persuade everyone to participate. I was a relative newcomer and not the dean so I was in no position to tell everyone to get involved — I just provided the idea.

The dean and I deferred to have our names on the books as he was too modest. Instead, the volumes carried the names of the separate editors only. They could have carried both of us as editors-in-chief.

However, one faculty member who was supposed to edit one of the volumes did not take his work seriously enough and Professor Tan took his name out. The person was quite well known but Professor Tan did not want anyone to delay the publication programme. I admired his integrity and courage.

Until then, I had not come across in my life so many academics jointly publishing so many books at one time. I regarded the whole thing as a pioneering effort in research and publication and it was a way of promoting NTU as a centre of research as well.

When I joined NTU, the School of Accountancy and Business had already set up a new division of economics with, later, Professor Chew Soon Beng, a former colleague of mine in NUS, as head. Economics, however, was not taught as a major discipline but as a supporting degree in the school.

So Professor Tan appointed me to head a committee to look into having economics accepted as one of the major disciplines for a degree. I made a report suggesting not only that economics be made a major discipline but I also recommended the institution of a PhD programme in the school by coursework and thesis. That was the beginning of the PhD programme in the school which was later renamed Nanyang Business School.

The dean then appointed me to head a school-wide committee to set up the vision for the new Nanyang Business School (NBS). Members of the teaching staff then were very young and they served on the committee. I was already retired so was the most experienced and certainly the oldest.

The secretary of the committee was a young lady, Dr Ang Soon, who later became a prominent full professor of accountancy in NBS. Another committee member was Dr Gillian Yeo who was responsible for putting up the draft for the research vision for the school. She later took on a very prominent role in the school not only as a full professor but also for many years as the *de facto* chief executive of the school.

Another who was active in our committee deliberations and submissions was Dr Tan Hun Tong, who later became a world renowned professor of accountancy in the school. The present Director of the Nanyang Technopreneurship Centre of NTU, Associate Professor Hooi Den Huan, was also an important member of the NBS Vision Team Committee as Head of the then Division of Marketing and Tourism Management.

This committee made a lot of recommendations for the future. The report was published in 1996 in a document entitled *Nanyang Technological University: Nanyang Business School's 21st Century Vision* by Lim Chong-Yah and associates, and edited by JJ Williams.

Change to American nomenclature

What then were our recommendations? Well, for a start, we proposed a change in nomenclature from lecturer, senior lecturer and professor to assistant professor, associate professor and full professor respectively; in effect, from the British to the American style.

The proposal for this nomenclature change from British to American terms originated from returnees that NUS had sent to the US under the Senior Tutorship Scholarship Scheme. They were of the opinion that the change in name would be more beneficial to the university and the country as a whole. They made a formal presentation for this change in the committee.

At first, I was stuck in the old nomenclature but later changed my mind after hearing them speak. So for NBS, this became an important part of the recommendations of our committee.

Interestingly, when the committee's view on this matter was submitted to the appropriate NTU authorities, they did not favour the proposal for change of nomenclature. However, later, when Professor Tan Teck Meng and some other staff members of NTU were appointed to start a new university — Singapore Management University (SMU) — they decided to adopt the American-style nomenclature. As soon as SMU instituted it, this was followed by the two older universities, first NUS and then NTU.

So NTU accepted the new nomenclature in a circuitous fashion, although the idea originally came from NTU itself!

Another recommendation was to have service apartment-type lodgings in NTU for short-term visitors. NUS by then had its Visitors' Lodge. I had suggested the idea based on my memorable experience in Kyoto University where I was housed in such a facility within the campus during my sabbatical.

Again, the NTU authorities did not accept this proposal giving a variety of reasons but they later changed their mind. I was told this was due to the persistence of staff from NBS, especially under its new dean Professor Neo Boon Siong. So we now have the 170-room Nanyang Executive Centre established in 2003 to provide housing for our visitors.

Role in selection of professors

I was the most senior member in NBS and the only full professor there, so I was given the task of identifying suitable people for promotion to the rank of full professors. I was appointed to be an *ex-officio* member of a committee chaired by the dean.

In recollection, I was glad that I played a useful role in the internal selection of staff for promotions. In fact, I supported decisively quite a lot of promotions of senior lecturers in the school's initial in-takes to be made full professors. They have turned out to be great full professors of international standing.

NTU in formation of SMU

I had mentioned SMU earlier in this chapter. Then Education Minister Tony Tan (who became Singapore's seventh president in 2011) was also responsible for universities and I had the privilege of meeting him occasionally at dinner functions hosted for me by his uncle Tan Sri Tan Chin Tuan. It was at one of these private functions, in a general off-the-cuff conversation, that I mentioned to Dr Tan that if he wanted a suitable local with a lot of pioneering spirit and energy and with knowledge of university enterprise, it would be Professor Tan Teck Meng.

I just threw up the name casually. Whether that suggestion made an impact on him, I do not know as the minister is also well known for exercising his own judgement. In any case, we found out later that Professor Tan was approached to start SMU as the provost. Professor Tan, whom I knew well, asked me if I knew what the functions of a provost were. I told him that it was a new term as we only knew then about the posts of vice-chancellor and deputy vice-chancellor. I said, "It's the equivalent of a chief operating officer while the president of the university would be the chief executive officer or CEO. These two posts would be the two most important positions in any university."

I asked, "Why did you raise the issue?" He confided in me that he was approached to become the first provost of SMU and asked for my advice. I told him to take up the challenge as he had the ability to deliver and would be able to give a very good account of himself to the minister. He left NBS shortly after bringing with him as lieutenants quite a number of able academics. These founders of SMU include, in random order, Professors Low Aik Meng, Leong Kwong Sin, Pang Yang Hoong, Low Kee Yang, Tan Wee Liang and Toh Thian Ser. Professor Pang Yang Hoong, a Professor of Accounting, is currently the Dean of the School of Accountancy.

New School of Humanities and Social Sciences

Before Professor Cham Tao Soon stepped down as NTU's president, he had proposed a new School of Humanities and Social Sciences (HSS) to be instituted and to have as part of this school the Division of Economics. He had obtained the support of the Ministry of Education on this matter.

The head of the Economics Division was then Professor Chen Kang who, like many of us then at NTU, had come from NUS. He was a young member of staff when I was head of department there.

I found out he was quite a consultative person by nature, as he would also consult his senior academic colleagues in important matters affecting the department.

He told me that NTU had decided that all of us in the department would have to reapply to join the new Division of Economics in the new school. The Division of Economics in NBS would be abolished.

He was upset by the decision of re-application as if all of us were new staff. However, we were given the privilege of applying first. I did not believe that the university would make such a stand until I was shown the minutes of the decision. Chen Kang showed me other minutes to prove that this policy was to be pursued.

It was my turn to be upset. Later when Dr Su Guaning took over as president of NTU, I discussed the matter with him and suggested it was an indiscreet move. Dr Su agreed and decided that we would be transferred lock, stock and barrel to the new department with no change whatsoever.

But the process leading to this was a traumatic experience for all concerned and unnecessarily time-consuming.

Head search for Economics

Not long after we all came on board to the new HSS, Chen Kang told me he would not like to continue as head as he wanted to go on sabbatical leave and when he returned he would not take up the headship.

An interim dean, Professor Eddie Kuo, had been appointed. I spoke to him about getting a new head. He asked if I had any suggestion of names to fill the vacancy. Eddie Kuo too came from NUS. I remember when I was the dean there that I played a role in appointing him as a staff member in the Department of Sociology, so we could talk freely with each other. I suggested to him to get Professor Euston Quah to come from NUS to head the division if he was willing to move over. Euston Quah agreed but I had to get different groups to agree before it was unanimously decided he could become the head. All agreed, and Euston Quah became our new head.

Dean search for HSS

However, the school being new, the president asked me to be the chairman of a dean-search committee. I did not understand why this was necessary as Eddie Kuo was the interim dean and could fit the bill of a new dean very well. The president replied that Eddie would become the founding dean of the School of Communications and it would be better not to have a person serving as dean of two new schools. So I took on the responsibility of finding a new dean with Eddie as a member of this committee. Professor Wang Gungwu of NUS was kind enough to help NTU in this global search.

Chairman, NTU Re-making Committee

But more challenging was the task of chairing the NTU Re-making Committee which would comprise senior staff members in the entire university. Under consideration was the proposal that the university be professor-centric and student-centric, a suggestion that Professor Su proposed for the committee's deliberation.

But another of the terms of reference for the committee was a sensitive one: Should the university be renamed Nanyang University?

A very competent management staff Ms Tan Sock Leng would serve as secretary to the committee.

We had divisions on how to handle the name change. We also had serious differences of view on the old Nanyang University Arch which served as the entrance to the old Nanyang University being transferred to the new road leading into NTU.

Two influential committee members said something to me that bothered me. They asked, "Why are you appointed chairman? We thought you were sympathetic towards the changing of name back to Nanyang University and that's why we persuaded Su Guaning to have you appointed chairman. We thought that you were sympathetic to the transfer of the University Arch to its proper place."

I was amused by their confession. In the end, the government, through Dr Tony Tan, then the education minister, rejected any notion of the change of name, or rather, it recommended the postponing of the decision to be reviewed 25 years later. The controversial subject was thus closed.

Some of the committee's recommendations were, however, implemented. One of these was to make foreign staff eligible for permanent employment in the university. This meant putting them on the tenure of the university. My main objective was that many of them might opt to become Singapore citizens. I was told I had "high hopes and wrong hopes" because our national and university working conditions were not so conducive that academics would opt for Singapore citizenship.

I was told that I was naïve in my thinking. Besides, said my detractors, "We are not America or Australia." My reply was that we needed very able people to teach and do research and if we did not offer them tenure, we would not be able to attract the right people and this would affect the research and teaching quality of the university.

The committee also recommended, *inter alia*, the setting up of a College of Medicine for NTU.

The restructuring committee's report was never published and I do not expect it to be made public because of the sensitivities involved. The committee members did, however, spend quite a lot of time in brainstorming to arrive at our recommendations on various policy issues of the university. I was even given the honour of presenting an interim report to the Board of Trustees, then called the University Council, at its specially arranged dinner function. One well-known senior member of the Board even told me that that was the first meeting of the Board that held special meaning for him, discussing the direction of change of the university.

Dean search for NBS

So other than doing my own writing, research and teaching, I was kept busy at NTU by serving on various committees such as chairman of the dean-search and restructuring committees. As an aside, I was to head the dean-search committee of the Nanyang Business School (NBS) as well. I enjoyed and appreciated the confidence that the university authorities, particularly its president, had in me to help the university in the best possible way. As I admired their dedication to their work, I was glad that I could help as a part of the university policy-making administrative team when asked to do so.

I particularly appreciated the contributions made by a very experienced head-hunter, Ernest Wong, from the University Council. Mr Wong was the President of UOB when I was a director of the bank.

Chairman of disciplinary committees

There were also two occasions when I had to serve as chairman of a disciplinary committee dealing with sexual harassment. These were unusual assignments to me.

The other members of the committees would include the head of the human resource department (Ms Angela Lim) who would serve as secretary, NTU's resident lawyer (Ms Tay Hsiu Chieh) and the dean of the school where the alleged harassment took place plus other senior academics from other schools (now called colleges) within the campus.

Case No. 1. A female staff member charged her male head of department for sexual harassment. She rejected his approaches and so consequently, she alleged that she was not placed on the tenure appointment. We spoke separately to both and also with people who might have connections to this case particularly in the department concerned. We later made certain recommendations.

Thank goodness, both parties accepted our recommendations and the recommendations were endorsed by the university administration. The president later told me when he appointed me to serve as chair, "I know you are a first class chairman of the National Wages Council and I know that you too would be a first class chairman in a case like this." I told him, "Mr President, NWC and sex — they are worlds apart. One deals with wages and wage policies. The other concerns humans and their sexual behaviour and morality."

But, my president is right, the role of chairman is still the same, that is, to adjudicate fairly. The case was handled successfully without any publicity in the media. I must confess the minutes of the meetings had the makings of a bestseller but they were never, and should never, be publicised.

After Case 1 was successfully resolved, it was unavoidable when Case 2 surfaced that I would again be approached by President Su to handle it.

"Do you have the indiscretion to turn down the president knowing that you could help," I asked myself; so since I could not back out, I might as well take on the task, was how I looked at it.

Case No. 2 involved a very talented and distinguished overseas staff. A charming and able PhD female student complained of sexual harassment. We interrogated both the alleged perpetrator and victim several times and also interviewed those closely connected with them. I had, as usual, the benefit of some staff members on the committee helping me. My main fear was that it might get out of hand and end up in a court of law resulting in permanent damage for them, their families and the university.

I later discovered that the student had discussed the matter with her lawyer. I became worried that if the case went to court, I would have to represent the university to present its case. Her lawyer was thrilled, I was told, with the idea of confronting me. I was close to 80 then, and I did not cherish the idea of a legal battle of this sort, being not trained in law myself. Somehow, we fortunately managed to persuade the two parties to take on a course beneficial and not detrimental to both. Thank goodness both agreed. And the matter was successfully contained within the narrower walls of the university as a disciplinary case and not into a wider public domain.

Fearing that I might be considered an expert in such disciplinary cases, I quickly threw my discretion to the winds and wrote a letter to the president to plead for another old professor to handle such cases. Thank goodness, he noted my plea positively, besides thanking me very much for my past services.

Later, the president, Professor Su Guaning, met me at times for lunch and I never had the occasion to remind him of his commitment nor talked about sexual harassment matters in the university.

Scandals in ivory tower

But there are consequences. My head of department, Professor Chen Kang, considers me his senior professor that he could always turn to for help. One day, he told me of a sexual harassment case affecting a visiting staff member in the department. I wanted to say, please, don't get me involved but I felt it would be discourteous to turn him down.

It transpired that this visiting staff member was infatuated with one of our female students who alleged that he could not control his impulses.

We did not know about the affair until the police telephoned the university and reported the case. I was worried that another court case might develop.

Thank goodness, it was resolved. I was the unofficial, off-the-record, advisor.

The case was such that the visiting professor was put in police custody for quite some time and as his visit was financed by the government of his country, we did not want it to develop into a diplomatic incident either.

One should not expect an ivory tower not to have scandals because academics are also human beings; the students too.

There was another case involving a young academic. He never told me about his troubles until it appeared to be too late. It was on Christmas Eve. He started to relate to me his problem — he had been accused by two students of sexual harassment, which was a shock to me. More frightening for him was that he would be given a suspension order by the university, so I thought I should have a talk with the person handling the suspension order.

By chance, I passed the room of the officer in charge of this academic. I discussed the case and learned that the matter was being handled by the police. I asked whether the police would charge our young colleague with the alleged offence. The reply was "not sure", because the Attorney-General's (AG) office had not given any reply and it was still investigating the matter.

I said, "What if the AG dropped the case after investigation, and what if the police did not want to charge him? Wouldn't our suspension be premature?" The reply was that a number of very important people in NTU had decided to give the suspension order. I appealed for reconsideration and to ring up all involved to say that the matter was being discussed with me. I knew the people involved and they knew I had some experience in handling the previous sexual harassment cases, so they might take my suggestion of not imposing the suspension order seriously.

I was clear and firm in suggesting that the university should allow the accused academic to go on leave, while the case was being investigated. The students would not be embarrassed since the academic would not be teaching while on a forced leave of absence.

The professor telephoned the higher authorities to get their agreement. It was on the eve of Christmas day when the call was made. Thank goodness they were all still in the office and they agreed to temporarily rescind the order of suspension. It had not been sent yet and the young academic could go on forced leave. I was very happy that my intervention was a timely one.

So although I was not appointed officially to handle this disciplinary case, I was still doing the work by chance and by force of circumstances. I was grateful that those behind the suspension order agreed with my approach, a more measured and fairer one.

A few months later, the whole case resolved itself.

Teaching role in NTU

The story of my life in NTU would not be complete, if I did not mention my teaching role.

During my time, the university established two outstanding post-graduate programmes in which I participated as a pedagogue.

The first was the Nanyang Fellows Programme while the other was the Master of Science (Managerial Economics) Programme for very mature students from China, both of which are still on-going.

Nanyang Fellows

The Nanyang Fellows Programme was mooted by Dr Tony Tan and launched by him in 1998 when he was then deputy prime minister. The programme is linked with the Massachusetts Institute of Technology (MIT) in Boston where Dr Tony Tan had studied and where, he told me, he had particularly enjoyed listening to the lectures of a senior professor, Paul Samuelson, who later was also a Nobel Laureate in Economics. The university later also arranged for the tie-up as well as with two other universities — Wharton Business School in Pennsylvania and the University of California, Berkeley. Students would first study in our School before moving on to these universities.

Dr Tan wanted to upgrade the Nanyang Business School and so initiated this programme with grants from the Totaliser Board. With these grants we were able to offer scholarships to promising middle level Asian officials targeted for leadership roles, who would be able to contribute on their return home.

I enjoyed giving lectures to these bright students. They were mature students aged between 30 and 45 and it was a great joy to teach them. My course was on the world economy with a focus on East Asia.

As was my style of teaching, I would get them to write papers on various topics and present them to the class for discussion. We had very interesting fellows as part of the programme.

One of them was a lady student from Jakarta who was sent by the Mayor of Jakarta to study under the Nanyang Fellows Programme. She was originally trained in medicine but decided to take up an administrative career. When she was a Nanyang Fellow, she wrote on Singapore's mass rapid transit (MRT) system as part of her academic exercise.

She told me thus, "We have decided to have an MRT in Jakarta and I have been given the honour to be in charge of the MRT programme!"

We had another student whose father was the prime minister of Vietnam although we did not know of it then. One day, when his father came to see him in Singapore, his father fell ill and was warded in the Singapore General Hospital. His mother had accompanied his father and they had to stay for a few weeks. His father recovered; as a result of the treatment, the student said that his parents too had developed a profound liking for Singapore. The father was with us incognito, as he preferred it that way.

Apart from the students from ASEAN countries, we also had other overseas students, who came from as far afield as India, Pakistan, Sri Lanka, Poland, Kazakhstan, Japan, Korea, USA, and Mexico. We also had local students from various ministries as well as from the army, navy, police and air force on the Nanyang Fellows Programme. What a privilege it was to teach in such a class.

I remember one day, a student who was with the Police Force telling me that he was in charge of the security of my neighbourhood that included my house. I felt very reassured.

Another, from the civil service, said he liked my EGOIN theory of poverty and affluence and would teach it to the civil servants.

There was a spirit of camaraderie among the students of the programme. To develop it further, I made it a point, after the end of the programme and after all the papers had been marked, to invite all of them to my house for dinner giving a chance to the overseas students to visit a Singapore home. They were grateful and they told me how the visit was one of the cherished memories of their stay in Singapore. So I was delighted when I was voted Best Teacher of the Year, for 2004/2005.

The Mayors' Class

Another post-graduate programme I am fond of is the Mayors' Class. Until NUS introduced the same course in later years, NTU held the monopoly of this unique programme. The Mayors' Class was pioneered by my economics colleague, Professor Chew Soon Beng.

Like the Nanyang Fellows Programme, the Master of Science in Managerial Economics, also launched in 1998, is a one-year graduate programme for mature students, in this case from China. It was later dubbed Mayors' Class as most of the students were government officials groomed to become mayors. At the beginning, several were mayors themselves. I have been told that often there were more people under each of their charge than the entire population of Singapore.

It all started with Chinese leader Deng Xiaoping's visit to Singapore in 1996. He was impressed with Singapore, which had developed from poverty into a showcase city-state. He felt that China could learn from Singapore, especially on how we managed our financial, fiscal, monetary policies and public administration in general. Mr Deng was impressed at the cleanliness of our city, the absence of slums and beggars, besides our achievements in public housing, the efficient management of our airport and seaports. My "students" too wanted to know more of our growth with equity policy and practice under the aegis of the National Wages Council (NWC).

In 1998, a request came from Hebei to train a dozen of their officials in administration and the Mayors' Class programme developed from there.

The original course proved so successful that the Master of Public Administration programme was introduced in 2005 for high-level officials primed to become China's new leaders.

When I first began to teach them, I had the students asking me to speak in Mandarin. I kept saying that my Mandarin was not up to the mark, as I had not studied Mandarin formally in school or university. In fact, whenever I speak Mandarin, I am told it has a bit of a Malacca Hainanese accent.

Their reply: "All of us speak with an accent anyway and we understand you and particularly your jokes perfectly."

I had some eminent interpreters, such as Professor Chen Kang, to help from time to time. He would help me to explain some terms of which I did not know the Chinese equivalents such as "elasticity of demand", "marginal propensity to import" or "Gini Coefficients". Chen Kang had no problem rattling out these terms in unaccented Mandarin.

I presume my students must have been quite happy with me as their professor, as they voted me for two separate awards: Best Teacher of the Year Award by the Mayor Class Master of Science (Managerial Economics) Programme in 2004, and Best Teacher of the Year Award by the Mayor Class MSc Programme in 2006.

One of the graduates of the programme, Ma Yufeng, was so jubilant over his experience in Singapore that he wrote a book *My Experiences as a Mayors' Class Student in Singapore* in which he devoted one chapter to former prime minister Lee Kuan Yew and another to me and my own growth theory for which I felt greatly honoured.

In 2001, the two Mayors' Classes produced slightly more than 1,000 graduates. Alas, today, the Mayors' Class or 市长班 as it is known in Chinese does not have the same glamour attached to it as before, partly because China has since started to set up its own training facilities in Beijing and Shanghai. This is to be expected. President Su told the professors that we could not have the honour to continue the exclusive programme *ad infinitum*. We knew it would slow down eventually.

My visitors' book

For a long, long time I have kept such a visitors' book. My visitors would be asked to honour me with their names and addresses. When I was at NTU's Nanyang

Business School, two most welcomed and most unexpected visitors called on me. They were His Excellency the Crown Prince of Perak, Raja Nazrin Shah and Professor Michael Spence, a Noble Laureate in Economics from Stanford.

The Scholar Prince

One day I received a call from the aide-de-camp to the Crown Prince of Perak seeking an interview with me by the Crown Prince. My reply was, "Sorry, you have got the wrong number." He said, "Are you Professor Lim Chong Yah?" I replied, "Yes." The caller said it was not a mistake. I thus later met the Crown Prince at my office.

To my surprise, he came alone to my office, unescorted. He cut a handsome, youthful and unassuming figure. He was about to complete his PhD from Harvard in Political Economy, having successfully studied PPE (Politics, Philosophy and Economics) earlier at Oxford. He was to write a thesis on the pre-World War II GDP of Peninsular Malaya. We discussed and I was most impressed by his knowledge on the subject. I found the book by Arthur Lewis on Tropical Development quite enlightening. He agreed and added, "It is a pity there is no chapter on Malaya." What a well-read man. He then honoured me with this remark: "I find your book *Economic Development of Modern Malaya* particularly most useful to the understanding of the economy of pre-war Malaya. I like your book so much that I have purposely sent it to London to be bound with the best leather cover and it is displayed on my office desk."

I escorted the scholar-prince out to the car park about 150 metres where I saw a number of bodyguards milling around as motor outriders. His chauffeur-driven car and his aide-de-camp were also there waiting for him. As expected, Dr Shah later succeeded his late father to become the 35th Sultan of Perak and in due course most probably he will become the Yang di-Pertuan Agong (Paramount Ruler) of Malaysia.

Professor Michael Spence

When Professor Michael Spence came to see me, he had already agreed to chair a World Bank-sponsored international committee of global luminaries on global development and underdevelopment. I had become fixed on my own explanation as found in my EGOIN Theory, the Triple C Theory and the S Curve Theory. Nonetheless, he honoured me so much by seeking my view on the subject. His call was completely unexpected. Probably he had been prompted by Mr Goh Chok Tong who was a member of his global commission.

He said, "I am surprised you asked me for help to get a new dean for your Business School. This is a senior management appointment. You should try to get one of your own people to take on this responsibility. I will help you to get eminent professors and researchers though." He made a profound statement that set my mind thinking up to this day. I did fail to convince my university on this approach at that time when I was given the job as Chairman of the Dean Search Committee for NBS.

A rare book buy

The biggest and the most famous bookshop in Oxford when I was a PhD student there was Blackwell along Broad Street. There was a book sale on. I browsed through some interesting books at the sale books section. Lo and behold, I saw an impressive classic-looking thick book by Frank Swettenham published in 1907 on Malaya, the economic and infrastructural development of Malaya, and pre-war Malaya. He, being the first British Resident-General of the then Federated Malay States had first hand knowledge of the country and indeed had played the most important role in its development. Besides, the book was sold at only two shillings and four pence, equivalent to our $1. I quickly grabbed it. It was a windfall. What's more, I saw a name John Anderson with the year 1908 signed on it. I was thrilled. John Anderson was the Governor of the Straits Settlement of Singapore with Anderson Bridge in Singapore named in his memory. Being not a shopper myself, my family's comparative advantage was with my wife and not me; the book was a great and memorable buy in my life.

More than half a century later in Singapore, in Eden Hall — the British High Commissioner's Residence — I chanced to mention to His Excellency Paul Madden whether he was interested in that rare book for custody and display. I was then the President of the Oxford and Cambridge Society in Singapore, and the Society often held its functions there. Because he was preoccupied with other matters at that time, he did not give me a reply. The NTU University Librarian, however, expressed a sure and positive interest, and I promised to give the rare book to the NTU Library instead. All's well that ends well, I hope.

Students' Emergency Fund

At NTU, there was at one time, a tremendous demand for my participation as a conference keynote speaker at many functions. I wondered how I should handle such excessive demand. I thought that if I was so badly needed to speak by commercial organisations, perhaps a fee should be paid. It would not be for me though. After all, my needs are rather limited — mainly buying second-hand golf balls which are not too expensive. When my wife and I go out of Singapore, our grown-up children, particularly Fern and Wun, would insist on paying for everything. Even when we travel on our own, they would often buy our air tickets.

So I decided it would be best to set up a students' emergency fund for the university to use, as it did not have anything like it at that time.

It started with Ernst & Young, who wanted me to speak, and the university replied that a sum of $20,000 was payable which would go to the NTU Students' Emergency Fund. The good and gracious company agreed. This was then established as my normal fee. Later, another well-known company, Canon, asked that I be their keynote speaker at a regional meeting in Sabah. From then on, it snowballed. I also channelled all my royalties from my published works into this fund.

The money came in useful for helping many needy students. For instance, there was one of my Chinese graduate students who was ill but did not have the money to go for an urgent operation. China was still very poor then, and most of the students who came here to study were also very poor.

So the NTU administration decided to dip into the emergency fund to help her. However, a rule in the fund was that if it exceeds a certain amount, the dean of the school would have to be consulted to make sure there would be no excessive use of funds by a particular person. Since I was still around, the dean turned to me for permission. I was thus asked to release the funds earmarked for the student. It was a one-off request. I usually do not know how it is used trusting that the funds will be used wisely by the university. Her operation was successful but several months later, she passed away. Her relatives were, however, ever thankful and grateful to NTU.

After that incident, the NTU administration insisted that all our graduate students should also buy health and accident insurance; undergraduate students had all already been insured.

Lim Chong Yah Bursary Fund

Another fund that NTU set up was a bursary fund in my name. It was patterned after similar funds in some Ivy League universities in the US where as long as a student could get in, he or she would be able to get scholarship support. We wanted to follow that model, and provide for any scholar who was able to enter NTU but was unable to pay his or her way through. Mrs Marina Harper, the director of the development office, insisted that the fund should be in my name to ensure its success. She had enormous experience in fund-raising.

The fund had its beginnings with the Palm Island Club (PIC) that was formed after I visited my forefathers' Hainan Island. When I first went there as a guest of the Chinese government, I did not meet a single person who was a native Hainanese; all top officials I met there were from "outside the province", that is, from the mainland. The only person who had been born and bred there was my coach driver.

I thought the native Hainanese needed help in the form of education to improve their lot so that they could stay and contribute to the island themselves. Thus the PIC was started, comprising English-educated Singaporeans whose forebears had come from Hainan, like me. It dispensed help to Hainanese in the field of education in one form or another. As Singaporeans, we would of course include help for Singaporean families of Hainanese descent or otherwise. PIC came in to raise funds for the Lim Chong Yah Bursary Fund, which was open to all NTU students.

There were also many contributors, big and small, from the entire campus, giving varying amounts of $10, $50 and more. From these thousands, the fund added up very quickly and benefitted many students in need.

I made a personal contribution of S$100,000 to the fund when I launched it in 2007 as I feared that it might not attract enough public donations. I believe my lawyer daughter Fern too came to the rescue with a donation of S$100,000 as well. Actually, I need not have worried as money started to pour in later. This fund led to NTU launching a Campaign for Accessibility to Higher Education, which today helps to support some 120 financially strapped students each year.

We held several fund-raising dinners. At one of them that was PIC-sponsored, NTU President Su Guaning went up to sing a love duet with me on stage to get people to donate — and the audience was very generous indeed. Among those who went on stage to sing was Ms Claire Chang, board member then of the Singapore Chinese Chamber of Commerce and Industry, who did so in Mandarin and even Cantonese and Hainanese. She was very well applauded. No one had expected her to sing in dialect. And among the guests who turned up to support this NTU fund-raising dinner was Mrs Tharman Shanmugaratnam (wife of the then Finance Minister) who came as a guest of Mrs Fang Ai Lian (Chairman of the Methodist Girls' School Board) and Ms Claire Chang.

So the bursary fund is in good form. If the amount to be dispensed is large, the administrators of the fund would seek my consent, in lieu of the dean's consent. There was a case of a bright Malay student in her third year of studies who said she had to leave the university because her taxi-driver father had an accident and died and she had to look for a job to provide for her mother and two younger siblings.

The university persuaded her to continue with her studies with a well-deserved bursary from the Lim Chong Yah Fund. She later successfully graduated.

Soon other universities in Singapore started their own funds after our experience but it is not under any professor's name. The honour given to me was unique and greatly appreciated.

After the successful fund-raising campaign, the development office of NTU in November 2009 sent me a list of donors of individuals and organisations that had donated "above $100,000" each. I was pleasantly surprised at the long list. I was more than pleasantly surprised that the list included religious organisations such as the Singapore Buddhist Lodge, the Jamiyah Singapore, the Taoist Federation (Singapore), and the Hindu Endowments Board. I have remained so thankful to the donors to the NTU students' bursary fund as well as to the eminent fund-raising committee headed by Mr Michael Lim Choo San, a very well-known and well-respected civic leader and a prominent member of the then NTU University Council, now called the Board of Trustees. Ms Fang Ai Lian topped the list of donors with a substantial donation. She did it as a trustee and on behalf of the estate of the late Mr Foo Hee Lim. Dr Tan Eng Liang on behalf of the Goh Cheng Lian Foundation also made an impressive donation.

Another Emeritus Professorship

Looking back, the extension of academic life in NTU for another 20 years after my retirement from NUS was totally unexpected. Instead of what I thought would be a humdrum way of life, I was very active in my new role. In 2012, the university conferred upon me the title of emeritus professor at the age of 80. What an honour, considering when I was appointed an NTU professor two decades before, my appointment was to have been on a year-by-year basis. The university appreciated the contributions I had made in research, teaching and university service to the development of the university. For this, I remain most grateful.

With this conferment, I thus became the only person in Singapore with two emeritus professorships, the other one having been awarded by NUS in 1992.

Today, these two universities have become two of the world's greatest in terms of global ranking. In Asia, NUS has been rated the best, while NTU is second best. Both are poised to go even higher globally with time. With Professor Bertil Andersson at the helm as NTU President and with his ability, energy and devotion, there is still an upper limit to go for NTU. Of course, NTU's rapid ascendancy had its foundation well-laid out by NTU's founding president, Professor Chiam Tao Soon, and his most-worthy successor, Professor Su Guaning. As an NTU professor, speaking for myself in appreciation and very likely also for all others, I am thankful for the pre-eminent role played by these three devoted and distinguished professors as president of the university, in transforming NTU into a world-class university, with unstinting government financial support of course.

So life in NTU for me has not been without memorable events. Well, life does not follow a robotic model — it has its own rhythm, its own patterns of sunshine and even isolated storms. But academic life in Singapore can continue to blossom at its best, both in teaching and in research.

13.1. Some of my MBA students at Nanyang Technological University. The prestigious Nanyang Fellows MBA programme attracts outstanding, mid-career civil servants from all over the world.

13.2. Fourteen books, written by around 140 professors, from Nanyang Technological University's Business School, were launched at the same time. This was a rare feat. The project was initiated by me as Director of the School of Accountancy and Business Research Centre (SABRE) to promote research and communitarianism among academics.

13.3. I was honoured by the visit to my office in NTU by the Nobel Laureate in Economics Professor Michael Spence.

13.4. Nanyang Technological University President Su Guaning and me singing an impromptu love song at a dinner to raise funds for the Lim Chong Yah Bursary Fund. The bursary fund supports NTU students who have difficulty financing their studies at NTU. April 2009.

13.5. At the dinner held in my honour on the occasion of the conferment of Emeritus Professorship on me by Nanyang Technological University in 2012. Clockwise, President NTU Professor Bertil Andersson; former President of the Republic of Singapore SR Nathan; former Cabinet Minister S Dhanabalan; founding NTU President Professor Cham Tao Soon; my wife Nah Nah; Professor Susana Andersson; former Cabinet Minister and Secretary-General of the NTUC Lim Boon Heng; former President of NTU Professor Su Guaning; former Chairman of the Council of Economic Advisors of the United States of America, Stanford University Professor Edward Lazear; myself; and Deputy Prime Minister Tharman Shanmugaratnam.

CHAPTER 14

PROBLEM PUBLICATIONS

As the saying goes, "The pen is mightier than the sword."

As reported in an earlier chapter, I had problems with thugs over one publication of mine on rubber replanting. That was when I was at Pantai Valley. Let us see what happened to me in Singapore over some publications. Little did I know that some of the articles I wrote as part of an academic's repertoire of research and published body of work could ignite so much interest and disputes in Singapore.

Central Provident Fund controversy

It all started in March 1984 with the proposal of the then Minister of Health Howe Yoon Chong to increase the age for the instantaneous withdrawal of Central Provident Fund (CPF) savings for the work force from 55 to 60 years. Very concerned about the greying population, he argued that pushing forward the withdrawal age would result in Singaporeans having more money to live on in their retirement. His proposal was contained in a report entitled *Problems of the Aged: Report of the Committee on the Problems of the Aged.* This report was compiled by a specially convened committee on the problems of the aged which Mr Howe chaired.

What was produced was a green paper on the CPF, not a white paper. This meant that no policy decision had yet been made and the proposal was open to the public for discussion.

But the general public reacted very badly. They disregarded the other proposals in the report. They only focused on the proposed withdrawal age. They were furious. Those nearing 55 were particularly upset over the proposed extension and felt that the government had broken its long-standing promise.

The protest was so bad that I was told by journalists, including my friend Dr Tan Chee Khoon from Kuala Lumpur, watching the December 1984 General Elections that all the opposition speakers needed to do was to raise the CPF age withdrawal issue and they would get rounds of applause. The government took notice of that and tried to find a way out.

Dr Tony Tan, then Minister for Trade and Industry, tried to save the situation by suggesting that maybe a university academic could be appointed to look objectively into the matter. His intention was presumably to defuse the issue.

A month after this, a colleague, Professor Chew Soon Beng, who was the designated press spokesman for the Department of Economics and Statistics in NUS was asked by the media for the name of the academic appointed. His reply, "None of us has been approached yet. But we would only be too happy to help in any way we could." In telling the truth, he unwittingly had stepped on some very sensitive toes.

The government apparently felt that his unexpected reply was unacceptable. It probably had wanted the subject to die out, to be forgotten.

I was having lunch at Goodwood Park Hotel with Professor Lord Peter Bauer, then external examiner in economics for our department when I received a call from Ms Ong Jin Soo, the head of the university's personnel department, to head back to the university immediately and to report to Vice-Chancellor Lim Pin.

Feeling it would be discourteous to Bauer, I did not disrupt the lunch and went back to the campus only after it was over. Although I did not tell him about the content of the telephone call, Lord Bauer could sense the unease I was facing.

As usual, the Vice-Chancellor's desk was clean and tidy and he was his dapper self. He went straight to the point asking me why Professor Chew Soon Beng had answered the press query without having it first cleared by the university.

I simply replied that the statement was in response to a media query and it was the decision of the department under my charge as head that we should reply truthfully that we had not received an invitation yet but were prepared to help if anyone of us was approached.

Professor Lim Pin said: "I went through the minutes of your meeting but nowhere was it written that he was authorised by you to make such a statement."

"Maybe the matter was not so important that it should be minuted," was my reply.

He asked if our department could work with the administration on such matters in future to which I readily agreed.

When I asked what the crux of the matter was, he replied that the minister in charge of university education would make a public statement censuring our department and he wanted me to give an undertaking that I would not reply to the minister.

I was not happy that the matter was taken so seriously and that it had been overblown, but I agreed not to respond. True enough, one or two days later, there was a censuring press statement from the minister.

All of us in the Department of Economics and Statistics, which was one of the biggest in the university then with 120 teaching staff, including two Members of Parliament belonging to the ruling People's Action Party (PAP), Professors Augustine Tan and Ow Chin Hock, all hoped the matter would fizzle out as soon as possible.

But it actually exacerbated as a result of an unexpected and unanticipated editorial in The Straits Times which questioned the minister for censuring the department. It also praised the department for expressing views of public concern especially on economic matters.

I was called up again to see the Vice-Chancellor. This time he wanted me to write a letter defending the position of the university especially on academic freedom. The letter was to be approved by my then dean, Professor Edwin Thumboo, who was also Professor of English. The letter was also to be sent to the university's press relations officer Peter Lim for his agreement.

I knew Mr Peter Lim quite well as he was closely connected with the Methodist Church in Singapore. In fact, he was the first pastor of Barker Road Methodist Church in 1956 and had been principal of the Anglo-Chinese School in Seremban before being appointed as the university's press spokesman.

Long before that, he was part of the teaching staff at Barker Road's Anglo-Chinese School. It was not known to Professor Lim Pin then that the good reverend under the name of Lim Seck Tiong had stood for elections in 1955 in Tanjong Pagar Constituency in a three-cornered fight against PAP's Lee Kuan Yew who later won, and in 1959 became our first prime minister. Peter was very articulate in election campaigns. In fact, he always had a reputation for speaking very good English.

So I was confident that with Professor Edwin Thumboo and Mr Peter Lim at the helm, my final letter would be well-crafted. They approved my letter. It was forwarded to the Vice-Chancellor for further action.

Days passed; nothing was heard of, and I had thought that the letter had been forgotten. But two or three weeks later, Professor Lim Pin called me up again to say that some amendments had been made and that the letter was now ready to be sent to the press. The minor changes were not about substance but involved substituting one word for another even though the new words conveyed the same meaning. But I thought that if the revised letter would bring peace and harmony between the minister and our department, so be it. I accepted it to be published in my name.

And so the letter was sent out by me. The Straits Times published it with my name in bold as having signed the letter, defending academic freedom in the university. We all hoped that would bring to a close that rather unhappy episode.

Setting up of CPF study group

After the letter had been published, I went back to routine work at the department.

Just when I thought the entire matter had been laid to rest, the minister issued a press statement that the CPF withdrawal age issue should be investigated into independently by our department and that the authorities would give support by way of statistics and information. So I decided to set up a committee to delve into the subject, asking for volunteers to participate. In 1986, after probing and consulting with various government departments, some of whom were cooperative while others were not, we came up with the CPF Study Group Report.

However, when the report was ready, we were told not to publish it. This went against academic thinking and practice as traditionally academics are expected to make public their research work. Academics also live in the world academic community. They like their research efforts to be published, as universities all over the world evaluate their staff based on their published works.

I wondered what the objections could have been. Was it because we had made some suggestions one of which was that we supported the view that the CPF withdrawal age should not be postponed or extended but that it should remain at age 55?

Or was it because of our suggestion of the institution of an insurance policy for catastrophic illnesses (not a comprehensive scheme as is now proposed under the current and far superior MediShield Life Scheme)? Or was it the proposal to have a minimum sum scheme of which the current minimum sum scheme probably came about?

I had sometimes wondered why our report stirred up so much controversy as I had actually regarded it to be the best antidote for insomnia. It was written in academic jargon and strewn with a lot of technical terms, thanks to the actuaries in our group such as Professor Lee Yong Seng.

A reporter from The Straits Times somehow got hold of our report and it was serialised in the newspaper, making almost daily headline news.

I asked the minister if, since it was already made public, perhaps our department could publish the report but he referred me to another minister who then referred me to yet another.

After being passed from pillar to post and not getting anywhere, I took matters into my own hands and published the report as a special issue (Vol 3, No 1, April 1986) of the *Singapore Economic Review*, an academic publication of the department and the Economic Society of Singapore, of which I was then the president.

To my astonishment, I heard through the grapevine that then Prime Minister Lee Kuan Yew told the members of his Cabinet to read the issue as "there were a lot of good ideas in the report."

So from something that was considered unpublishable and problematic, the report had made it to the "must read" list for Cabinet Ministers, much to my delight and amazement.

What even made the whole event a little bizarre was that one of the volunteer members of the CPF Study Group, Professor Hank Lim, was invited to become a special advisor to the then Ministry of Labour (today's Ministry of Manpower) for consultation in the implementation of our report.

Thank goodness, all was well that ended well. My guess is that that was how the minimum sum scheme came about — from our CPF Report and also the health insurance scheme against catastrophic diseases.

Economic policy options

In 1985, Singapore's economy registered a negative yearly growth rate — the first time since independence in 1965. Then Minister of Trade and Industry Lee Hsien Loong was appointed to head a specially set up committee to find a solution to this malaise. The National Wages Council (NWC) of which I was then still the chairman came out to support the recommendations of this committee which recommended the cutting down of wage costs for employers. Serious tax cuts were also proposed.

The Department of Economics and Statistics was also interested independently to study different facets of the new economy, so I again asked for volunteers. Twenty-six stepped forward and we met three hours a week for a year to brainstorm.

At the end of our research and deliberations in 1986, we came out with a book on the major economic policy issues facing Singapore: fiscal, monetary, full employment, role of government, population, land utilisation, manpower, foreign investments, foreign trade, income distribution and the limits to growth. For each policy we mapped out our own sets of recommendations for the future.

As I had worked as a civil servant before, I knew the advantages of first clearing with the Civil Service on different aspects on our policy recommendations, to get their feedback and reaction. So we submitted copies of our work to the various ministries. All reacted well and welcomed our recommendations except the Ministry of Education. I suspect they were sensitive to our recommendations on introducing compulsory education and perhaps also the changing of the name of Nanyang Technological Institute (NTI) to Nanyang Technological University (NTU). For whatever reasons, the ministry was against our publishing the book which we had entitled *Policy Options for the Singapore Economy*.

The book ran into 499 pages and considering the amount of collective time and effort that had been spent on the project, I thought it was unfair to the researchers involved, including myself, not to publish it. Besides, we did have a number of policy recommendations that we genuinely believed were viable and would be of interest to the public and policy makers.

We were not expecting consensus for our suggestions and we believed that differences of view were normal in the course of brainstorming. Our society seemed to be afraid of exchanging views, which we felt should not be the case. It was in this spirit that we decided to get our book published.

The publisher was McGraw-Hill. Somehow it got wind of objections from a ministry regarding the book and they explored the possibility of backing out. I was shocked. I assured them that they would not get into trouble for publishing the book. I stood firm because the contract to print had already been signed.

While printing was under way, I reflected on what might have been the objections against the book and why was it only the Ministry of Education that had voiced reservations on having it published.

I could only think of three policy issues we had raised that might have rankled some authorities. One of them was our recommendation to revise the Land Acquisition Act to pay adequate compensation for land being acquired instead of the previous take-it-or-leave-it form of payment which was more akin to the confiscation of land.

But this had nothing to do with education and the ministry concerned with land acquisition did not take issue with us on the subject.

The other two policy recommendations we had made concerning education was, in our view, for the public good. One was the suggestion that the then Nanyang Technological Institute (NTI) be converted into a full university to be called the Nanyang Technological University (NTU). Why would this be an objection for the Ministry of Education? We could not fathom it out on this matter.

Another recommendation was our proposal that compulsory education be introduced for boys and girls up to the age of 16. This might have bothered some officials.

The book finally saw the light of day in 1988. Fifteen years later, I received a call from then Prime Minister Goh Chok Tong to go to the Istana for lunch. Over *yong tow foo*, I asked him what the meeting was all about.

He told me that the government had accepted the proposal to have compulsory education introduced. So that was the reason for the invitation to lunch — to share the good news.

My purpose for bringing up the problems we faced in getting our books published is not to show that we had been proven right when the government accepted some of our suggestions but to highlight how sensitive it was in the past to make public policy suggestions. Ministry officials have since relaxed their stance and are more open to other — sometimes opposing — views. We have definitely evolved for the better.

Permanent invitation to visit China

The year was 1979 and China was starting to open up its economy to foreign investment and foreign trade as part of economic reforms instituted by its far-sighted and pragmatic leader Deng Xiaoping.

I was curious to find out about the changes in China, so one or two years later, I led a delegation of members of the Economic Society of Singapore, of which I was then still president, to familiarise ourselves with China's new economy. We visited various cities and on my return, I gave a public lecture at NUS on my impressions.

Soon after, I published the lecture as a series of four articles in the form of editorials in the then Chinese daily Sin Chew Jit Poh which would in 1983 amalgamate with Nanyang Siang Pau to become today's Lianhe Zaobao.

The editorials appeared a week apart and were published on the front page.

In the four articles I tried to convey what China was like at that point in time. For instance, I wrote about how we were different in our dressing and behaviour when compared with the Chinese. In fact, we were quite conspicuous and we had curious people following us. Since then, China has developed almost beyond recognition. The Chinese are very well-dressed today especially in cities like Beijing and Shanghai.

I also brought up a point that was considered then critical of the Chinese government. I mentioned how I could not understand why portraits of Stalin and Karl Marx were often placed side by side with one of China's greatest leaders, Chairman Mao Zedong. I questioned why was it that no other Chinese leaders such as former premier Zhou Enlai were honoured, or some of China's greatest scholars such as Confucius, Mencius or Laozi? Similarly, why were there no portraits at all of ancient heroes like Wen Tienxiang, Yue Fei, or Lin Zexu who had stood up against the British in the First Opium War in 1839?

I was told my four articles were sent by the Bank of China in Singapore to Beijing. A year later, I received an open invitation from a Chinese government agency to visit any part of China that I wished to go, anytime, at my convenience and that I could bring along my wife and four supporting staff as special guests of China.

I took up their invitation, and travelled to Hainan Province in 1994 and 1996 and to the three North Eastern Provinces (Manchuria) giving lectures where appropriate. One or two officials from Beijing would accompany our delegation each time, not to impose any restrictions on us or to keep us in check but to ensure we would be well looked after. Indeed, I was free to speak wherever I went and to give press interviews as I liked.

Fifteen years later, while on a private vacation visit to Yantai in Shandong Province, I chanced upon portraits of some of China's greatest leaders in history all on public display. It seemed as if the Chinese authorities had shared my view on the subject. I also noticed they had removed Karl Marx, Lenin and Stalin from public display. Their own leaders, of course, remain.

Income inequality debate

In 2012, I discovered that our Gini coefficient, which is a measure of income inequality, had been deteriorating rapidly in Singapore in the past decade. Yet, this was not the case in the 1970s and 1980s when the Gini coefficient in fact registered a downward trend.

I found this new development alarming, so I decided to highlight this in a paper presented at the *Distinguished Speaker Public Lecture* organised by the Economic Society of Singapore in April 2012 and a follow-up paper at the Singapore Economic Policy Forum 2012, co-organised by the Economic Society of Singapore and the Division of Economics of NTU, in October 2012.

In the years after independence, under NWC's guidance, our Gini coefficient had improved. However, later it started to deteriorate but the NWC did not sound the alarm then as it was not a big decline. In part, this was due to the influx of large numbers of lowly-paid foreign workers.

In my papers, I suggested ways to stem the widening income inequality gap. It stirred a controversy with the newspapers highlighting my proposals as "shock therapy". One of my suggestions was to hike up the pay of the lowest-paid workers earning less than $1,000 per month by 50 per cent over a period of three years.

Another was to have voluntary restraint, for three years, on further pay increases for those earning more than $1 million per year. Quite a number of Singaporean CEOs were reported to be earning from $2.5 million to $5.5 million a year, or S$208,000 to S$458,000 a month.

Shock therapy it might have been but I found some support among the public on my stand to raise the pay of the lowest income groups. And even though the NWC had been noticing since 2011 that the income growth of low-wage workers had been lagging behind that of the rest of the workforce, I guess my statement must have spurred them to finally do something about it, as Chairman Lim Pin alluded to in the book, *The Story of NWC*, authored by Tan Chung Lee.

For its guidelines governing the period from 1 July 2012 to 30 June 2013, the NWC recommended that workers earning less than $1,000 a month should be given an increase of at least $50. A similar recommendation was made by the NWC in 2013, 2014 and 2015 to raise the wage income of the lowest income group in Singapore by a quantitative guideline.

Thanks to this initiative by the NWC headed by Professor Lim Pin, the Gini coefficient has since improved as I have noted in my book *Singapore's National Wages Council: An Insider's View* (2014).

CHAPTER 15

SETTING UP INSTITUTIONS

At the time of writing (2015), were one to be a young academic in Singapore, one would be expected to give research top priority. Not only that, one's research would have to be published in top global journals.

During my time as a young economist, although research was equally emphasised under the heading "publish or perish", publications then took on a wider perspective to include books and regional academic journals. There was also some push towards nation building and community service. That made sense then for newly independent nations like the Federation of Malaya and later Malaysia and Singapore. We had to build up economic institutions from scratch at the same time. This had already been built up in the rich, developed world where academics there had rightly a different orientation and emphasis.

Despite the imposition on my time, I would like to think that my contributions to national and regional institution-building were not futile. We are all creatures of our circumstances.

Four of these institutions in particular stood out: The Economic Society of Singapore (ESS), the Federation of ASEAN Economic Associations (FAEA), the East Asian Economic Association (EAEA), and the Pacific Economic Cooperation Conference (PECC), later renamed the Pacific Economic Cooperation Council.

Economic Society of Singapore (ESS)

It began as the Malayan Economic Society established by students of the Economics Department of the University of Malaya (in Singapore) in 1956. I became its treasurer (1958–1959) while the university's vice-chancellor Professor Lim Tay Boh became its president. Its ideals were to bring together academics, government officials and business leaders to discuss economic issues and problems affecting Malaya (including Singapore) and the region and to conduct independent research. The society was also known for its publication, Malayan Economic Review.

After the University of Malaya was renamed the University of Singapore in 1962 and after Singapore's independence from Malaysia in 1965, it was thought that the society and its publication should also be renamed. So the Economic Society of Singapore (ESS) came about in 1969.

From 1973 to 1991, I served as president, and it was during this period that I decided to also rename the society's journal to the *Singapore Economic Review* to better reflect the changing realities of the political and economic alignments of Singapore and Malaysia. I served as its editor from 1978 to 1991, after which I became its editorial advisor. When I retired from the National University of Singapore (NUS) in 1992, the Society appointed me as an Honorary Fellow, together with other very prominent personalities like Dr Goh Keng Swee.

In 2005, the journal, under Professor Euston Quah, launched the bi-annual Singapore Economic Review Conference to which international economists such as Nobel Prize winners in Economics and other world luminaries in economics are invited to participate.

Part of my academic life was thus greatly involved in the activities of the ESS and its antecedent Economic Society of Malaya.

Federation of ASEAN Economic Associations (FAEA)

In 1976, ESS became a founding member of the Federation of ASEAN Economic Associations (FAEA).

I initiated the move when I was President of ESS as a means of bringing together academics of the countries in ASEAN (Association of Southeast Asian Nations). Its aims were to promote better understanding among ourselves, to foster *esprit de corps* and to build up regional cohesion and identity. The main platform for this would be through an annual conference which member countries would take turns to host. The presidency of FAEA would also be on a rotating basis with the head of the host country's economic association serving in the role. Professor John Wang then was the Honorary Secretary of ESS, and he helped me to draft the constitution of the Federation.

Thus, for the first three occasions that Singapore hosted the FAEA annual conference, in 1980, 1985 and 1990, I served as its president.

In 1987 when Bali was hosting the FAEA annual conference, the Indonesian Economic Society deemed it fit to confer upon me the "FAEA Founder's Distinguished Award," in recognition of my work in founding the Federation. The Indonesian Society also conferred the same title on Dr Emil Salim for hosting the first conference of FAEA in Parapat, Indonesia.

Thank goodness, I was still fluent in the Malay language so when the governor of Bali had completed his citation on me, I replied in the main in Malay, to which the Indonesian language is closely related. My response, with a well-known Malay pantun (a poetic form) as support, was particularly well received by the Indonesian hosts.

Till today, 38 annual conferences have been held by FAEA, and because of the rule of hosting by rotation, all of the member countries have been hosts, sometimes several times around.

East Asian Economic Association (EAEA)

Despite the rapid transformation of the economies of East Asian countries since World War II, there was no grouping to bring together economists from this region and those interested in this region.

When I was a visiting professor at the University of Kyoto in 1983, I was approached by my host, Professor Sinichi Ichimura, for advice in forming a regional association. I read through the draft constitution of the East Asian Economic Association (EAEA) that he had prepared.

Actually, I was more in favour of a federation based on the Federation of ASEAN Economic Associations model, but my friend Sinichi concluded that it would be difficult since there was no grouping in East Asia that was similar to ASEAN. Besides, Japan itself did not have a national economic association as existed in each of the ASEAN countries.

So I went along with what he proposed — the setting up of an international academic organisation to focus on the economies of Northeast and Southeast Asia. The first meeting was held in Hong Kong in 1987 with Sumitro as President while both Ichimura and I were appointed vice-presidents.

EAEA hosts a biennial conference and publishes a quarterly Asian Economic Journal. There is active participation from countries outside East Asia such as from the US, Australia, New Zealand and Europe.

I am still active in EAEA as a senior advisor.

Pacific Economic Cooperation Conference (PECC)

I have written in an earlier chapter about my involvement in the setting up of the Pacific Economic Cooperation Conference (PECC) in Canberra, Australia and the establishment of the Singapore PECC chapter so I will not dwell on it here.

However, I would like to mention here some of the very distinguished and interesting personalities that I have met over the past 34 years of my involvement with the PECC.

Membership in PECC is on a trilateral basis with countries sending representatives from the government, business and academia. Each year, the plenary session of PECC would be held in different parts of the Pacific.

It was in such annual conferences that I came to know Dr Nam Duck Woo. He was the former Prime Minister of South Korea (1980–1982). He went on to become the International Chair for PECC from 1983 to 1985. However, because he was a former vice-chancellor of the Korean National University, he took a great interest in academics like me who were members in the PECC.

I became good friends with him, and had the privilege of hosting him and his friends for lunch whenever he visited Singapore *en route* to Indonesia on his business trips. He too came to know my colleague and friend Dr Hank Lim well in the PECC gatherings.

Representing Japan at the inaugural meeting was another eminent politician Dr Saburo Okita who was, at one time, the foreign minister of Japan. He was reputed to play an important role in the early economic transformation of Japan.

On one occasion when I was in Japan on sabbatical, visiting the Tokyo Foundation for Advanced Information Research (FAIR) in 1987, it was Okita who introduced me to Niigata University. I gave a talk there on the economic challenges facing Southeast Asia, and thanks to Okita, I got to discover Niigita's famous rice and rice *sake*. Later, I was able to send one of my graduate students there on a study programme.

In February 1993, Okita was due to visit Singapore. I arranged a lunch meeting at Shangri-La Hotel with some of Singapore's luminaries from the Civil Service such as Mr Ngiam Tong Dow. Okita was due to pay a courtesy call on the then Senior Minister Lee Kuan Yew after the lunch. This, I did not know at that time.

Alas, the meeting never materialised. I received a call the day before from the Japanese Embassy in Singapore to say that my friend would not be able to turn up but that this would be confirmed later within an hour. I was worried; was something amiss, I wondered?

Thirty minutes later, the embassy called to say my friend Dr Okita had died suddenly. I found out that, being his usual conscientious self, before leaving for his scheduled visit, Dr Okita had been speaking with an influential American scholar who was trying to get him to pester the Japanese government to revalue the Japanese Yen. His demise was certainly premature and a great loss to Japan, East Asia and the Asia-Pacific region.

Okita was so well known that when China's Deng Xiaoping first visited Japan he sought him out to be a special advisor on economic matters in China. Okita had been born in Dalian, the northeast province of China that was formerly Manchuria, later occupied by Japan.

What was remarkable was that although his PhD was in engineering, Okita switched his focus to economic planning and financial matters. In 1953, he was appointed to head the economic planning agency of Japan with a view of doubling the country's per capita income in six or seven years.

Dr Okita was also the writer of an article in Euston Quah's festschrift "Development, Trade and the Asia-Pacific: Essays in Honour of Professor Lim Chong Yah". It was Dr Okita's last article before he passed away.

Then there was Dr Koo Chen-fu of Taiwan with an amazing, albeit tumultuous, family history. He was a well-known businessman and diplomat and was unusual in many ways. He was head of a thriving cement company in Taiwan.

When I was in Taiwan as a visiting professor in 1987, he took pains to play host to me. It was at a lunch meeting he had organised that he confided in me that his former surname was Lim (林), just like mine, but that he inherited the name Koo (辜) due to a family quirk of history. "Lim" means "forest" in Chinese while "Koo" means "guilty".

He said, "Long ago in ancient China, my army general ancestor lost a major war and the emperor was so annoyed that he forbade his family and descendants to use the surname 'Lim' and told them that they had to call themselves 'Koo'."

He added that in his family, they would never marry a Lim, as this would be incestuous, according to Chinese tradition, at any rate.

He spoke good Japanese. He would at times consult me on the speeches he intended to make at PECC meetings. I felt very flattered.

PECC and APEC headquarters in Singapore

An important point about the PECC was that it established its headquarters in Singapore, a path-breaking measure at that time, as the official policy in Singapore then was not to have international bodies based here.

From what I understand, the authorities were then afraid of having locals being lured to work for international bodies, as they offered much higher salaries then, and also officials from international agencies might insist on having diplomatic immunity. All these fears came to nought. For one thing, our salaries had become much higher than the PECC officials of similar standing and grade.

And it was thanks to PECC that the Asia-Pacific Economic Cooperation (APEC) got to be based in Singapore as well.

When PECC was first formed, there was no problem of how to organise meetings. Member countries took turns to host the annual conference. Later, Japan and Australia suggested the setting up of a coordinating secretariat to handle some PECC matters.

Pak Jusuf Wanandi from Indonesia supported having a secretariat, if it was to be based in one of the capitals of ASEAN. Japan had indicated that it would be happy to finance it, if it was based in Tokyo. South Korea indicated that it was not ready to host the secretariat, while the US declined as it did not want to show its dominance. Australia did not wish to show its card yet.

At a meeting later at Hotel Equatorial in Singapore, I found on the agenda the location of the PECC secretariat. I quickly secured the support of Pak Jusuf Wanandi and Dr Mohammad Noordin Sopiee, the head of the Indonesian and Malaysian delegations respectively to consider Singapore as the location.

To my delight, all present voted in favour of my proposal. And that was how we managed to get PECC based here.

It was only after the meeting that my dear colleague from the Economics Department, Dr Hank Lim, who was my chief helper, pointed out to me in private that I had not been given the nod by the Singapore government to have PECC based in Singapore. He asked, "What if the government disagrees? Would it not be embarrassing?"

I said, "Sure, the government has the authority to decide, because it might incur costs and it would have to find a place to house the secretariat. But it would take six to nine months to get the decision if I asked the government first. I did not want to miss the chance of having the secretariat based in Singapore."

"What would you do, should the government turn us down?" asked Hank.

I replied, "I would then eat humble pie, and say to the rest that I did not succeed in getting government support, and pass the secretariat to a new bidder."

Hank remarked, "Prof Lim, you are a risk taker, an academic entrepreneur."

Sure enough, I was later approached by a senior civil servant on this issue. He said, "Professor Lim, I went through our earlier minutes on PECC but nowhere was it found that the government had given prior approval to have the secretariat based here. How come it is now based in Singapore?" I explained to him the circumstances.

I added, "Let's be thankful for this. Do you remember Thailand later was asking to be considered and the Philippines too? But it was then too late for them."

The senior official then assured me that he would push to get this, and later, the to-be-formed APEC Secretariat to Singapore. He succeeded and, in the latter case, with prior government agreement.

On hindsight, I think I did the right thing despite not having sought government approval first which later came when it gave a house (No. 4) on Nassim Road for use as the PECC International Secretariat.

I hope we will continue to support and nurture institutions such as these as it would be to our advantage to have such international connections. The last thing we should aspire to is to be a small island unto ourselves.

Fellowship across the seas

Speaking of interesting and important personalities that one meets as a member of international associations, I would like to relate the story of Dr Arifin Siregar, the governor of the Bank of Indonesia and a former minister who was one of FAEA's presidents. When an annual conference was held in Jakarta, Siregar invited heads of attending delegations to his house for dinner, in accordance with FAEA tradition that whoever plays host as president would have to invite the heads of delegations to his house for a dinner get-together.

When I arrived, I noticed an extremely attractive young lady among the guests. I asked Arifin, "Did you invite a film star here tonight?" When I discreetly pointed out the lady in question, he laughed and said, "That's my wife!" I made his day. We have remained good friends to this day.

Before I left Jakarta, he gave me a signed copy of every denomination of the Indonesian currency. The notes had his signature as bank governor and he countersigned each one of them, so the currency notes now had two signatures, one freshly penned and the other printed.

I kept the notes as souvenirs but they disappeared when my house was burgled.

When I met him again in Bandung at one of the FAEA meetings, I told him what had happened.

"That's not a problem," he said and went to the reception counter of the historic hotel where we were staying and asked to be given Indonesian currency notes of all denominations. He paid for them and signed the notes, handing them to me. I still have them and treasure them so much that I have kept them in a safe deposit box in a bank.

This story shows how close a rapport my generation of Southeast Asian scholars have with one another and I am sure present and future generations will strike up similar friendships. In my view, there is value in being a member of regional and international associations as it helps to foster fellowship across the seas. I am glad that I did not remain as an ivory-tower economist. My circumstances did not allow this to happen anyway.

I had remembered what John Hicks had told me early in my academic career, "I don't think you should do pure theoretical economics; instead, why not do something more useful for the development of your country and the region?"

Despite my many extra-curricular activities, I have been blessed that I could still find a respectable place, mainly through research, publication, teaching and university administration, in both NUS and NTU. And I must hasten to add that NUS and NTU have featured among the very top universities in the world. I cannot but be very proud of my close associations with both universities.

Presidential Council for Minority Rights (PCMR)

Apart from the regional stage, I have also been active on the domestic front. I have made voluntary contributions in time and effort to the National Wages Council to which I have devoted 29 years of my life and the Methodist Girls' School Board on which I served as member and later deputy chairman for 40 years.

I have also been a member of the Presidential Council for Minority Rights (PCMR) for 20 years from 1992 to 2012.

Singapore's constitution provides for a council to represent the interests of minorities in two important areas: The protection of religious freedom and the protection of ethnic minorities.

All laws passed by Parliament in Singapore have to come under the scrutiny of the council to ensure that there is no discrimination against ethnic or religious minorities. So too with all legal rules and regulations made under these laws.

We have diverse representation in this council with members drawn from the Malay, Indian, Eurasian and Chinese communities and with religious figures such as the archbishop of the Catholic Church. All of us, however, are appointed in our personal capacities.

For instance, the invitation to become a member was made in my own name. I was not told if I was representing any particular group.

I may be a member of the majority ethnic group in the council, but as a protestant Christian, I am in the minority, and as a Hainanese Chinese, I am also in the minority among ethnic Chinese.

Invitations to become a member are issued by the Singapore President. All ordinary members are appointed for a three-year term and all have to be sworn in by the president at The Istana. All Council meetings are chaired by the Chief Justice.

I must add that this minority rights council was the brainchild of Mr Lee Kuan Yew when he was Singapore's first prime minister.

National Science Council (NSC)

In the early 1970s, Dr Toh Chin Chye, the then vice-chancellor of the University of Singapore and also the Minister for Science and Technology, appointed me to be a member of Singapore's National Science Council. I must report my own disastrous first meeting.

I felt greatly honoured to be among the top scientists in Singapore. But I found tabled on the agenda a discussion on a science contest for school children that was aired on television at that time. Questions would be asked, and students from various competing schools would give answers. The members of the Council would be the judges during the show.

Correct answers to the questions would be given by the Council to the judges. If a not-absolutely-correct answer was given but was considered to be in a "grey area", the emcee for the quiz would refer to the chief representative member of the Council present at the show for a final judgement.

Before the quiz went on air, the members of the Council would spend hours and hours on drafting the questions and answers and on matters such as phraseology. I am generally a patient person in many ways but in some ways not, and at my first meeting I should have had patience and observe the much-acclaimed rule that "silence is golden".

Instead, I questioned the basic function of the Council. I said that the Science Council should not run a national quiz for school children and that it should be left to junior colleges to do so.

Our role, I said, should be to establish contacts with other scientists in the world and to find out the latest discoveries and advances made and see if we could apply them to uplift our economy and quality of life. The other members were not happy with my outspokenness and my blunt statements, particularly from a newcomer.

I could see that I was stepping on the toes of some very well-respected and extremely well-known scientists of this country.

Some of them might have even thought I was *kurang ajar* (insolent). Why should I be telling them what to do when I am an economist and not a scientist?

I knew that after that meeting, they would never invite me again. That in fact happened. But I also noted that soon after, the national quiz programme came to a halt. It was cancelled. The Council did not give it to the junior colleges to run either. In the meantime, I hoped the members had forgiven and overlooked my seeming presumptuousness. Maybe they agreed with me when they suspended the quiz. The point I was making then was that they should have gone for higher things and that even among scientists, a division of labour might be necessary. And division of labour is very much an economic concept, one of the fundamental bases of Adam Smith's evergreen book on *An Inquiry into the Nature and Causes of Wealth of Nations*.

I have nonetheless continued to advocate the critical and important role of science and technology in the development of a country, and Singapore cannot and should not be an exception. No country can grow and develop in the modern world without science and technology which, incidentally, is the view of all development economists.

15.1. Chairing a meeting of the Pacific Economic Cooperation Conference (PECC) in Singapore. Second from left is Dr Koo Chen-fu, Head of the PECC delegation from Taiwan, and second from right is Dr Saburo Okita, Head of the PECC delegation from Japan. The PECC was the precursor for what is now the Asia-Pacific Economic Cooperation (APEC).

CHAPTER 16

THE LIGHTER SIDE OF LIFE

Mountain trekking

Academic work, in addition to my university duties as a dean and head of the economics department plus serving as chairman on the National Wages Council (NWC) on top of other responsibilities such as chairing the Skills Development Fund and sitting on the committees of various national and regional organisations, ensured that I had a lot on my plate.

But fortunately in the academic world, there is a long vacation of some three months which allowed me ample time to take a breather from work. I made the most of these long vacations to indulge in my love for mountain trekking and exploring new places outside Singapore.

My interest in trekking probably stemmed from my childhood days in Malacca where I developed a love of hiking to St Paul's Hill on top of which are the ruins of St Paul's Church, originally built by the Portuguese in the 16th century and also to St John's Hill where the 18th century St John's Fort, built by the Dutch, still stands.

I made it a point to go hiking whenever I travelled and if possible, scale mountains too. Apart from being a healthy pursuit because of the physical exertion involved, it dove-tailed well with my love of discovering nature as hiking is often done amidst landscapes of exceptional beauty with forests, lakes, rivers, green valleys and blue skies.

What's more, hiking — and mountain climbing — is therapeutic. It is a time when you can shut out economics from your mind. In fact, you are cut off from the outside world with not even the sound of a car to penetrate the stillness of your surroundings. My wife and I have sometimes not seen anyone else when mountain trekking; there would be just the two of us in the wilderness. It can be a strange, yet wonderful feeling. When the mountains are high, the sky seems lower and the stars bigger and almost within reach. You are simply lost in the great wilderness of God's creation.

So for me, mountain climbing is the true sabbatical, where you can forget about arguments in economics and finance.

Of course, climbing has its dangers especially when it comes to high altitudes where you can develop mountain sickness. There are precautions to take such as avoiding alcohol consumption and trekking slowly. There is a sense of achievement in reaching the summit and when you do meet people along the way, you feel a sense of connection. And there were times at some places when we would start as early as 3 am to reach a peak at 7 am just to watch the glorious sunrise.

Mt Fuji

Every time we visited Japan, we longed to climb Mt Fuji (3,776 m) but work was always the barrier to the sacred mountain.

Then on one occasion, we purposely managed to take time off to climb the holy mountain. It was outside the official climbing season of July and August, and the weather was bad. Our Japanese friends advised against it as they said the hotels there would be closed. My wife and I went anyway.

The hotels were shut as our friends had said, but one mountain hut was still open. We managed to find accommodation in that hut named Sato, where we slept on hard bunk beds in a dormitory.

That night there were eight of us at dinner having *shabu-shabu*. We sat around a huge cauldron in which we would throw in thin slices of beef and vegetables to cook then dipped into sauces before eating with rice. The people we met were so different from the city folk we knew. They looked very rugged and definitely hailed from the wild countryside. All the men had beards and they were all polite.

I noticed a young man among the eight who looked like an urbanite. After dinner, he in broken English and I in my broken Japanese struck up a conversation. He was there to trek and I asked if we could all three go together since it would be safer. I assured him that my wife and I were properly attired and had torches and walking equipment. The hostess of the hut prepared food and green tea for us to bring along.

So the next day, we got up very early and set out. It was still dark but the trail was good. There was a full moon that lit part of the way. I walked a little ahead and waited for my wife to follow closely. That was how we usually trek; I would go first and she follows my trail.

However, the Japanese man accompanied my wife all the way, stopping whenever she did to rest and making sure he brought up the rear. He never overtook my wife. Whenever she stopped, he stopped.

As soon as we all made it safely to the summit, he politely asked if he could take his leave when he was assured that we could go down by ourselves. It was 6 am and the sun had not risen yet. I asked what he did for a living. His answer: In the fire brigade in Tokyo. He said *sayonara* (goodbye) with a polite bow and we never met again.

We had thanked him for his help — my wife remarked to me that he was like an angel who guided us all the way from the downhill Sato hut to the summit of the sacred Mt Fuji.

His presence added to the exhilarating and unforgettable experience of the hike itself.

Ben Nevis

This mountain in Scotland is the highest peak in the British Isles.

Because of its relatively low height (1,344 m) compared to other peaks elsewhere, Ben Nevis was among the first mountains that we scaled since we knew we could accomplish the climb quite easily.

It was in 1976 and prior to our hike, I consulted Professor Lee Yong Leng, the former Singapore High Commissioner to the United Kingdom on climbing the peak. He knew the area well and gave suggestions on how to get there as well as which route to take to go up — even where to eat at a Singapore restaurant with *char keow teow* (fried noodles) in the foothills!

On our way to the top, we noticed three young European women walking behind us; soon they overtook us with a wave. We waved back and said we would see them at the top. They said they came from Switzerland. We replied that we came from Singapore.

We took ages to arrive, but we found the trio at the summit patiently waiting for us. They had been there for an hour but wanted to make sure that we would arrive safely. They were happy to see us and we chatted for a while before they made their way down.

It was meeting people like the three women that made mountain climbing so pleasurable for us; trekkers tend to look after one another.

Ben Nevis was strewn with craggy volcanic stones spilled over from an ancient eruption.

We finally made our way down to one of the small towns at the foot of the mountain, where true enough, the Singapore restaurant as recommended by Yong Leng was located.

Jade Mountain

When I happened to be in Taiwan on sabbatical leave in 1976, we had the opportunity to climb Mount Yushan or Jade Mountain, so called as its peak in winter shines like steely jade in the sun when covered in snow.

The timing was fortuitous as until then the mountain had been closed to the public. The Taiwanese government had used the mountain as a military hideout since 1949. There were also fears of infiltration by China in the jungles of the mountain. Over the years as the threat lessened, the decision was thus made to open up the mountain to the public.

We joined a local group of Taiwanese for the climb. They sang happily throughout the climb, stopping now and again to rest and snack, sharing their food around. My wife and I had only brought sufficient food for ourselves so were unable to reciprocate.

They are very communitarian, she observed, while we have become individualistic.

Only dormitory accommodation was available in a mountain lodge near the summit and my wife and I found ourselves sharing a room with 16 other women.

One of the girls shouted cheekily in Chinese in the still darkness of the room, "Professor, how do you feel sleeping in the night in the same room with 16 young women?" I was too nonplussed to reply. My wife said, "He is having fun."

After our descent to the bottom of Jade Mountain, we decided to try out what is called mountain pot holing, a new sport to us. This involves descending deep into the earth below the surface with only a rope and torch. We saw people entering into a hole like rabbits and emerging 45 minutes later. We decided to give it a go.

Mid-way though, a thought suddenly struck me. What if there was an earthquake? Would it not be dangerous? This I discovered later was less dangerous than going on a roller coaster ride and fortunately anyway, nothing happened during our pot holing episode.

The Himalayas

In 1986, we made it to the Himalayas, a dream destination for mountain trekkers. Our goal was to climb up to the Mount Everest base camp where Sir Edmund Hillary and Tenzing Norgay had started off for their epic 1952 conquest of the world's highest peak. It would take us a total of 10 days.

It was amazing to discover that the person handling our trip in Kathmandu had actually once worked as chief assistant to Hillary.

We flew from Kathmandu, the capital of Nepal, to Lukla (2,860 m) to start our hike.

It was a beautiful start to our trek as we flew over an awesome landscape of pointed peaks draped in snow.

It was at Lukla that we would stay a couple of days to acclimatise, as we would be proceeding to still higher altitudes later.

When we were ready, we set off with seven porters to carry our luggage, tents and food. We also had a cook. Our first stop was Namche Bazaar (3,440 m), a two-day trek from Lukla and we were expected to stay a couple of days here to acclimatise.

From Namche Bazaar, we would be climbing up a very difficult stretch of mountain to Khumjung (3,970 m). Our guide, however, overestimated our ability and my wife began to develop a serious headache. She was suffering from altitude sickness. The best cure was to retreat and go down immediately but the weather was changing making it difficult to do so. Then a few hours later, I too started to have a headache and diarrhoea. It was no good; we simply had to descend.

We were able to do this only the next morning when the weather improved. The moment we went down to a lower altitude, both our headaches cleared up. It was a relief. We walked back to Lukla to try to catch a flight back to Kathmandu. There was a queue of passengers who had waited for three days to leave but our guide managed to get us aboard the only flight out to Kathmandu that day. He had "connections", he said. We discovered later that he was able to get us out by passing us off as locals as we looked like Nepalese!

When we arrived back in Kathmandu the thought crossed our minds that we were quite foolhardy to have gone on this trip which was tougher than what we had thought it would be.

Although we had to call off our mountain expedition, our time spent in Lukla and Namche Bazaar gave us a glimpse into life in the Himalayan mountains. Lukla and Namche were both mere villages; there were no hotels and trekkers had to sleep in tents. Although they were well appointed and the surroundings were incredibly beautiful with snow-clad peaks soaring above, the poverty was beyond belief. Children had running noses and it seemed that people there hardly changed clothes. My wife gave out some scarves for which they were grateful.

They were poor, I thought, because they had an exploitative government which was self-serving and looked only after itself.

One evening, I wandered to a tent nearby to talk to other trekkers. In it was a man who said he was head of the economics department in the University of Sacramento.

What a coincidence, I exclaimed as I had just been there to deliver a lecture at the invitation of the university's president and had even arranged for a friend's daughter from Singapore to study business administration there.

My mind was ticking, "What a small world!"

What the man said after that was even more surprising. He introduced himself as Lind, originally from Denmark, which means 'forest' he said. I introduced myself and said my name is Lim and Lim also means 'forest' in Chinese. Both of us were economists and both "forests" were trekking through the snows of the Himalayas.

At the Himalayan mountain, the sky is so low that one could be forgiven if one were to claim that one was closer to God. At a Pacific Economic Cooperation Conference (PECC) in Mexico City some time ago, I presented a paper on the importance of economic cooperation among Pacific Basin countries. A distinguished Mexican professor told the audience that the real Mexican problem was that, "Mexico was too far away from God, and too close to the USA." If the good professor had been with me in the Himalayas, I might have told him, "Professor, you are now closer to God, and too far away from the USA." I must leave this hallucination from the rarefied air of the Himalayan mountain top, and descend quickly down to earth, but get frightened with the earthly problems of Nepal, in particular its extreme poverty.

Huangshan and Mount Kinabalu

There were other mountains that we scaled including one of China's most famous peaks, Huangshan, literally 'Yellow Mountains', the subject of many a Chinese water colour painting of serrated granite peaks, pine trees and low clouds. There is a famous saying in Chinese among mountain trekkers that after climbing the Yellow Mountain, all other famous mountains in China appear to dwarf in beauty and grandeur: 五岳归来不看山，黄山归来不看岳. My English translation is not the official one; some poetic license is used.

We went with Cheng Cheng, my wife's younger sister and her husband, Yeh Yong Hua. The trip was a great success, because of good time-consuming planning on their part.

The other was nearer home — Mount Kinabalu in Sabah in 1980. We even brought our two younger children — Lynn and Ron — with us. This was prior to Lynn going to Cambridge. Ron later took part in several Ironman marathons.

It was quite an experience to move from dense tropical jungle through varying layers of vegetation to a temperate climate and even a place where no trees grew — all in a day! This is what climbing Mount Kinabalu is all about.

We stopped for the night to wait to get up the next morning to see the sunrise but my wife developed altitude sickness in the meantime. I sensed I would soon get it too. I stayed put to accompany her while our children continued hiking with the guide to reach Low's peak. We both missed the summit by just one hundred metres!

Gardening passion

For me, on weekends, there is nothing more pleasurable than pottering about in my garden. I started out gardening as a child during the Japanese Occupation in Malacca but this was born out of a necessity to survive, as our family had to plant our own vegetables to eat and also to sell in the market. I learnt how to grow best-selling items such as *kangkong*, sweet potato, tapioca and papaya on a plot of land behind our house. I planted for practical reasons then; now I plant for fun. But there was one thing in common — I had to have a little plot of land to indulge my passion.

Plants also need a gestation period, water and lots of care. So you need to stay put for a long period if you want your plants to grow. My living in Caldecott Hill for the last 35 years gave me plenty of time to grow plants that needed a longer gestation period.

In fact, I now have such an amazing array of plants that I probably need someone to catalogue all of them and my garden, if unattended, can become a veritable jungle!

Take palms, for instance; I have eight types at least. There is lacquer, a red palm that grows slowly but majestically, planted next to the yellow palms as they offset each other beautifully. Another is the Macarthur palm — which grows easily — as does the fish tail palm, fan palm and another, the slender lady, so called because it is thin and elegant.

The *pipit pinang* or betel-nut palm was planted in the hope that the lovely sparrow-like pipits would make a nest there. Alas, I have found none to this day but the tree is very decorative. Then there is the magnificent royal palm, which grows tall very quickly so I had to plant it well away from the house.

I even have a little herb garden where I have planted culinary herbs such as pandan, lemon grass, turmeric, galangal and the *limau kesturi* shrub which yields small limes.

I enjoy gardening for the physical exercise it provides and its therapeutic nature. Plants need nurturing and if a plant falls ill, you have to find out what ails it and try to restore it back to health. Sometimes they do not bear fruit and you have to delve into the problem to find an answer. So gardening can be quite a challenge.

In a book I wrote on the NWC, I penned for the preface a poem about a perfect garden that was so only because the plants inside were imperfect — with thorns, droopy flowers or wilting — because that was their very nature.

I also go for flowers in my garden such as the lovely Indian bay flower, a fantastic plant that flowers all the time.

I even have bonsai trees, growing them in miniature by planting them in containers. I manage to cultivate even bonsai species that are said to be difficult to miniaturise. Among my favourites is a pineapple bonsai which yields a sweeter fruit than the regular pineapple shrub.

Some plants can get quite unruly and cause problems. One of them was an oil palm that grew so well that it attracted squirrels and rats which in turn attracted snakes so I had to get rid of it.

My wife is just as crazy about gardening and it is the hobby that we work on together.

I even try to bring a bit of the garden into the office with a few potted plants to add a soothing touch of greenery.

My house is near the Macritchie Reservoir. Behind it is Bukit Brown Cemetery. So the relative green surrounds means we have, from time to time, some welcome and some not-so-welcome visitors. On one occasion, a Brahmin kite came and perched on the dividing wall between my neighbour's dwelling and mine, always facing our side of the wall. It was a huge bird but was tame in temperament.

We found the visit unusual and exciting. For a month, it was a resident, flying off in the day and coming back to roost at night.

My wife would go out to buy beef to feed the bird. We even gave it a name — Albert. But later when construction work started in the neighbourhood, it sensed danger and flew away permanently.

Every time we see Brahmin kites in the sky above us, our minds would go back to Albert. Other birds that frequently visit us are the brightly hued kingfishers, which sometimes dip into our swimming pool and then clean their feathers.

We also have visiting bats, which would hang upside down on our fruit trees and some of them would even fly into the house. They are quite a sight.

And because we have plenty of trees, we would find many a bird's nest, with eggs. We would of course leave them alone.

What wealth this show of wildlife has brought to me and my family.

A friend said, "They are like children, leaving when they are big. Then they come back from time to time."

Some visitors are unwelcome, though, such as macaques. But these mischievous monkeys are a source of delight for our grandchildren. We tolerate them if they do not enter the house and create havoc.

On one occasion our domestic helper wanted to test her theory that the Singapore police were among the most efficient in the world. This happened when she saw a cobra in the swimming pool's pump room and dialled 911. She was right — in 15 minutes the police were there. They were three young men, probably doing their national service but they appeared more frightened of the cobra than it was of them.

They were scared off when they tried to confront the cobra and it reared its head. We then called a wildlife group — Acres — which caught it and took it away.

On one occasion, when we were on holiday, our son-in-law, who was house-sitting for us, told us he saw a huge python in front of the house. It disappeared the next day.

The only animals we have not seen in our garden are wild boars which are visible elsewhere in the neighbourhood.

I must add that in the last few years my dear wife has taken over almost completely the management of our garden, leaving me only as an obedient assistant and the management of the compost.

Golfing

With their green and beautifully manicured surroundings, golf courses are like gardens with a plethora of plants and trees to create a sense of tranquillity. Many golf courses enjoy scenic lake and mountain settings. So whenever I golf, I indulge in two passions at the same time — the sport itself and my love for nature.

Yet, I only started golfing late in life, picking it up in 1989 after my open-heart surgery. My doctor advised me to exercise regularly to keep healthy and to do it at a gentle pace. Golfing seemed to fit the bill. You play in the outdoors amidst greenery and walking around an 18-hole course was equivalent to covering a distance of about five kilometres. Trekking required a lot of planning and I could only enjoy it a few times a year whereas golfing was simpler as I could make my way to a golf course whenever time permitted.

My wife picked up the sport as well and we soon developed a routine. Every Monday, Wednesday and Friday, before sunrise, we head for the golf course to play nine holes, returning home by 8 am in time for me to get ready to go to Nanyang Technological University (NTU).

And whenever I travel these days, I try to put in a round of golf as well. I have discovered some unusual courses such as the one at the foot of the 5,596 m Jade Dragon Snow Mountain in Lijiang in China's Yunnan province where oxygen tanks are on hand in case altitude sickness strikes.

It may sound incredible but sometimes when the annual haze coming from Sumatra's forests become unbearable, my wife and I would fly to Hong Kong to play golf on the Fan Ling golf course near the Chinese border for a breath of fresh air.

I have also discovered that unlike here where golf tends to have an elitist status, it is a sport that has fans from all walks of life in many countries especially those in the West. In Iceland, it is a family sport attracting even the very young.

When I learnt to play golf I decided to replace the traditional champagne popping every time the NWC guidelines were successfully concluded with a golf game instead so as to allow our Muslim colleagues to participate, which they did most happily.

Sightseeing holidays

Over the years especially after my second retirement at the age of 80 and after whittling down my attendance at international conferences, I have taken advantage of my available free time to travel the world before failing eyesight becomes a problem.

I am also blessed by having four grown up children with families of their own. As it was not possible or desirable for all of us to vacation together, my wife and I would holiday with whichever family happens to be free.

Perth has always been one of our favourite destinations because of its pleasant climate and it is not so far away from Singapore. The other is Chandolin in the Canton Valais of Switzerland. It is a place where our children and their offspring will go skiing while my wife and I would go walking in the mountains.

The drill is routine; if we are not back by 5 pm, they would get help to locate us but we have never had to use emergency services.

Then there is Japan with its multitude of *onsens*, which all of us enjoy and China with its varied attractions.

Apart from family holidays, we also travel with a group of church friends at least once a year to Europe, to revel in the beauty of its myriad countries and to understand their history. Then there is a golfing group of friends who organise annual golfing trips to Malaysia. We have even played golf at the Black Forest Golf & Country Club, situated in the very far north of Peninsular Malaysia, near the Thai border.

In travelling with these groups we give vent to our vocal chords singing golden oldies or hymns, mostly when we were in the confines of a coach.

So that is how I pass my time now that I have reached the autumn — or is it winter? — of my life.

Whenever I travel, at times I think of a Chinese proverb — "读万卷书不如行万里路". It means "It is better to travel ten thousand miles than to read ten thousand books."

You cannot know the world through books alone; in my view, it is better to see it in reality despite the ugliness and poverty in some places. But there is also beauty. Besides, as they say, "All work and no play makes Jack a dull boy."

So even if we live in the little red dot that is Singapore, we should not be confined to it. The world is our hinterland, not just for trade but also for tours and knowledge transfer.

Fond memories of holiday places

Thanks to the growth of modern technology in transportation and communications, my wife and I, in our autumn years, have been able to visit places we had never dreamed of having the opportunity of visiting. These special places in the Old World include sailing from Aswan Dam to Cairo via the Nile, the Yangzi River cruise from Wuhan to Chongqing, the Danube River cruise, the Rhine River cruise, and the Baltic Sea cruise. The unforgettable sights in the Old World that we have seen must include Petra of Jordon, the Dead Sea of Israel, the 'fairy chimneys' and underground city of Cappadocia in Turkey, the Taj Mahal of India, the Stone Forest of Yunnan, China, the Forbidden City in Beijing and, of course, the Great Wall of China and the Leaning Tower of Pisa and the fjords of Norway.

What about the New World? As an occasional traveller, the Old World is already very big for me: Too many wonders and beautiful sights to see and many more on my wish list. I need only to thank God for the creation of both the Old and the New World, and thank God again for an affluent Singapore that has enabled travel-crazed Singaporean retirees like my wife and I travelling together to see and enjoy the beauty of the world; the Old and the New. Thank God that we still have the health and some savings left for travelling.

Technological handicap

Although I own two iPads and use two desk-top computers, I cannot type. Really, I have not learned how to type. Dependence on a good typist for connection with the outside world becomes an absolute necessity, a rather embarrassing confession. My dyslexia, though mild, at times can also be an embarrassment to any new helper, with my unexpected frequent misspelling of some words.

Besides, I write out my books and articles in pencil, and my helper/helpers will have to read my handwriting to get them in typed form, often after several revisions, to the publishers and editors of journals. My Achilles' heel thus becomes more obvious.

16.1. This flower is called Queen of the Night and we had a very prolific plant that gave us more than 20 blooms in one night. The photo was taken by my wife, Nah Nah, on her iPad.

16.2. After my quintuple bypass, open-heart surgery in 1989, I took to golfing to keep me healthy. I even got a hole-in-one in New Delhi several years later. It is a feat I have not been able to repeat, unfortunately.

16.3. Up on the famous peak of Huangshan in China with my wife, Nah Nah, her sister Cheng Cheng (second from left) and our brother-in-law, Yong Hua. Photo taken by a friendly passerby as we were having a break during the trek with some delicious bachang and Chinese tea.

CHAPTER 17

A NATIONAL CALLING

In February 1972, I was approached to chair a newly formed National Wages Council (NWC) that would be made up of representatives from the government, employers' associations and trade unions.

The representatives would be of the highest level — permanent secretaries in the case of the government, presidents on behalf of the employers' associations and the heads of trade unions.

I was not sure of accepting the invitation at first as I was not even a citizen then — I was still a passionate Malaysian — but I was told that I would fit in well as a neutral person. Besides, there would be other non-citizens in the Council — two Americans, two Germans and two Japanese nationals, all representing their respective chambers of commerce.

I was not given any terms of reference for the Council, only that it would have to deal with wages and wages policy.

The NWC and I

After some consideration, I decided to say yes to the invitation to chair the NWC. Apart from viewing it as a national calling to serve Singapore, with which I had developed many close ties, I also thought that I had a reasonable chance of being successful as an honorary chairman. There were three reasons for this personal optimism of myself.

First, I had worked in the Singapore Civil Service before so I still knew some people in its upper echelons. I was also familiar with Civil Service practices and their approaches to the Cabinet.

Second, I had been a trade unionist myself, having held a union management post (as president of the academic staff association) in my early years as a senior lecturer in the University of Malaya at Pantai Valley. And in the National University of Singapore (NUS), I was holding a management position as Dean.

Third, and most important of all, was that as a professor of development economics, I gathered that perhaps I could have something to contribute in the economic development of Singapore. NWC gave a unique chance and opportunity that I should not miss. The NWC would be handling a lot of development matters of which wages are an integral part. Tax issues, economic issues such as inflation and recession, and equity issues such as income distribution, would be discussed and evaluated in the Council. I guess my familiarity with public economics too was an added advantage that I could handle economic, labour and management matters reasonably well.

Later, it came to pass that these three attributes played a critical role in my successful and much-appreciated handling of NWC affairs.

Awards as a stamp of approval

I must have served the Council to the satisfaction of not just the government and trade unions but also employers, and served it long enough for 29 years that each of these groups showed openly their recognition of my contributions when I stepped down in 2001.

There were three awards from the government, given out on National Day — the Public Service Star (*Bintang Bakti Masyarakat*) in 1976, the Meritorious Service Medal (*Pingat Jasa Gemilan*) in 1983 and the Distinguished Service Order (*Darjah Utama Bakti Cemerlang*) in 2000.

I was also bestowed with three awards by the National Trades Union Congress (NTUC), the umbrella organisation of trade unions in Singapore. The first was the Meritorious Service Award in 1985 followed by the Distinguished Service Award in 1999 and Special Recognition Award in 2011.

Looking back, I cannot help but be imbued with a sense of pride as I view the conferment of these awards to be no mean achievement — and despite the occasional hiccups that occurred in my relations with the government arising from my problem publications as I have discussed earlier. Few academics earn this kind of rare honour.

As for the employers, there might not have been awards but they showed their appreciation with their fundraising efforts to set up the Lim Chong Yah Professorship in Arts and Social Sciences at NUS. Launched in February 2003 with contributions from companies and individuals, it was set up to engage overseas eminent professors to lecture and do research at NUS.

The importance of tripartism

Right from the NWC's inception, I tried to ensure its success by securing the support of all the Council members to accept two principles to guide our deliberations.

One was that of consensus for any decision to be adopted by the Council rather than by majority vote. The latter would have been very divisive apart from being unworkable since any two parties could try to impose their will on the third, while consensus means that all three parties would have to agree. Any decision made by the Council would reflect not just the view of the government but also that of the trade unions and employers. Without a doubt, this principle of consensus sowed the seeds of tripartism practised today to the benefit of not only Singapore's workers, but also the employers and government.

At the Council's first meeting I also pushed for the acceptance of the principle of non-attribution, dubbed the Chatham House rule. Members would be absolutely free to express their views within the Council but after deliberations have been made, they are not permitted to reveal the prior stands of individual members. This was to allow members to change their minds without having to be burdened by their initial stands.

Although we had not been advised of the objective of the Council, from the outset, when we held our first meeting, all present agreed that the NWC goal should be to promote "growth with equity".

In other words, the Council should not just be pre-occupied with income distribution between employers and employees by raising the wages of workers only but that it should always bear in mind and consider if this would be detrimental to growth, or would it promote growth? We all held the view that the two objectives have to be upheld simultaneously.

And I am proud to say that in my 29 years with the NWC, we have achieved this much-treasured objective of growth with equity. Real wages during my tenure as chairman grew at an average of 4.6% per year and this was achieved with unprecedented impressive GDP growth rates.

The importance of tripartism cannot be overemphasised. The International Labour Organisation (ILO) calls it "Singapore's competitive advantage."

As Cleopatra Doumbia-Henry, director of the International Labour Standards Department of ILO put it after a study visit to Singapore in January 2010: "This tripartite culture has enabled Singapore to create a climate of industrial harmony leading to a favourable investment climate, economic growth, social and political stability and a higher standard of living and better quality of life for Singaporeans."

NWC is unique

As my academic colleague, Professor Chew Soon Beng, has pointed out, the NWC institution is unique to Singapore, and difficult to emulate elsewhere despite the efforts of other countries to do so. Few people also know that the NWC was formed without a law being passed by Parliament. It was a purely advisory body set up by the government.

Yet, it managed to carry out its role very well.

Its success has also been well documented by many observers. American economic historian Hilton L Root put it succinctly in his chapter on the workings of the NWC in his book *Small Countries, Big Lessons: Governance and the Rise of East Asia*:

"NWC allowed Singapore to overcome labour unrest, thereby transforming a liability into an asset. Labour relations have improved to the point where firms can respond efficiently to economic indicators without the typical strife that accompanies rapid economic transformation in both developing and mature economies. Moreover, the council is an outstanding example of how consultation can promote growth with equity."

The history and workings of the NWC has been amply written about in books such as the very readable *The Story of NWC* by Tan Chung Lee so I shall not dwell on it here but I will touch on a few of the sticking issues faced by the NWC.

I also wrote a no-holds-barred book myself entitled *Singapore's National Wages Council: An Insider's View*. Through the book I hope I was able to show that although I have been neutral in all my years in the NWC, I have always been pro-Singapore, to me, a pre-requisite of being its chairman.

In his review of my book, Professor Bhanoji Rao, member of the governing board of GITAM University in Hyderabad, India wrote: "In 1965, the just born city-state had a per capita GDP of US$516. In nominal terms, it rose by 100 times to US$51,709 in 2012. In this accomplishment, the most crucial role was played by the country's only resource — manpower. Guiding the pricing of that resource, ably and humanely, was the task carried out by Prof Lim for three decades as the NWC Chair. Many manpower-rich developing countries will benefit from a reading of this insider's account of NWC and its contributions to Singapore's success story."

NWC guidelines system

In the early years of the NWC, there were questions raised among the public as to why the Council issued yearly guidelines only. They wanted a compulsory wage increase system. They failed to understand that we were operating an industrial democracy and not a command economy. This means that the Council could not force employers to pay, nor could it mandate the quantum to be paid. It could only suggest guidelines — whether quantitative or qualitative. From the time of its formation up to now, the NWC has been expected to only give yearly wage increase guidelines.

In the first 15 years, quantitative guidelines were issued giving employers the flexibility to implement according to their circumstances. But the spelling out of recommended amounts to be paid affected the pay of the public sector from the president and chief justice down to the most humble of public workers. After 1985, qualitative guidelines were issued giving employers even more flexibility as they were open to wider interpretation. Because of this latitude, less and less attention was paid by the public to the NWC recommendations.

At times we introduced changes to the Central Provident Fund (CPF) rates but since CPF is compulsory we had to make our suggestions with care and through the government.

It was never expected that the NWC should play a role in economic crisis management nor was it expected that it should play a critical role in the economic restructuring of Singapore from 1979 to 1981.

But circumstances were such that the NWC had to step in to try to moderate the hyperinflationary pressures of 1973 to 1974 caused by huge increases in imported food and fuel prices. Our inflation rate for these two years was 20 to 30 per cent per year. It was frightening and since many societies have been destabilised before due to global hyperinflation, the NWC had to recommend the raising of wages to raise money income, and CPF rate increases to mop up increases in money supply. It turned out to be a successful strategy.

Later, I noticed that writers of various hues and authority did not factor this hyperinflation crisis when discussing the crisis management of Singapore's economy. They concentrated on GDP fluctuations as the only criteria for measuring whether or not a crisis exists.

It is not GDP growth that is the only yardstick. There are other factors such as increases in fiscal indebtedness, unemployment rates, balance of payments deficits and exchange rate instability.

Economic restructuring and crisis management

When it came to restructuring during 1979 to 1981, the NWC's recommendations were made in very close consultation with the government. One feature in this restructuring was to substitute capital for labour; a moratorium was also placed on the increase in foreign labour input which enabled restructuring to go on effectively. At that time in Singapore, there was surplus domestic labour, especially in the female sector.

Another aspect of the restructuring process was the establishment of the Skills Development Fund (SDF). I had wanted to call it the Restructuring Fund but then Finance Minister Hon Sui Sen said no one would understand it and suggested instead the Skills Development Fund, saying that he had the support of the then NTUC's Secretary-General Devan Nair, our economic advisor Dr Albert Winsemius, and the then permanent secretary at the Finance Ministry Ngiam Tong Dow.

What should be noted was that for a fund like this to be effective it had to be legislated. So in September 1979, the Skills Development Levy Bill was passed in Parliament. The levy was a sort of economic tax imposed on employers who fail to wean off their over-reliance on cheap labour or to improve their work processes. The levy was intended to help promote Singapore's economic restructuring which would involve a shift from labour-intensive, low-skilled, low-wage industries to technology-intensive, high-skilled and high-wage industries.

Thus, with the Act passed, the SDF could instigate, facilitate and promote the training and retraining of workers in the process of upgrading. It also provided monetary incentive for the mechanisation, robotisation and computerisation of our economy. On these two fronts, the SDF was exceedingly successful.

And so three years later, I stepped down as SDF chairman as I considered I had done my part to put in place rules and regulations on how the fund should operate. I must not neglect my academic work as a professor of economics at the university.

Dealing with recessions

One fallacy about the NWC that I never succeeded to dispel was how the economy went into a recession in 1985. This was the first recession experienced by the country since independence in 1965. Real GDP growth rate went negative in 1985, at –0.7 per cent.

Some government officials maintained that the recession was caused only by excessive wage increases consequent on economic restructuring in 1979–1981. I maintained that it was largely due to regional recession especially in the neighbouring maritime countries of Southeast Asia, particularly Indonesia and Malaysia. I pointed out that these two countries had no economic restructuring and no wage increases for a long time yet they were also burdened with a serious recession in 1985.

Indonesia and Malaysia attributed the recession to the serious collapse in commodity prices. As main exporters of commodities such as fossil fuel, rubber, tin and palm oil, when prices fell a lot, their economies went into a tailspin. Though Singapore was not a producer of these commodities, we were an important exporter and trader. Many well-known regional palm oil companies are based in Singapore. We also had a very important oil refinery centre in Singapore.

Being an open economy, Singapore is always exposed to externally induced changes or external shocks.

In 1997–1998, we had the so-called Tom Yam Crisis caused initially by the collapse of the Thai baht which in turn had a drastic effect on the exchange rates of other Southeast Asian countries.

While the NWC took appropriate measures to combat it so successfully that the crisis vanished as quickly as it had appeared, other economies in Southeast Asia were more badly affected. In Indonesia, this culminated in the overthrow of the Suharto government.

In the US sub-prime crisis of 2008, state reserves in Singapore were used for the first time to deal with our declining economy. The government paid back what it had borrowed from the reserves immediately after the crisis was successfully resolved.

One of the things I did in the NWC was to have a yearly review of the economy especially the wage side of the economy. This was a way to keep tabs on the direction of the growth of the economy. If there was unhappiness over the speed and direction of growth, it would be discussed and brought to the immediate attention of the high-level government representatives in the council.

This kind of tripartite approach also gives some sort of protection to the interests of workers, employers and government. The interests of the nation as a whole would also be safeguarded.

Commenting on this approach, Dr Ng Gek Boo, former ILO Assistant Director-General and Regional Director for Asia and the Pacific said: "The ILO has been impressed by the NWC mechanism which ensures tripartite participation and tripartite dialogue."

Stepping down as chairman

After several attempts to do so, I was finally able to step down from the chair of NWC and in April 2001, I handed over its reins to another academic, Professor Lim Pin. Confident of his capabilities, I made a conscious effort not to interfere or comment on any future NWC recommendations.

But alas, in 2003, I found myself wading in by calling for a review of the efficacy in implementation of the wage system in preventing retrenchments during a recession. Some companies had actually cut employment first, instead of across-the-board cutting of wages first.

Out of sheer necessity, I was to speak up again on several other occasions.

Reluctant post-chairmanship interventions

Professor Lim Pin, my former vice-chancellor, is a very worthy and distinguished person who has given prestige to the position as chair of NWC but alas, he is not trained in economics or the social sciences.

So there were limitations to what he could do; of this he was aware himself, but the government assured me that they would have enough economists on the NWC to look into important economic issues and problems.

I had once thought of suggesting that perhaps one or two eminent government economists could be with Professor Lim Pin when he announced the NWC recommendations to the press to lend credence but thought that might be misconstrued as an affront.

My first outburst in 2003 was during the SARS (Severe Acute Respiratory Syndrome) crisis which was followed by an economic downturn in the West, affecting us. So what lingered on was a kind of *hidup segan mati ta mau* — a kind of limbo; our economy slid into a limbo and we went into recession.

Before this, there had been pressure to seek a suitable time to raise the CPF contribution rates into workers' accounts but the conditions were not conducive. The contribution rate for employers had been cut from 20 per cent to 10 per cent in 1999 when we went into recession following the fallout of the Asian currency crisis in 1997. It was partially restored to 16 per cent in 2003 before the SARS crisis.

I was chairing a bi-annual forecasting meeting at Nanyang Technological University (NTU) in July 2003 when a newspaper reporter asked me for my comments on the CPF issue.

I totally forgot about the pledge to myself not to interfere. I replied that it was a good idea in the circumstances that the employers' CPF rate be reduced by three percentage points as this would reduce employers' total wage bill and help save jobs. This was given wide publicity in the media but I did not think that my suggestion would be given due consideration. So imagine my surprise when the government made an announcement in October 2003 that the employers' CPF contribution rate would be cut by three percentage points in 2004.

Still, I treated the news as a mere coincidence, although some friends were convinced that the government had taken my remark seriously.

I was further surprised when the economy took an upturn with the stock market among the first to react very favourably. So I thought that perhaps my intervening remark was not completely misplaced after all.

Then in 2008/2009 there was the global sub-prime crisis. I remember one of our best run and very high profile banks — DBS — proposing retrenchment to cut costs. It was its then CEO, an American, who made the proposal.

That got me very worried as previous cases had proven that when retrenchment was practised, it would prolong rather than halt an economic crisis. This also went against the principle of crisis management. I was worried that if DBS started to retrench, others would follow and the situation would worsen.

So I wrote a letter to The Straits Times to say that retrenchment should only be used as a last resort and not as a first initiative. I said that in Singapore the practice was first to cut wages across the board from the CEO to the bottom ranks. Our practice was not like the American practice of firing and retrenching people as a first resort.

The bank was not happy with my suggestion.

But I had widespread support from the man-in-the-street and public figures. I had people writing in to quote even Mr S Dhanabalan, DBS' former chairman who had stepped down in 2006. Mr Dhanabalan had said in previous recessions that the bank followed the NWC lead in cutting wages across the board during recessions, and that retrenchment was to be resorted to only as a last resort.

Not long after, the government announced a wide-ranging proposal to cut wages. Again, I thought, thank goodness that my intervention had salutary effects on public thinking.

Then came the Gini coefficient crisis in 2011/2012 and I had to speak up again when I noticed that it was rising rapidly. Indeed, the Gini coefficient had been deteriorating in the last 10 years up to a point that became obvious that something had to be done.

I gave two talks organised by the Economic Society of Singapore not just to bring the attention of the public that this tendency is not good for us as it would create an even more serious imbalance in income distribution. The first was in April 2012 and the second, six months later, in October.

I spoke about growth without equity. I argued for reforms to raise the salaries of low-wage workers as they were clearly being grossly underpaid.

I was worried that the further deterioration in the Gini coefficient would be detrimental to the social and economic stability of the country, hence my intervention on the subject.

I suggested a few remedial measures to take. One was to raise the pay of the very low-income workers, which received tremendous support from the public. I said that all workers' pay, local and foreign, below $1,000 per month should be cumulatively increased by 15 per cent in year one, 15 per cent in year two and 20 per cent in year three.

I also suggested that those who received $1,000,000 or more a year will have their wages or salaries frozen for three years, voluntarily of course. This can work in Singapore through tripartite consensus.

The reaction of some of our government political leaders and top trade unionists was very negative. However, it generated a great deal of positive support from the public particularly on social media. Eventually, our political leadership had second thoughts on the matter. They soon also expressed concern over the phenomenon of the deterioration in income inequality.

Finally, in May 2012, to my delight and relief, low wage workers were given due consideration when the government pledged its support to reduce income inequality. The NWC adjusted its wage policy to that proposed by me to have a quantitative guideline system that those paid less than $1,000 a month would get at least a $50 raise. The next year, the NWC repeated this and increased it to at least $60. They used $1,000 as a benchmark, as that was suggested by me as a minimum wage proposal. The third year carried the same quantitative guideline approach. Nowhere was there a hint of my original proposal.

So yet again, I found my intervention had some fruitful effects in the management of wage policies in Singapore. I am impressed by the pragmatism and rationality of our leaders, including trade union leaders.

17.1. I served on Singapore's Presidential Council for Minority Rights for 20 years from 1992 to 2012.

17.2. Calligraphy presented to me by then National Trades Union Congress Secretary-General Lim Boon Heng. The Chinese characters are an elegant word play on my name and the role that I performed in the development of the economy.

17.3. As consultant to the Mauritian government I presented a wage reform report in 2002 to the Prime Minister of Mauritius, Sir Anerood Jugnauth. The Mauritian government was at the time very concerned about the international competitiveness of the Mauritian economy.

CHAPTER 18

BUILDING BRIDGES

During my time with the National Wages Council (NWC), I had the opportunity to visit several countries as a consultant to help set up similar councils or to advise on economic issues. But as some of the following examples show, it can be quite difficult to replicate the success of the NWC elsewhere.

United States of America

The first of such visits was in 1975 after Singapore had successfully overcome the 1973–74 economic crisis.

I was invited to visit the US by the State Department under its special "International Visitors' Program".

I was told I could go anywhere and meet anyone I wanted. It was to be my first ever visit to the beautiful country as the Chinese call it (Mei guo, "美国"), two years before I would go there for my sabbatical.

Discovering another book by me

In the two weeks that I was there, what I saw such as the Grand Canyon in Colorado and the city of San Francisco certainly made the country live up to its Chinese name.

I also visited the impressive Smithsonian Institution and Library of Congress in Washington DC. To my pleasant surprise, I discovered that most of my articles and books were available in the Library of Congress. However, I also saw an additional book under my name although I did not recollect writing it. I wanted to ask to see it but did not have the time, so I thought I would try to solve the mystery at one of my other stops — Chicago — which also had a world renowned university and library.

But initially I had a shock when I visited the Chicago Public Library as I could not find any publication in my name when I did a search. It suddenly dawned on me that I should search under "Yah" my first name and not "Lim" which to them is our first name, and to us, our surname.

True enough, I saw all my publications there. I also saw the book that was published by the University of Tokyo Press on regional economics. I started to find out more of this mystery publication bearing my name but did not remember writing it. After all, no author can forget what he has written just as no father can forget his children and how many he has.

As I reflected, I remembered having gone to a conference some time ago in Hawaii. The theme was regional economics. After the conference, upon my return to Singapore I received an invitation from two eminent professors at Tokyo University asking if I would be good enough to go through some selected manuscripts to pick out 12 to 14 publications for a special issue. They sent me the articles and I made suggestions. They accepted them although I never heard from them again. Perhaps they might have sent a letter to let me know what they did but I never received it.

In any case, there it was, the book with my name listed under editorship. I must say it was a nice surprise. I tried to get in touch with the two Japanese gentlemen at the university after that but I was told they "had gone" (passed away).

Me, as president

On my maiden visit to the US, my wife accompanied me. However, my host in each city was surprised that she and I would not be on the same flight. I would usually arrive first and wait at the airport for three to six hours for her flight to land.

One of them said this kind of arrangement was time-consuming and inconvenient. He added, "In the USA, only the president and vice-president would not be allowed to travel together."

My wife replied, "In my family, my husband is the president and I am the vice-president. We have four young children back home who still need us."

He was quite taken aback.

On our trip, I only chose to visit some of the Ivy League universities to meet some of the world's famous professors there. The three Ivy League universities I visited were Massachusetts Institute of Technology (MIT), Harvard and Chicago. I also dropped in, on my own, at Brown University and Columbia University.

Samuelson, the Great

In MIT, I met for the first time, in person, Professor Paul Samuelson. I told him, "The most appropriate Chinese expression I should use is *chew yang* which means I have heard so much about you that I am glad that I can meet you for the first time."

The two words are so precise and summed up succinctly my encounter with him. I only knew of Paul Samuelson only because my professor at Oxford, Sir John Hicks knew him well.

He once said to me, "Paul had to write his textbooks to get enough money to feed his many children." He had six.

When I met Paul, the first thing he wanted to do was to take a photo with me and my wife. So we did before we talked.

Fast forward to two to three decades later, when we sent our Nanyang Fellows to MIT. They met Paul who by then was quite advanced in age. Yet, the first thing that he would do was to request a picture to be taken with them. They were thrilled.

At Harvard University, I had lunch with the dean and professor of economics James Duesenberry. I knew him before through his writings. He was well known for his demonstration theory which means within a group of people, if one of them is influential and starts to overspend on goods and services it would cause a spill-over or contagion effect on the others and this would help to lift the consumption level of a society.

I also remember that Duesenberry had been an external examiner in economics during the colonial days at the University of Malaya (in Singapore).

Duesenberry, the external examiner

On my visit, Professor Duesenberry and I had a walk in the campus. He told me, "You know, Professor Lim, you have come at the wrong time. I am now serving my sentence."

I asked him to explain his choice of words. He continued, "It has become my duty to become the dean. Each head of department, appointed every three years on rotation by full professors, has to take on the burden of important administrative duties. In truth, they are more interested in their own scholarship than in administrative tasks. But for the fact that I am serving this sentence I would like to spend more time with you." Despite the shortage of time on his part, he and I managed to discuss a range of economic issues.

To round up my visit, I took the Potomac River walk around Harvard's women's university of Radcliffe.

Milton Friedman on Singapore

From Harvard I moved to Chicago where I managed to get to the root of my mystery publication as mentioned earlier. The Chicago University arranged for me to meet Milton Friedman, one of the world's most influential economists and later a Nobel laureate.

He was a man of short stature but has received heights of recognition for his ability and intellect on economic matters. Nobody could outwit him.

He spoke of two things at our meeting. Although he was a great admirer of the economic rationality for many of Singapore's policies, he told me he could not understand, however, why we had free public hospital services, at that time. He asked me, "What do you think will be the demand curve?" I replied that it would be a horizontal straight line from zero to infinity. He replied that if the demand is infinite then the policy would be unsound. I agreed that it was unsound but culturally people would not go to the hospital unless they were seriously ill. That was the tradition then.

Well, he informed me, "If the same policy were to be implemented in the USA, most of the workers would be on sick leave."

Though there were cultural differences at work, I accepted his point that public services should not be free because infinite demand would be wasteful and lead to unnecessary overconsumption. Later, our Singapore government wisely accepted the co-payment system in most of our public services, including hospital services, to pre-empt any potential wastefulness.

Another topic he brought up during our first meeting was how he could not understand why I had accepted my appointment as dean of the faculty of arts and social sciences. He asked me, "Why do you want to be the dean and take on the administrative work that comes with being a dean? Don't you think you can contribute more to Singapore and to society at large if you were to concentrate on economics?"

A similar remark was later made by an eminent professor in Thailand when I went there to give a lecture to professors of universities in ASEAN (Association of Southeast Asian Nations) at Chulalongkorn University. The Thai gentleman urged me to stick to my profession rather than take on administrative responsibilities. This reminded me of what Friedman had said, so after I had served two terms as dean I requested my vice-chancellor at the University of Singapore to appoint a successor as I wished to step down.

Friedman had also talked to me about the need to stick to a fixed exchange rate system that could be guaranteed by a country's currency board.

I told him that we were still under the Currency Board System, although we had by then a sort of central bank, which was the Monetary Authority of Singapore. He made a surprise remark about my colleague SY Lee whom he knew personally. SY, who has been referred to in an earlier chapter had advocated having a floating currency.

Professor Harry Johnson

When I left Chicago, I regretted that no arrangements had been made for me to see Professor Harry Johnson.

I had thought that Johnson was at the London School of Economics (LSE) in England then. I knew he had dual appointments across the Atlantic as a full professor in the University of Chicago and LSE.

I did not mention to the organisers of my visit that I would like to see him. And alas, years later, I was told he had passed away. Professor Johnson was an external examiner at the University of Malaya (in Singapore) and a regular contributor to the *Malayan Economic Review*, later renamed as *Singapore Economic Review*. On one of his visits to Singapore, we had dinner in Johor Bahru. He challenged all of us to use chopsticks the way he could and to walk back with him to Singapore. He won in both challenges. Nobody could take up the challenge to walk back to Singapore.

But at least during my visit, I had some opportunities to discuss with several US economists on how we had successfully handled the stagflation crisis in Singapore in 1973–74. This success had impressed them and must have contributed to their decision to invite me as a state guest. Our Public Service Commission, then under Dr Phay Seng Whatt, too must have put in a good word for me.

New Zealand

The success of the NWC in Singapore invariably evoked interest in other countries to institute a similar institution. After a particularly fruitful economic restructuring programme initiated by the NWC between 1979 and 1981, I was invited as an informal consultant in 1982 by the New Zealand Government under the helm of Robert Muldoon, the prime minister, to look into the possibility of setting up a National Wages Council there.

New Zealand troops in Singapore

Prior to my visit, I had on a number of occasions met up with then New Zealand High Commissioner to Singapore Judith Trotter in my own private capacity to discuss ways and means to delay the departure of New Zealand troops based in Singapore since 1969. Like the withdrawal of British troops in 1971, there would surely be an adverse economic impact, other than psychological strategic considerations. The troops were in Dieppe Barracks which were then the New Zealand military headquarters. But she informed me that the New Zealand government was determined to withdraw its forces and it eventually did so in

1989. I was also told that for many Kiwi soldiers, the attraction to join the army was because of the chance to be posted to Singapore!

New Zealand NWC?

On my visit to Wellington, the New Zealand capital city, the government had set up meetings with businessmen, politicians and trade union leaders to exchange views with me about the intricacies of tripartism, which is what the NWC is all about. I discussed with the three groups separately in Wellington and found that essentially they were positive in having a tripartite alliance similar to that of our NWC. I had been told a different story before I left for New Zealand that the unions were against this kind of set-up especially the left-wing unions, which had caused many sleepless nights for government officials. But when I was there, I was assured by the left-wing unions that they would totally support the idea of tripartism *à la* Singapore.

I remember my wife and I being checked into a neat and tidy hotel in Wellington. At dinner, I paid my hosts a compliment, saying how well managed the hotel was and also spoke highly of its cuisine. My New Zealand hosts quickly told us that the hotel was owned and run by Singaporeans.

We were assigned a driver who acted as a tour guide during our entire stay. The gentleman was from the Foreign Office and had a first degree and a higher degree, both in law, from Oxford University. He brought us to as far as South Island including taking us to Milford Sound which is not very far from Queenstown. We went to a mountainous area where he drank the clean water straight from a stream and urged us to do so.

I had no doubt about the water's cleanliness but my wife and I did not have the courage to enjoy it with our quite delicate stomachs and we found that the stream's water when boiled was equally exquisite.

I made a blunder though. In my friendship with this charming young man, I had spoken to him about Singapore and how open we were, especially our universities, in recruiting foreign staff. When I went back to Wellington with him, a host from the Government headquarters told me that this man appeared to want to apply for a job in Singapore and said I should not have interested him in this kind of venture as I was a guest. I was taken aback and apologised profusely, saying that it was not my intention to steal staff from New Zealand to Singapore. I assured him of how much I valued their hospitality and friendship.

After all my positive discussions with the business leaders, politicians and trade-union honchos, I was quite sure that the NWC would be set up after my return to Singapore. A name had even been chosen — National Wages Council, New Zealand.

Alas, that was not to be. The reason? There were too many political leaders in the proposed council each representing different parties. After the first meeting, they were interviewed by journalists and asked what they had talked about. Each leader would state his stand, thus catering to his constituency. It soon developed into a public debate which became difficult to handle when it came to what kind of guidelines to adopt with each leader pandering to his own group.

So the NWC idea was called off. What a disappointment!

In Singapore, we did not have any public debates because all the members of the Council stuck to the Chatham House principle of non-attribution very seriously.

South Korea
South Korean NWC?

Like New Zealand, South Korea was equally intrigued by how the NWC operated in Singapore. It was thanks to a book published by the International Labour Organisation (ILO) about the NWC written by one of my PhD students Rosalind Chew that had been translated into the Korean language as well.

Indeed, so keen was South Korea in pursuing the idea of having an NWC of their own that they sent one of their professors to our Department of Economics and Statistics for six months to find out how we managed the operations. He wrote about it in reports sent back to South Korea and I was invited in 1983 by the Korean Federation of Employers to go to Seoul to meet with various groups to discuss the possibility of setting up a National Wages Council there.

I was brought to the deputy prime minister's office and I even saw my photo in the Korean newspapers reporting on my visit the next day. Since my host was the head of the Korean Employers' Federation, I was checked into Hotel Lotte, which he owned.

It was not my first time in Korea as I had been there a few times before. I witnessed its transformation from a backward economy to a first class economy. I marvelled at its efficiency; its intercity trains such as that from Seoul to Pusan (renamed Busan) were clean, orderly and very exact in their timings as in Japan. They also did not have any graffiti.

Yet, despite all its efficiency, the institution of NWC did not get off the ground — all because its trade unions could not agree to recommendations put forward by the other social partners representing the industry and government leaders in annual wage negotiations. Instead of compromising and practising give-and-take, the other two social partners declared their wage increase guidelines without the agreement and support of the trade unions. Several unions went all out to get what they wanted by going on strike. The tripartite alliance broke down.

Egypt
Public lecture at Cairo University

In 1989, I was invited by the Department of Economics of the University of Cairo to deliver a keynote address on employment and unemployment at an International Conference on Unemployment. I accepted it without hesitation. My paper was entitled "Employment Policy and Strategy: A Search for Options".

However, a week before leaving, I still had not received the conference programme. So I arranged for lunch with the Egyptian ambassador to Singapore to discuss the problem. He assured me that all was in order as the conference programme would be given as soon as I arrived. There was enough time for everything, he said, and told me not to get too anxious.

But I was used to being prepared way ahead of time and was keen to see the programme first.

When I arrived at the airport in Cairo, the person who met me — to my pleasant surprise — was the first secretary of our embassy in Egypt. He was the son of our then registrar of the University of Singapore.

He told me that he had taken the trouble to examine the accommodation the conference organisers gave me at the quarters for visiting professors. He did not like it, saying it was uncomfortable and not up to standard. So he decided to book my wife and me at the Hotel Sheraton by the Nile instead. He did not tell me that I needed to pay for the transfer though.

That night, Singapore's ambassador to Egypt hosted us to dinner. There was a VIP guest in the Attorney-General of Singapore who was then visiting. I was told the ambassador's wife had scoured all over Cairo for rice and other appropriate food to serve us, as food suitable for us was not in plentiful supply in Egypt, especially the kind of ingredients they wanted to serve.

At dinner, I learnt that Dr Goh Keng Swee had been invited to be economic advisor to Egypt some time ago. He did not receive any prior schedules of meetings either. When he arrived at the airport, no one met him except the personnel of the Singapore embassy. When he had meetings with various ministers the timing was so flexible that he did not feel at ease. Dr Goh was more used to the Western style of meetings with its stress on punctuality.

I was told that Dr Goh sustained a cut or abrasion and was sent to a hospital. But when he was there and saw the conditions, he asked to be flown back to Singapore.

This story worried me somewhat, but thank goodness, nothing untoward happened and my stay in Egypt turned out well.

I soon learned that I was the only foreigner at the international conference, though simultaneous translation facilities were there for all.

In my presentation at the conference, I advocated that Egypt should aim at full employment. To get out of serious unemployment, I said they had to make conditions attractive to foreign investments and that they should also encourage more tourists to the attractive country.

I found there was a division of views among the audience. Those who were older disagreed with my suggestions; they said it was global exploitation and imperialism that had caused the situation of serious unemployment and underemployment in Egypt.

However, I found support among the younger participants at the conference. During the tea-break, they sat with me and told me they agreed with my views and that the older generation was behind the times.

I had also advocated family planning for the Egyptians against the background of their population explosion.

After the conference, I was given a tour. My guide pointed out several buildings. One had been built by donations from Japan, another by funds from USA and yet another by money given by Britain. He said that no building had yet been donated by Singapore. I took the hint but kept quiet. To me, there was a tremendous reliance on aid to develop the country but in my view development should be by the bootstrap method, that is, you must have the will and know-how to develop a country. Aid is just a bonus but should not be the first pre-condition for development.

Years later, I read that Egypt was in big trouble, all due to poor income distribution, general poverty and serious unemployment. Sigh, I wished that they had followed my recommendations. That was to be wishful thinking on my part.

Pakistan
Dashing the hopes of ADB

I was approached sometime in the 2000s by the Asian Development Bank (ADB) to confer with the top leadership of Pakistan and Sri Lanka to discuss their respective countries' economic development.

While trying to work out the logistics of such meetings, I noticed to my delight that the then President Pervez Musharraf had taken the trouble to send me a box of some of the country's world famous mangos to my home address at Caldecott Close.

Most unfortunately, by the time the mangoes arrived, the fruits were overripe and although we ate some of them, my family and I could not enjoy the mangoes in their best form. Worse still, I discovered that I was in no position to accept the ADB's very flattering invite to have an exchange of views between the Pakistani leadership and me on economic matters.

I knew that I had to do a lot of homework before I could go there and I was not sure of my usefulness to Musharraf for whom I have the greatest respect and liking or to his cabinet colleagues whom ADB expected me to confer with as well.

Much to the disappointment of ADB, I had to decline its invitation.

Sri Lanka
Again, dashing the hopes of ADB

As many of us are aware, some of the most outstanding and able leaders in Malaya including Singapore were of Sri Lankan origin and nearly all were ethnic Tamils.

Indeed, Sri Lanka has had a rather chequered history.

After independence from Britain, Sri Lankan Tamils were persecuted by the majority Sinhalese population which left many very capable Sri Lankan Tamils with no choice but to leave the country for a more secure future elsewhere. Civil war would later break out in the country in 1983 and rage for 26 years before it ended in 2009.

I had a tremendous amount of sympathy for the Sri Lankan Tamils as their condition reminded me of the condition of the Chinese and Indians in Malaya/Malaysia though certainly not to the same extent of gravity.

So when ADB invited me to go to Sri Lanka, I was very hesitant. I discussed the invitation with my wife and children. My children, who were grown up by then expressed their reservations like my wife about the security of the visit and its usefulness. So I had to decline again ADB's flattering offer. The official handling the matter asked me whether it was ideological. I most reluctantly had to say that that constituted an important element.

I had also discussed the potential visit with two friends in the Nanyang Business School and they had both discouraged me from accepting the invite because of the civil war. Later, when I met Professor Jayakumar, our then foreign affairs minister, and told him of this, he replied that if he had known of it, he would have encouraged me to go and he would have made sure that I would be taken care of in such a way that I would be happy to be there. But it was too late.

Speaking of Sri Lanka, I remember what my former civil service boss, Dr Frederic Benham, had said of the country in one of his books, *Colombo Plan and Other Essays*. He had also told me that Sri Lanka was at one time, a much better developed country than Singapore especially in terms of education. I had been helping Benham when he was economic advisor to the Singapore government in the 1950s to make a study of the Sri Lankan education system in the 1950s when it was still called Ceylon with a view of having Singapore emulate it or part of it.

Mauritius
Great honour to be consultant

In 2001, I was approached by the Mauritian Government to be a consultant to solve their economic problems especially with reference to the country's wage structure and wage adjustment system. At that time, its balance of payments was in trouble, the country's exports were declining in competitiveness and labour relations were very problematic. Although strikes were outlawed there, a lot of illegal strikes were taking place.

My younger son Ron was in Mauritius around that time on an assignment with Accenture, the management consultancy company he worked for, and he had brought his family there as well. My wife and I decided to join them. Somehow the Mauritian Government knew about our visit, and it wanted me to discuss some of their troubling economic and labour issues with them. But I was not keen as I was on vacation. Whilst on holiday, my wife and I even brought with us Shaowu, then still a little boy. Shaowu is the third and the youngest son of my elder daughter, Fern.

When I came back to Singapore a few of our ministers were approached by the Mauritian Government with a view to persuade me to accept the offer.

Milton Friedman had told me before that the price mechanism would be a good gauge of the seriousness of one's intent, so I put up a rather high consultation fee, hoping it would be turned down. I did not expect the Mauritian Government to accept it, but it did and I had to make preparations to work on the project, which kicked off in January 2002. My brief, from the Mauritian Ministry of Labour and Industrial Relations, was to examine the legal, institutional and regulatory frameworks governing wage determination in Mauritius and to recommend reforms.

I decided to get the support of two colleagues, Professor David Reisman, a very senior member of our academic staff at the Nanyang Technological University and a young lecturer, Dr Sng Hui Ying. Professor Reisman made an advance trip in February to conduct some interviews while I did some background work in Singapore.

In the first week of May, all of us left for Mauritius to conduct more interviews and discuss with officials from the relevant ministries and other important social partners.

We were met upon arrival by the drivers of two cars despatched by the Ministry of Labour. One car was for my wife and me, while the other would ferry Reisman and Hui Ying and her husband, Lawrence, who was accompanying her.

During the transfer from the airport, I learnt that should there be a flat tyre our driver would not be allowed to change the tyre. He would have had to call his ministry and the designated person for doing the job would be despatched. I also found out that there were 134 minimum wage systems — each for one sector of the industries. There were many other problems providing the rationale for our being there.

Even though we arrived at night, the rooms at our hotel were not ready. We found out that we had to wait for the next shift of chambermaids to begin before our rooms could be cleaned. That was the inflexibility of their system and it left a bad impression straightaway.

We were, however, well treated throughout our stay and the weather was very invigorating too. The hotels were also excellent — five-star and above. Indeed, the country was more interested in high-end tourism and did not cater to backpackers. The country was a "paradise with problems".

At the end of my fact-finding mission, with the help of my two colleagues, I began work on my report, entitled "Wage Determination in Mauritius: Recommendations for Reforms". Before submitting it to the Mauritian Government, I had asked for permission to reproduce it if the occasion arose. They had given me the go-ahead, and the report has since appeared as a chapter in my book, *Singapore's National Wages Council: An Insider's View* published by World Scientific in 2014.

Although our trip was overall smooth, there was a potentially marring incident.

During our visit, I was asked to give a public lecture entitled "Singapore: Its Problems and Successes". Publicity on my talk was given along the following lines: "Come and listen to a lecture from Professor Lim Chong Yah of Singapore, a country that has no cows but exports milk".

Prior to the lecture, I received a telephone call from a Mauritian friend of Chinese extraction who warned of possible demonstrations against me because some unionists were not keen on having an institution similar to the NWC in the country; only the employers and the government were keen. The unions were in two camps — one that was for it and the other against it. The opposing group planned to demonstrate at my lecture.

Nearly all the Mauritian newspapers were in French but we managed to get someone to go through them and translate for us any negative reports on the impending lecture.

Lawrence was so concerned about events turning ugly that instead of using his precious leave to go sightseeing he decided to help. Ever so enterprising, he told me that my wife and I should stay in a room while he would monitor the situation and let me know if it was safe for me to appear for my talk. Lawrence was a senior member of an international consulting company with an important branch in Singapore.

After a while, he came to the room to give the all-clear signal to turn up.

He said, "It's all right to go now; there are no demonstrations. There are only a few trade unionists but as there are quite a lot of top ministers present and top officials from the Labour and Finance ministries, the probability of trouble is very low."

True enough, his assessment was correct. There was no disruption when I gave my talk; only the newspapers had been afraid of the possibility of demonstrations.

So this Mauritian paradise did not have too serious a problem, after all, but it had serious enough problems that should and could be solved.

Because of the high fee Mauritius had to pay me and as my intention was not pecuniary but to act as a deterrent, I set up a scholarship scheme for a Mauritian each year for several years to be part of our Nanyang Fellows programme. A year later, the Mauritian who won the scholarship studied at NTU for a year and a half. He was successful. NTU gave him his well-deserved Master's degree.

China
Guest professor at Beida (Peking University) and Renda (Renmin University)

I received two official invitations to visit China. The first was in the early 1980s to deliver a series of lectures at Beijing (Peking) University and at Renmin University to talk about the workings of a market-oriented economy against the global setting.

When my wife and I arrived at Beijing's airport we were received by 10 officials. They noted that we were dressed in Western-style clothes while they were still all wearing Mao suits even though they had already started to open up.

They were surprised at our style of dressing. They must have noted that we were probably delicate creatures, not toughies. They quickly conferred with one another at a separate meeting and told us that we would not be put up in the lodge for professors at Beijing University as had been originally intended. Instead, they decided that we should instead stay at the upmarket Xiangshan (Fragrant Hill) hotel built and donated by the world-renowned IM Pei, an American architect of Chinese descent.

The Fragrant Hill hotel was new. It was located on the outskirts of Beijing and we were shuttled back and forth from the hotel to the universities.

Economic and social conditions in China then and now are very, very different. For instance, my wife and I wore many layers of clothing, because no heating was available, and the temperature could fall well below zero.

And when I met top officials and shook their hands, I could feel their hands were rough like those of manual labourers. Indeed, many of them said they had come back not too long ago from looking after pig farms. This was just after the Cultural Revolution when many intellectuals were sent to the countryside. My sympathies were with my Chinese academic colleagues. And I was so happy that they were opening up. They were embarking on a new and, to them, uncertain road to development. My wife and I gave them our sympathising tears when they related to us their sufferings during the Cultural Revolution.

Professor Chew Soon Beng, my colleague at NUS, accompanied us. This was at my request. Fluent also in Chinese, he did his undergraduate studies at Nanyang University when the medium of instruction was Chinese and he had also studied in Chinese-medium primary and secondary schools in Singapore.

He also gave a series of independent lectures at the University of Beijing and Renmin University.

One day, he went shopping as he wanted to buy a woollen dress for his wife Rosalind. To his amazement, he was brusquely told by a store assistant, "If you want to buy, you just buy, don't ask me to show you the clothes; you are not the king." China, thank goodness, has metamorphosed since then.

Goods, especially clothing, in China were apparently in very short supply, so it seemed that they were doing a favour by selling to visitors and not the other way around. What a difference this was to market systems where the customer is king and at times behaving like a rude king.

One day, a male worker came to the hotel and entered our sitting room. My wife was shocked to see the stranger. I was then in the bathroom but heard the conversation.

She asked him, "Why did you not knock on the door before coming in?" The man said, "Must I? What happens if you don't reply?" She said, "Then you don't come in." He continued, "Oh, I did not know this; I am sorry, so shall I go out now and knock?"

They were exposed for the first time to the outside world.

Now Beijing and much of China has changed 180 degrees and the country and its people have become quite modern in their dressing. There seems to be no lack of the supply of goods either. Actually, China has become the factory of the world for manufactured goods and in such a short span of time; what a miraculous achievement!

Hainan University and me

On my second invitation to visit China, I went to Hainan. It was my first trip there. I had never been to this province before but was keen to go there because my parents had hailed from there when they were very young.

I was invited to give a public lecture at Hainan University. The topic I picked was "The Causes of Rapid Development in China". It was widely publicised. After the talk, as requested, I wrote the following poem in Chinese brush:

"五指山下是故乡
天涯海角过南洋"

It can be roughly translated to:

"Below the awesome Five Finger Mountains lay our beloved villages.
From the Edge of the Sky and the End of the Sea, we left for Nanyang."

("天涯海角", literally translated as "Edge of the Sky and End of the Sea" are places at the southern-most tip of the island of Hainan and Hainan is the southern-most province of China.)

It is not easy to translate poems, even one's own, with its rhymes, idioms and metaphors but that was the gist of my first two lines.

Years later I discovered the full poem, with my Chinese name inscribed, was adopted by one of the counties in Hainan and reproduced in the City Hall of the Wan Lin County located between the northern and southern parts of the island. That was where my beloved parents had come from.

My own university, NTU, carried the news in the January 1997 No. 23 issue of NTU NEWS under the heading "Professor Lim Chong Yah receives highest honours from Hainan academia". This was followed by, to quote only from the first paragraph:

> "In recognition of Professor Lim Chong Yah's eminent scholarship and distinguished career, and for his invaluable service to Hainan

province and Hainan University, the Hainan University Council, in a public ceremony on 13 December 1996 conferred on Professor Lim the Honorary Professor of Hainan University and the Honorary Chairman of the Hainan University Council. Both awards are the highest honours from the Hainan academia, with the latter conferred by the provincial government."

Israel
My first visit to the Holy Land

With advancing age, I longed to visit Israel as a pilgrim as both my wife and I are Christians. Finally, the opportunity came. Originally, some friends were supposed to travel with us but they withdrew at the last minute. But my wife and I were determined to go through with our plans.

We had to be given special visas by the Israeli Embassy in Singapore. The ambassador, a gentleman called Zvi Kedar invited me to have lunch with him. He welcomed our visit but he also wanted me to visit the universities in Israel with a view to establishing ties with economists and educators there.

I had to explain to the learned ambassador that my objective was very simple and personal — it was to be a pilgrimage. I said that it had to be free from work and that it had to be nothing to do with work. He understood and did not push any further.

He ended, however, by saying, "Do you know you and your prime minister (then Mr Goh Chok Tong) share the same birthday on 20 May?"

I said, "Yes, but the prime minister is much younger than I am." Curious, I added, "How do you know that we share the same birth date?"

He said, "You forget that you are talking to the Israeli ambassador." By that I gathered he meant that the Israeli ambassador must be a particularly well informed person. I was bemused by his remark.

My wife and I had a meaningful and memorable visit in Israel. After visiting all the holy places, we swam in the Sea of Galilee, played with fish in the sea that were not afraid of people, ate enough of St Peter's fish, and went to the Dead Sea to have a good mud bath.

When we were about to return home, our guide said, "Do you know, Professor Lim and Mrs Lim, throughout the journey, I had carried with me a gun at all times?" I was taken aback. He carried on, "I could not tell you that there was a shotgun in my backpack for your protection and mine so as not to frighten you but this is to let you know that we did take all necessary precautions for your safety."

I later asked my wife that if he had told us this earlier, would we be worried? She said yes.

As an adjunct to our visit, we had travelled overland from Cairo. When we reached our hotel in Israel, we discovered that our passports were missing. We telephoned our guide and told him of our problem. He said he would see us the next day.

He turned up to give us back our passports. He said, "You are in Israel; there is nothing to be afraid of."

There had been so many checks wherever we went that we forgot to keep tabs on our passports but what he had said was very reassuring indeed. We must have left them at the immigration department.

Of course, we had always said in our prayers that Israel and her Muslim neighbours could and would one day, in the not too distant future, live in peace and harmony. We often pray for the happiness of both Muslims and Jews. In Jerusalem, the Muslims and Jews are both descendants of Abraham, their common ancestor. Have religions divided them?

The Chinese Civil War has ended

There was a big global conference on Chinese entrepreneurship and development held in Singapore and organised by the Singapore Chinese Chamber of Commerce. It was in 2002. More than a thousand delegates from all over the world participated. China had already successfully started the process of opening up. The conference was meant to be bilingual, with simultaneous translation between Chinese and English. The Singapore Chinese Chamber of Commerce insisted that I should chair the conference, and I agreed. Some participants from Taiwan were particularly vocal and from time to time rather abusive to the budding entrepreneurs from the Peoples' Republic of China (PRC). They openly called them "communist bandits". I was fully aware of the words they used in the Civil War years in China. Some mainland Chinese, in retaliation, would call the Kuomintang Chinese "black crows", insisting that black crows would remain black (meaning corrupt) wherever they were found.

I did not want the international conference to become an exchange of abuses between some Chinese from mainland China (PRC) and from Taiwan, the Republic of China (ROC). Other ethnic Chinese present too were quite embarrassed.

Cao Zhi poem helped

I was at my wits' end in stopping the abusive exchanges. My Mandarin was quite a handicap. But I must use it, as the protagonists were using it very effectively.

I reminded the audience that both the ROC and the PRC had displayed most praise-worthy economic achievements. Both economies had very enterprising people. As for the quarrels, I took the opportunity to remind the audience of the very well-known poem among the Chinese-speaking community. The poem pleaded for the stopping of quarrels and antagonisms among members from the same family, actually between brothers. My recitation of the poem worked. They stopped their exchange of abuses. I moved on to another facet of entrepreneurship and development.

The famous poem recited by me at the opportune moment reads thus:

煮豆燃豆萁,
豆在釜中泣。
本是同根生,
相煎何太急。

When President Xi Jinping of China and President Ma Ying-jeou of Taiwan met in Singapore recently (November 2015), they both adopted a friendly attitude towards each other, a far cry from the posture in the Civil War years. The good cross-straits relationship, however, remains a problem.

Company directorship
More than one aberration

When it was sure that I would step down as the Chairman of the NWC, it became easy to get the permission and blessing of the government and the NTUC to accept directorship positions when offered to me by the chiefs of private companies in Singapore. My university, in principle, welcomed the private sector appointment as part of the enriching experience for staff in the Nanyang Business School in particular. Over a period, I thus became a director of the newly formed Délifrance, the old and well-known United Overseas Bank (UOB), the Straits Trading Company (STC) and prior to these, the Industrial and Commercial Bank (ICB) of Singapore.

One day, I received an unexpected call from a senior executive of the Monetary Authority of Singapore (MAS) extending an invitation to me to join the Board of Directors of MAS. He continued that I must first resign from the directorship of UOB in order not to have a conflict of interest. I sought and received the permission of Mr Wee Cho Yaw, the chairman of UOB, to resign in order to take on the new public service job. I informed the MAS senior executive of this. A week later, he rang me up and said that it was decided that I must now resign from all my directorship appointments. I was shocked by the new demand, and decided not to accept the offer by MAS, perplexed by the turn of the unexpected outcome. More perplexing was the later appointment of a board director of the Development Bank of Singapore (DBS) on the Board of MAS. I had to let things take their course and let the mystery remain a mystery, to me at least up to this day.

Another mystery or aberration still lingers in my memory up to this day. Most unexpectedly, a government-linked corporation came to buy over Délifrance which was a fairly profitable new French food chain in Singapore. I was one of the founding directors of the company. I also served as the chairman of its audit committee. After the purchase and change in top management, Délifrance slid into non-profitability. It had to be sold back at a considerable loss, now to a Swiss private company. Délifrance became non-listed. I lost my paid appointment as a director and chairman of the audit committee. The whole buying over of the company by the government-linked company has remained a mystery to me. I had to be content to let sleeping dogs lie. Where ignorance is bliss, it is said, it is folly to be wise.

Dr Goh Keng Swee's faith in me

While on a holiday in Perth, I received a long teletext from Dr Goh Keng Swee asking me to consider replacing him as an overseas director of the National Electric Company (NEC), Japan. The perks were good and the position challenging. NEC then was to me the best known, probably the biggest electronics company, in Japan. I also discovered that there were several globally well-known personalities from Western Europe and the USA serving on the Board. I accepted the offer but as to why Dr Goh would pick me to replace him remains a mystery as well. I never asked him about it. To me, I remained grateful to this elderly Singaporean as a promoter of other Singaporeans and as the most prominent and important economic founding tsar of independent Singapore. When he approached me to replace him, he no longer held any official position in Singapore.

18.1. Banquet given by the Hainan Governor, His Excellency Ruan Chongwu in my honour. Hainan University conferred an honorary Professorship on me, and the Hainan provincial government awarded me an honorary Chairmanship of the Hainan University Council in 1996.

CHAPTER 19

MY FAMILY

How I met my wife

It was in 1953 when I was a third-year student at the University of Malaya and residing at Dunearn Road Hostels. My two friends from Malacca and I decided not to return home to celebrate the Chinese New Year festival that year.

The duo — Chia Tiow Kim and Ng Tiam Chua — had just qualified as teachers. They had been my classmates in Anglo-Chinese School and had been invited to a colleague's home on South Bridge Road on Chinese New Year's Day. They asked me to go along. Their colleague was a fellow teacher in Pearl's Hill School, still undergoing training at the Teachers' Training College. She was introduced to me as See Nah Nah. I playfully called her N^2 and later shortened it to Nana, the name she goes by today.

I took an immediate liking to her. I found her to be lively, good looking and pleasant and I thought she would be a good lady friend to have. She was young, two years my junior. I must confess at that stage I was looking out for suitable steady female companionship but I did not date her because I was too busy with my studies and university co-curricular activities.

A year later, at my request, my two friends took me to visit her again. I had just graduated with a good honours degree in economics and had landed a job with the then Treasury, now the Ministry of Finance. I had more time, and now that I was earning some money, I could afford to date.

I asked her out to see a movie that was showing at the Capitol Theatre opposite St Andrew's Cathedral on North Bridge Road. I remember the film was called "Twenty Thousand Leagues Under the Sea" based on the science fiction novel by Jules Verne. I tried to keep myself afloat after the show and took her out for dinner at the nearby now-defunct Satay Club along Beach Road. It was a lovely location, right by the shoreline where you sat on doll-size stools and tables on a sandy beach to enjoy the barbecued meat on wooden skewers freshly cooked over a charcoal fire.

That outing was followed by many more outings to come. Queen Elizabeth Walk became our meeting point at night where we would stroll on the waterfront promenade. It was — and 60 years later still is — a very charming place at night but I think it was a lot more romantic than it is today.

We would also meet at Polar Cafe on High Street for tea as it was close to my Empress Place office. On weekends, we would wake up early in the morning to make our way to Changi Point to swim or to Merdeka Bridge (where I got into trouble with the traffic police) for a picnic.

I discovered that we had quite a few things in common. We had a fondness for literature and some knowledge of the Bible (she had studied at St Margaret's School). We both had also benefited from double promotions during our schooldays.

She loved poems while I loved composing them, so I took the opportunity to pen some verses to woo her. I still remember the first poem I wrote for her:

Beauty is the night
So lonely and quiet
I see the sweet white moon beaming coyly in the sky
I think of my darling dear
And would that she is here
Together with me
To the heavenly moon and her celestial light
Sing praises high
Entangled in the lullaby
Of God's unheard music which no mortal words can describe.

And being an economist, I could not resist introducing economic jargon in one particular later poem:

My love for you multiplies
As the days go by
My love for you is the multiplicand
And yours the multiplier
And let the multiplier and the multiplicand roll into one
To produce a new product
Closer to the Divine.

When she fully qualified as a school teacher and with me holding a secure job in the Administrative Service, we started to talk about our future. It was not long before we decided to start a new home together.

In those days it was the custom to get engaged first before a marriage could take place. The advantage of getting engaged for me was that her mother, Madam Goh Siang Tao, would give her more freedom for us to be seen together. Times were a bit more puritanical then.

On one occasion we decided to go upcountry to Johor with some of our friends. Her mother asked her younger brother Ah Puat to go along as chaperone. Chia Tiow Kim and Ng Tiam Chua joined us as well.

The second car was driven by Tiam Chua who also brought along three other friends.

When we reached Kota Tinggi, Tiam Chua's car developed engine trouble. By the time he had it fixed in a motor workshop, it was getting dark. We decided to continue our journey to Desaru, instead of returning to Singapore.

The year was 1955. Security was still a problem in Malaya. The Malayan Emergency was on. When we arrived at a police station to obtain a permit for Desaru, we were warned not to go, as it was a "black area" where Communist insurgents were active. We had to sign a document that we were going to Desaru of our own volition. If anything were to happen to us, we would not be able to hold the police responsible.

I remember it was about 6.30 pm. The roads from Kota Tinggi to Desaru were flanked by primary forest. We had the feeling we were entering no man's land and hoped that we would not encounter armed insurgents.

The road we were travelling on was quiet and deserted. Darkness was gradually enveloping the place. Occasionally, we saw some wild boars. Believe it or not, most unexpectedly, I saw in the semi-darkness a tiger with two cubs in front of me at the turn of the road. My full-beamed light was ignored by them. I sounded the horn to try to get them to leave. My legs were trembling. At the same time, I told everyone to wind up the windows. Cars had no air conditioning then. We were driving with our windows down. Ours was the only vehicle on the road; the other car driven by Tiam Chua was a long way behind but we had no means of alerting our friends to the danger.

To be honest, as we proceeded, I was very scared, but I had to be calm for the sake of my passengers. So I drove slowly sounding the horn again and again. Much to my relief, I saw the mother tiger getting up slowly and reluctantly. She then nonchalantly moved into the jungle. The two cubs followed. When we arrived in Desaru and met up later with Tiam Chua and our other mutual friends, I recounted what we had seen. They laughed it off, saying I had concocted the story. Never mind that I had three witnesses to verify the incident. Fifty years later, they were all still convinced it was a hoax. It was not. Nana, who sat next to me, could bear witness to this.

We had our engagement in 1956 at The Great World on Kim Seng Road. Great World was a popular amusement park in those days along with two others: New World and Gay World. Alas, all three are no longer around. Great World had cinemas, restaurants, *ronggeng* (a Malay dance), and fun rides to provide family entertainment. The site is now occupied by Great World City, an office, shopping and residential complex. We now go there for Japanese buffet meals.

It was at our engagement dinner that my family from Malacca met Nana and her folks for the first time.

A year later on 11 May 1957, we went to the Registry of Marriages to register our marriage. It was followed by a tea reception at Robinsons located then at Raffles Place. The department store, which was very popular among the European community, was burnt down in a huge fire in 1972. I did not know it then but it was owned by Tan Chin Tuan who later became a good friend.

My boss, Dr Frederic Benham, presented me to the gathering. Nana's much younger sister Cheng Cheng was the flower girl, while her brother, David, was my best man. The bridesmaid was my wife's first cousin, Lay Nee.

Lay Nee was the eldest sister of Goh Lay Kuan, a dance pioneer and Singapore's foremost famous ballet teacher who later married Kuo Pao Kun, the playwright and a theatre pioneer.

After the tea reception, my wife and I drove to Malacca for a dinner reception. My younger brother, Chong Wah, received us at the Malacca-Johor boundary with a team of relatives including my nephews and nieces. Our dinner reception was held at the clubhouse of the Hainan Association on Jonker Street in the heart of Malacca's Chinatown. It is still there today. On that joyous occasion there was even a local band to provide entertainment. I had to make my speech and toast in Hainanese. I survived the test. My wife, the bride, who is Hokkien, did not know what was said. She survived too, joining in the clapping, nonetheless.

My wife's family background

When my wife's father, See Hong Peng, died in 1988 and we went through his personal documents, we discovered that he had graduated with a first class honours degree in law in Shanghai, China where he had been living in what was known as the French Concession, a neighbourhood that was under French jurisdiction then.

Originally, his family hailed from Xiamen. When he left China for "Nanyang" (南洋) he decided to settle in Singapore. The term "nanyang" means "South Sea" and refers to the countries in the South China Sea region to which many Chinese had emigrated for work or to trade or as refugees. British Malaya, particularly

Singapore, was considered to be its hub. We also discovered that he had been the founding principal of Singapore's well-known Tao Nan School.

While Nana's family in Singapore could still speak Hokkien, one maternal side of her family lived in Shanghai, thanks to an uncle who moved north from Xiamen to settle there. As a result, as we found out, when we visited Nana's relatives in Shanghai decades later, they no longer could speak any Hokkien, having been well-assimilated into Shanghainese society.

Setting up home

There was a housing shortage in Singapore in the 1950s, so we rented a room in a house of a Peranakan family on Exeter Road. The room had actually been the servant's quarters in a sort of outhouse that was separate from the main house but it suited us fine as the rent was reasonable and there was tremendous privacy, being an independent housing unit. Our kind host family would sometimes come by to offer some Peranakan food.

Later, we found a double-storey house with a small front garden on Jalan Chengkek in the Macpherson area. A couple of my colleagues in the Civil Service like Tan Cheok Kian also rented houses along Jalan Chengkek.

It was here that we welcomed our first two children — a daughter, Fern, born in 1958 and son, Wun, one year later.

Looking back, the early years of our married life had its hilarious moments. We were both working and usually Nana would take a taxi to get to her school to teach while I would set off for my office at Empress Place in my Ford Prefect which had to be cranked up to get started. There were times when my car would not start and she ended up pushing it while I tried to jump start it.

We had a black and white *amah* so-called because of the black trousers and white samfoo tops worn by these traditional domestic helpers who came from China to work in Singapore from the 1930s to 1970s. Our *amah* insisted in showing my wife and me the stools of our children every morning. She had been trained by the British in Singapore to do that and the habit died hard. To oblige her, we went with it.

Suet Fern

I shall never forget the day in May 1958 when Suet Fern, my first child, was born in Kandang Kerbau Hospital (KKH). Apart from being a momentous occasion in itself, it also marked the first time that I was involved in a road accident. I was so excited when driving to the hospital that I knocked into a car that was in front of me. Fortunately, the driver was unhurt although his car sustained some damage.

That was the first — and fortunately the last accident — in my 60-odd years of driving in a number of countries including Malaysia, the United Kingdom, Australia and the USA.

Fern's academic talents showed at an early age. When I went to Oxford University for my doctorate, I brought my family along. Fern was four when we enrolled her in the South Oxford Infant School. Its headmistress, Ms Wigmore, personally took an interest in her and gave her special tuition in Mathematics and English. She explained that Fern was far too good for her class and it would not have been fair if she was not given extra lessons. Our son Wun also attended the school. They were the only two Asians in the school and attracted a great deal of attention.

We lived two years in England and she began to develop the Oxonian accent in speaking; whatever dialect she had picked up from her maternal grandmother was soon forgotten. It was reminiscent of me forgetting English completely during the Japanese Occupation of Malaya.

Years later she was back in England to study law at the University of Cambridge, completing her degree with a double first, and scooping up most of the prizes for law students.

It was in Cambridge that she was very thick with Lee Hsien Yang whom she came to know when they were both studying in Singapore's National Junior College (NJC). Yang was a year her senior.

I was told during her final examination, he would queue up for her in the snow for the exam room to open, an episode that showed they were in a serious relationship.

Fern completed her dining terms at Gray's Inn in London as a top prize-winning student as well before she returned to Singapore to take the local Bar exam. She confessed to us that she found it boring as it was a matter of memorising procedures and facts. She might have found them boring but she aced the exam. The chief examiner, a high court judge, confided in me that she was by far the best student of the class.

Fern now runs her own law firm, Stamford Law Private Limited, as senior partner. She and Yang have three sons — Shengwu, Huanwu and Shaowu. The older two are studying in universities abroad and are proving as talented as their parents. Lee Hsien Yang read engineering at Trinity College, Cambridge and he too won a double first degree. He was a President's Scholar and a Singapore Armed Forces (SAF) Scholar.

The youngest boy, Shaowu, is in National Service and my wife and I often send him back to his military camp at Sungei Gudang at night when his parents are not in town. My wife and I were fond of taking him out for holidays with us before school and military commitments tied him down. He is talented in bridge games and his team from the Singapore army not too long ago was featured in the local press for winning the global championship, after beating the formidable Chinese runners up in China.

Shengwu, their eldest son, has, in my view, inherited his parents' outstanding academic talents. But unlike his parents, he chose to go to Oxford University rather than Cambridge, to read PPE — Politics, Philosophy and Economics.

People might surmise that I had perhaps some influence on his selection of university and economics as a subject but the choice was purely his.

One evening in 2010, I was attending a dinner held in honour of Chris Patten, the former governor of Hong Kong before its handover to China. He was in Singapore on a visit as the Chancellor of Oxford University. The event was hosted by Dr Melanie Chew who had published her well-regarded book, *Leaders of Singapore*, in which I had also been profiled.

Addressing the guests, Chris Patten said, "I would like to report to you folks that one of your students was the top student in a big class of PPE students in Oxford, scoring a double first honours and winning several coveted prizes."

Dr Chew piped up, "Sir, this student is actually the grandson of Professor Lim Chong Yah." I happened to be sitting beside our most distinguished guest-of-honour. Patten was taken aback; he apologised for not knowing beforehand that I was Shengwu's maternal grandfather.

Shengwu went on to do his D Phil in economics on a scholarship at Oxford. He again topped the list in his M Phil class, that being the degree on the road to a D Phil. He has since moved to Stanford University for an American exposure in a PhD course, also on a university scholarship. The latest news my wife and I heard from him via his email to us is that he has accepted an Assistant Professorship in Economics at Harvard University to be preceded by a research fellowship for two years at the globally prestigious Harvard Society Club in Harvard University.

His younger brother Huanwu has taken a different path, graduating from the Wharton School at the University of Pennsylvania with a business and engineering degree. He is currently working in a private equity firm in Singapore as an investment advisor.

Yes, the latest news about Fern is that, as The Straits Times of Singapore dated 9 April 2016 captioned, "Singapore lawyer wins lifetime achievement award", with the sub-caption, "Lee Suet Fern is 1st female lawyer in Asia-Pacific to get Chambers and Partners honour". She is now the managing partner of Morgan Lewis Stamford in Singapore.

Suet Wun

Suet Wun was born on 31 August 1959, a date that is impossible to forget as that was the day when the Federation of Malaya, my birthplace, became independent in 1957.

I had enrolled Wun at the Anglo-Chinese School here as I wanted him to benefit from the same all-round education and nurturing environment as I had. Like Fern, he went on to NJC where he also excelled in debating. In his first year at NJC, he and his team-mates of three clinched a national debating prize for which they were awarded a trip to Japan. Coincidentally, Fern also won a trip to Japan for being part of a top debating team one year earlier.

I accompanied Wun on his trip incorporating it with my own visit to Agikan, a national research institute in Tokyo in 1976. Wun was just 17 and the trip was an eye-opener exposing him to a very different culture.

Wun, at my urging, studied medicine at the University of Singapore but after completing his housemanship, he decided to change tack. Instead of continuing to become a specialist doctor, he decided this was not the path for him. So he changed course, refusing to tell me his plans although he did consult his mother. He had developed an interest in university administration and won a fellowship to study in the US at UCLA (University of California Los Angles) for which he was awarded a master's degree in public health and a master's degree in hospital administration in the same year.

His wife, Christina, had earlier won a scholarship from the National University of Singapore (NUS) to pursue a PhD degree in management at UCLA and Wun decided it was an opportunity for him to further his own studies at the same time.

It was there that Wun's first child, and my one and only granddaughter, was born. Shimei was born just as I was about to be wheeled into the operating theatre of the National University Hospital (NUH) for a quintuple heart bypass surgery. That day was June 1, 1989. As you can imagine, I was in a state of trepidation. However, when Wun called to announce the good news, my anxiety lessened and I thought how wonderful it would be if I could survive the surgery so that I could see my granddaughter.

To this day, I have always been grateful for that timely call.

After his return from the US in 1991, Wun was appointed the chief operating officer at Kandang Kerbau Hospital (KKH) where he had been born. In 1966, the hospital had earned a name for itself in the Guinness Book of Records for delivering the highest number of newborns within a single maternity facility.

After KKH, Suet Wun was at the NUH as its CEO (chief executive officer) before he was transferred to Tan Tock Seng Hospital (TTSH) as its CEO in 2002. A year after his appointment, Singapore witnessed the outbreak of the deadly SARS (severe acute respiratory syndrome). It was a terrible time for Singapore when 33 people succumbed to the illness. It took a toll on the economy with a decline in tourism as flights into Singapore were curtailed and hotels suffered a drastic drop in room occupancy. People dared not venture out because of the fear of getting SARS. Measures had to be put into place to prevent the disease from spreading.

Wun, Christina and their two children Shimei and Shiquan were actually on a family holiday at a seaside resort on Bintan Island when the outbreak occurred. My wife and I had joined them and we had planned to stay for five days.

On our first day in Bintan, Wun received a call from the then minister of health who told him to cut short his holiday and return to work, as TTSH had been designated as the hospital to contain the SARS epidemic.

My wife and I lived in fear that Wun would be exposed to SARS. Wun, on the other hand, was more worried about something else — the possible exodus of doctors and nurses from TTSH. This was what had happened to hospitals in Hong Kong and Taiwan, two other countries that had been badly gripped by the SARS epidemic. He tried to be transparent as well as boost morale as an administrator of the hospital. He held frequent meetings with his staff, gave them reminders to practise infection control and gave daily updates on the SARS situation.

The mass resignation did not take place. I was proud of Wun for having provided the leadership at that critical point in our medical history. Singapore as a whole came out very creditably in the SARS crisis.

Quan, Wun's son, is a six-footer as was my paternal grandfather (Lim Teng Mao). Quan is an undergraduate at the Singapore Management University.

Mei, the only girl among my seven grandchildren, went to NUS to study in the Department of Communications and New Media. Today, she works in the Ministry of Defence. She is patriotic and would have been happy to do national service if this was mandatory for women. Early in 2015, she got engaged to be married to a Singaporean lawyer by the name of Benjamin Smith whose father is British and has worked here for many years as an engineer. Ben's mother taught English literature at Raffles Institution.

Christina, our daughter-in-law, is a full professor at the Nanyang Business School, Nanyang Technological University (NTU). She also heads NTU's Division of Information Technology and Operations Management.

Suet Lynn

Suet Lynn was born in the John Radcliffe Hospital in Oxford which made its name as being the hospital where pencillin, which was discovered earlier, had been used in 1940 for the first time to treat patients.

Lynn was born in winter during my second year in Oxford University. We were staying in Boars' Hill. Two doors away lived a professor at Oxford by the name of Nicolls. His three children were constant playmates with Fern and Wun, being of similar ages. When I drove my wife to the hospital to deliver, Mrs Ann Nicoll came around to babysit Fern and Wun.

When I left for England to study, I went with two children but returned with three and a D Phil to top it off — all within two academic years. For this reason, I always proclaim Hallelujah whenever I think of it.

Lynn's arrival was very welcomed. I remember Nana having to scrimp on herself in order to save money to buy a good pram and warm baby clothes due to the cold weather.

When we returned to Singapore, I managed to enrol Lynn in the Methodist Girls' School (MGS) where she received her primary and secondary education. It was partly because she studied there that I accepted the invitation to be a member of the school's board of directors and later was appointed the board's deputy chairman. And I guess this was partly because I was a *de facto* Methodist because of my years of study at the Anglo-Chinese School in Malacca and a *de jure* Methodist for 44 years when my wife and I and our four children were baptised at Barker Road Methodist Church in 1969. It was Reverend Richard Ong, who was then the superintendent (now called bishop) of the Methodist Church in Singapore who asked me to be on the board.

I served for over 40 years before stepping down a few years ago. In fact, I had been the oldest member of the school for a long time since its days when it was located on Mount Sophia to its current location on Blackmore Drive. I treasured the opportunity of being able to play a part in the school's changes, growth and development.

Lynn is a natural story teller, taking part in story telling contests from a young age. She even won a contest once for which she won a plane ticket to Japan. It was about the same time that Fern had won a prize ticket, also to Japan, as part of her college's top debating team and so I took them both as I had to go to Japan to present some research work.

Singapore's ambassador to Japan then, Wee Mon Cheng, a personal friend, picked us up from the airport. It was cherry blossom time and on one occasion, he took us to a beautiful park to view the pretty blossoms. The girls were thrilled. When Mon Cheng published his book, *Economic Diplomacy in the Land of the Cherry Blossom*, he invited me to pen the foreword.

Years later, he was appointed chairman of the Singapore Broadcasting Corporation (SBC). On one of my trips to Japan during this period, I saw "Oshin", a superb Japanese movie, and recommended to Mon Cheng to air it on local television. The serialised drama proved to be one of SBC's most memorable programmes.

After MGS, Lynn studied at Hwa Chong Junior College, winning a scholarship under the school's humanities programme at a time when students were encouraged to study not just the hard sciences but also the soft sciences such as social science, literature and law.

She was supposed to go to Oxford University to study English literature but changed her mind and did law at Cambridge instead. After graduation, she went to London to do her bar exam. She went on to work as an equity reporter for Dow Jones Newswires and later became its Scandinavian Chief Correspondent.

She is now an executive producer and hosts a regular interview series called "Conversation With" on Channel NewsAsia (CNA) in Singapore. Many of the luminaries she has interviewed include Indonesian President Joko Widodo, IMF Chief Christine Lagarde, and US President Barack Obama.

It was on National Day in 2007 that she hosted an interview series "A Few Good Men" on CNA, featuring separately Tommy Koh, Ngiam Tong Dow and myself. She had to obtain my permission to be interviewed by her. I was proud of how she carried off the programme. Both of us adopted a professional stance and there was nothing to hint of our father-daughter relationship on the 'live' airing.

She is working to publish a children's story book which shows she has not abandoned her story telling streak.

Suet Ron

Our youngest son, Suet Ron, was born in Kuala Lumpur in 1968.

In naming our children, I adopted the following format: The boys' names comprise three letters while the girls' names have four. And all the four children's names end in "n" which is the first letter of my wife's name.

I have been told that I have two "hao" ("hao" means good in Chinese). Good or "hao" is written with the same character for girl and boy (好). So what people have been telling me is that I have been twice blessed.

Ron is an ACS boy through and through and has studied in both the United States and Australia. He and his wife Clair graduated from the University of Western Australia.

Their two children, Shiwei and Shixuan, are the youngest of my grandchildren and all four of them join us for dinner every night except Sunday. I am grateful for that as with them, the old couple are not left alone. We also go on year-end holidays together, trekking through mountains in many beautiful locations.

During the week in between, our other children and grandchildren, who are much older, join us as well.

Ron is known as the Ironman in the family. He thrives in taking part in triathlons which require participants to swim, run and cycle — over long distances. In one event in Southern France, we were so worried even though his family went to support him. He got a medal for finishing the event. He is always enjoying bike rides in Malaysia, Indonesia and Australia, taking part in triathlons from time to time.

He works in the financial services industry.

My two sons and younger daughter Lynn love cycling. I always muse over this that they cycle for pleasure whereas I cycled out of necessity in my younger days in Malacca.

To lull my children to sleep

There were frequent occasions, such as when our babies were teething and generally to give my wife a much-needed break, I took on the duty to lull our babies to sleep. My favourite lullaby song, my version that is, was:

Lullaby, and good night
My baby's delight
Sweet angels, around her/him
My baby goes to sleep
Lay thee down, now and rest
May thy slumber be blessed
Lay thee down, now and rest
May thy slumber be blessed.

This lullaby song had to be repeated until the child fell asleep, while I rocked him/her with my arms, often walking back and forth in the room. My babies have now families of their own. My recollection is that of yester-years, long past, but no less endearing, no less a part of my life as their doting father, their dad, in nostalgia. The four of them shared, *inter alia*, this lullaby song in common, when they were babies.

My greatest blessing

I came to Singapore alone. Now I have 18 members in my family. That is my greatest blessing. Yes, with my granddaughter married to Ben recently, the number increased to 18. My wife and I look forward to being great grandparents one day.

Our 60-year journey (by See Nah Nah, wife of author)

The very first time I met Chong Yah, I must admit I didn't actually notice him. It was at a crowded gathering to celebrate Chinese New Year and he was one of the many faces there.

He didn't even actually come up to me at that gathering. I found out later that he had noticed me and in fact got one of his schoolmates, who was a mutual friend, to bring him round to my house for a visit later. And that was the start of our 60 years together.

Now we have four grown-up children, seven grandchildren, and have lived a very eventful life. Many have asked the secret of this long and successful marriage. I must admit I do not know myself but it is probably because of our many shared interests — a love for literature and books, hymns, poetry, travelling, plants and gardening, and a deep interest in the events of the world around us.

The first major upheaval was when Chong Yah decided to leave the security of the civil service and start his journey in his life as a professor. For me, I had to leave my pensionable teaching career so that we could make the move to Kuala Lumpur. It was a time of some trepidation. We had two young children and Kuala Lumpur was a new city for me as a Singaporean.

Later, we would travel even further. We moved to Oxford for his PhD. It was one of the worse British winters when we arrived in 1962. It was a society that has since disappeared. A place where newspapers and magazines could be left on the roadside — people dropped the money into a little box — and where little babies could be left in their prams outside the supermarket unattended, including my own newborn daughter. It was a society of safety and trust that no longer exists.

My husband's career and the children and their upbringing have always been first in my life. And he has depended on me for friendship and companionship. I have always taken care of all his needs. His partial colour-blindness means he has always consulted me about his clothing. After his quintuple heart by-pass, I have never liked him to travel alone. And so we have been constant companions on all his sabbaticals, conferences, and lectures abroad.

We always have meals together and enjoy a glass of wine and a cup of coffee. We eat all kinds of cuisine — so even at home we eat Peranakan, Italian, Japanese and Chinese food.

Yes, we still call each other "darling" till this day. We love to play golf together and we also have a church golfing fellowship. We have been attending Barker Road Methodist Church for more than 45 years.

The garden has been a constant pleasure for both of us. Going shopping for plants, finding new species together, is very amusing.

Are all these the ties that have bound us together as husband and wife for the past 60 years? Yes, all these and more than I have the space to recount here. In all these years, I must confess we did make sure that we stayed together at all times in this life's blessed journey.

As an aside, I think after serving devotedly — with no payment at all, *pro bono* — at the National Wages Council for nearly 30 years, it seems a pity that his healthcare needs could not be taken care of by giving him a civil service card or some such similar thoughtful gesture.

I have been blessed that I have him as a life-long partner and I presume he considers himself similarly blessed to have me as his wife.

We pray that the good Lord will make us a blessing to others.

19.1. Our engagement in Singapore. Nah Nah had just graduated from the Teachers' Training College and I had started my first job in the Financial Secretary's Office at Empress Place.

19.2. Nah Nah and I got married on 11 May 1957. This is the reception at Robinsons at Raffles Place, Singapore.

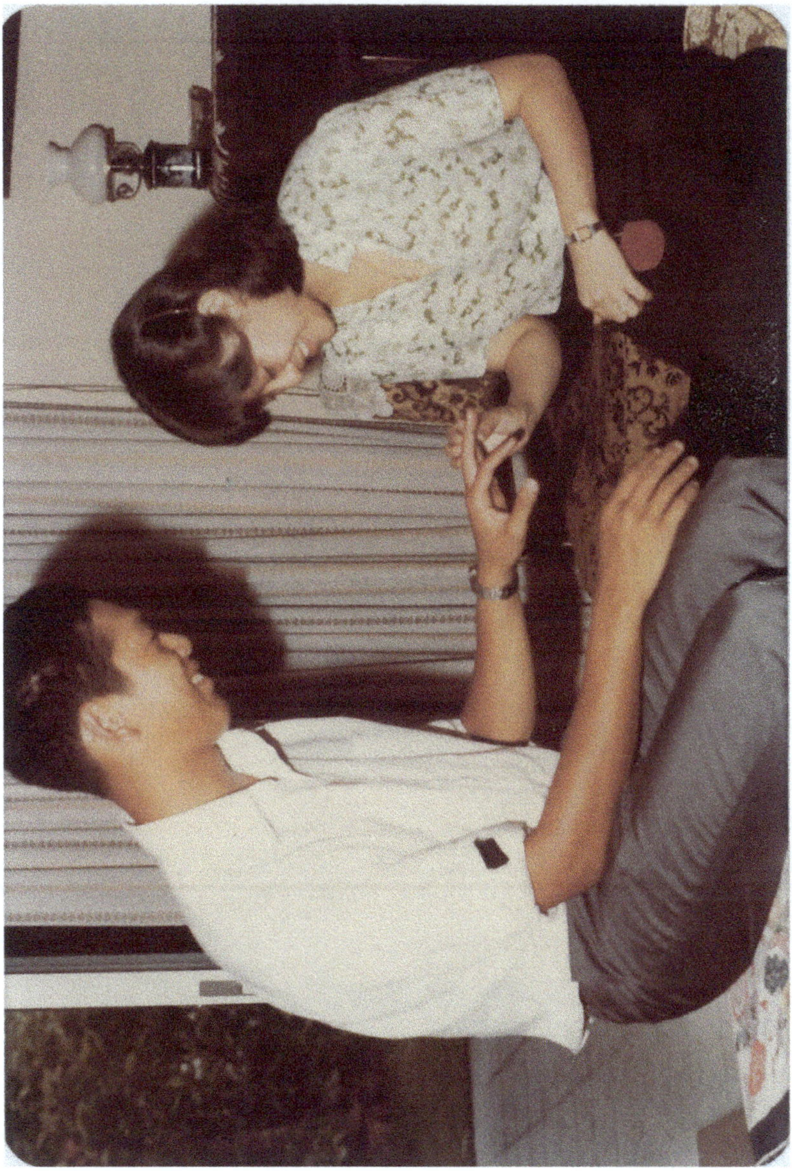

19.3. My son-in-law, Yang, and my elder daughter, Fern, at their engagement at our house in 1980.

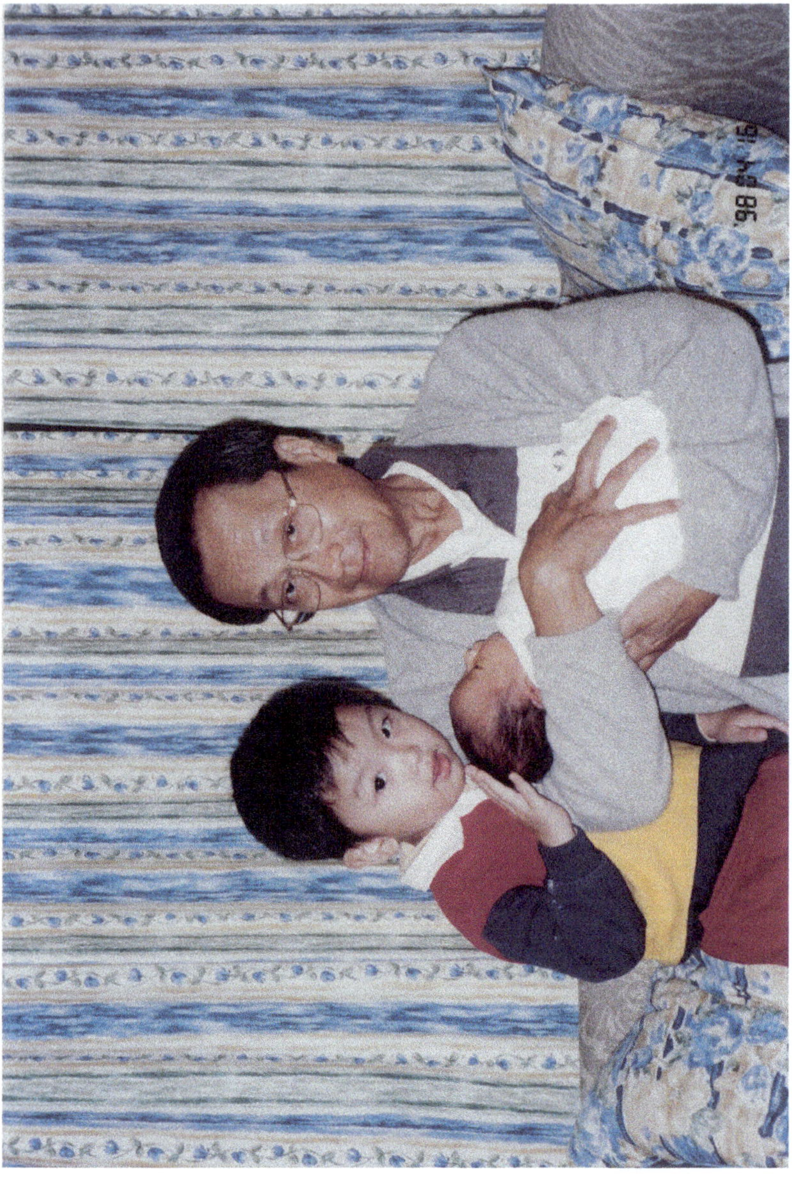

19.4. My grandson, Shiwei, was born in Perth, Australia. Beside him is his cousin, Shaowu. We all still enjoy going to Perth for holidays.

19.5. Pictured here are, from left, Ron, Shiwei, Clair, Nah Nah, me and Lynn with Shixuan, in front, at Tokyo Castle's beautiful gardens. We continue to take pleasure in trips to Japan and I remember my various sabbaticals at Kyoto University and Soka University very fondly.

19.6. Life in the Dead Sea, Israel. My wife and I made a trip to Israel in 1990. The mud there is supposed to be therapeutic.

19.7. My lovely granddaughter, Mei, together with her husband, Benjamin on the day of their wedding, 11 July, 2015. Standing from left to right are my son, Wun, my daughter-in-law, Chris, and my grandson, Quan.

19.8. This picture was taken at my granddaughter Mei's wedding dinner in 2015. Some of my wonderful Malacca and Kuala Lumpur family can be seen here with whom my wife and I are still in close contact. Seated beside me on my right is my dear brother, Chong Wah.

19.9. At the congratulatory dinner by Nanyang Technological University in my honour for the Emeritus Professorship, 2012. On my left is Shengwu, my first grandson and on my right is his younger brother, Shaowu. The photographer is my son, Wun.

19.10. My grandson, Huan, on his sixth birthday. He is even more handsome now as a young man.

CHAPTER 20

PERSONAL HEALTH PROBLEMS

As a young boy growing up in Malacca, I was extremely healthy, the result ironically of the difficult conditions arising from the Japanese Occupation and the difficult conditions for some years that followed.

After the war, I cycled many kilometres a day in the morning all over Malacca town distributing bread to coffee shops before going to school. And because we needed to grow our own greens to meet the food shortage, I was often busy after school working in the vegetable plots behind our house. I had thus plenty of exercise in those days, though I lacked protein food for a growing boy particularly during and immediately after the war years.

It was my oral health that suffered most. With no toothbrush, toothpaste and the lack of means to see a dentist then, I lost most of my teeth during the Japanese Occupation.

When I started student life in the University of Malaya in Singapore in 1949, I often had migraines, and skin boils on my buttocks. I found out later that these were caused by stress but at that time, I attributed them to poor nutrition caused specifically by the lack of vitamins in my diet.

The food at Dunearn Road Hostels where I stayed was below par, but as a hungry young man, I ate everything on my plate. The Hainanese cooks actually doled out special treats to me from time to time. I remember that when I was down with a cold or flu, they would cook rice porridge specially for me. I think they did it because I could empathise with them and spoke their dialect.

The boils and migraines were irritating, especially around the time of examinations, but were not life-threatening. In any case, the boils cleared up and I stopped having migraines soon after I graduated. For more than 30 years since then, I never had cause for worry where my health was concerned. No more boils and no more migraines.

It thus came as a shock when I was found to have blocked arteries during one of the regular medical examinations that heads of the departments of the university were required to undergo then.

I was on a treadmill when the technician doing the reading of my workout stopped the machine and said I should not continue as there were strong signs of blockages in my arteries.

I was sent to the National University Hospital for a further check-up and the cardiologist there, Dr Maurice Choo, confirmed the presence of five blockages. He recommended immediate surgery. The year was 1989 and I was 57 years old.

Dr Choo rang a personal friend of his in Australia, Dr Douglas Baard, to ask if he could come to Singapore to perform open-heart surgery on me. Experts in this area then were in short supply in Singapore. "He is an experienced heart surgeon and very dependable," said Dr Choo reassuringly. I was grateful that Dr Baard was willing to come and operate on a helpless me.

The day before I was wheeled into the operating theatre, I heard the cry of my son's (Suet Wun's) first-born, my granddaughter, and my first Lim grandchild on June 1 after she had just been delivered in a California hospital. My son had let me hear her birth cry so as to boost my spirits. Indeed, before being operated on, I was hoping that I would be able to see my granddaughter in person.

I was given this blessing. I felt that God must have given me a new lease of life when I woke up after surgery in a regular ward surrounded by flowers — one bouquet came from then Prime Minister Lee Kuan Yew and his wife — and well-wishers, one of whom was Tan Sri Tan Chin Tuan.

Dr Baard must have done a fabulous job as until now in 2015, after 26 years, I have no need for further heart surgery, despite the popularly held view that the surgery would probably last not more than 10 years.

Perhaps the fact that I took up golf in a bid to keep fit might have helped. Proper diet too must have played its part, besides cutting down on an excessive workload.

Heart problem

Although I was happy to have had a successful quintuple bypass, I was at the same time determined to find the cause or causes of my blocked arteries. I put it down to stress, which probably stemmed from the multifarious duties that I was juggling at that time.

So immediately after the operation, during my recuperation, I made up my mind to step down from some of these responsibilities. At the first opportunity,

I resigned as chairman of SINPECC (Singapore Chapter of the Pacific Economic Cooperation Conference), which I had co-founded in 1980.

I also wanted to resign as head of the Economics Department at the same time, but for some reason, it was not feasible. We had then about 130 academics in the department, the biggest in the university and perhaps even in the world. Tradition then dictated that departments would not be given managerial support; instead, only secretaries and clerical officers would be provided.

The result then was that many of the senior staff in the department, like me, had to do double duty — this enormous managerial burden, I believe, was partly responsible for my heart problem.

When we established the Economics Department based on the model in British universities, it was intended that there would be six or seven people among the teaching and research staff — not the 130 that we had. Fortunately, the university at a later stage instituted a reform programme that had senior staff members taking turns to be head. This was a tremendous relief for me, as I was frightened that a heavy administrative workload, which was what I had before my bypass, would have driven me to a relapse.

Thank goodness too that I had supportive academic staff in my department, in particular Associate Professor Chia Siow Yue, who took over the economics segment of the department while Associate Professor Lee Yong Seng took charge of the statistics section. They became the *de facto* deputy heads of the department even though the university administration then did not approve of such posts.

As for the National Wages Council (NWC), it had then moved into a qualitative guideline system which required much less brainstorming, so my workload was much lightened. But I hinted that they should look for a successor as I was determined to step down as chairman.

For about 10 years now, the heart specialist, Professor Tan Huay Cheem of the National University Hospital, has been happy with my heart condition.

Prostate problem

Fifteen years ago, in 1999, I was told in a routine health check that I had prostate cancer. The normal PSA (Prostate Specific Antigen) test for a healthy individual is below 4 nanograms per millilitre of blood. My PSA test went haywire at 54. The doctors attending to my case, Professor Foo Keong Tatt and Dr Edward Yang Tuck Loong, were also confounded.

I was told of the treatment options available. One favoured by my two older children, Fern and Wun, who wanted me to get the best treatment possible, was to go to the renowned Mayo Clinic in Minnesota, USA for radiotherapy. And Wun, being a doctor, could accompany me.

I weighed my options consulting then Chief Justice Yung Pung How, who was also chairman of the Singapore Council for Minority Rights of which I was a member. I had known him prior to this, as his daughter and my younger daughter, Lynn, were both studying in Cambridge around the same time. And he had come to my office in Bukit Timah to discuss about the recruitment of some of my graduates for the Monetary Authority of Singapore which he was heading.

The Chief Justice kindly shared with me his thoughts, having successfully gone through radiotherapy treatment at Mayo Clinic himself. He was of the opinion that the radiotherapy should be done in Singapore, assuring me that whatever could be done would be done here. Besides, he said, I had my family and friends here while I would be isolated and cut off in the US. He also shared with me the pros and cons of having an operation or radiology treatment. He said he would prefer the latter as there were inherent risks in surgery.

If not properly done, I could end up having incontinence, I was told and in the case of radiation therapy, the risk was to end up impotent. Either way, I told myself, this would be unacceptable to any patient, but a choice had to be made.

Finally, I decided to go for radiotherapy. To reassure myself, I went to the physicist who was in charge of working out the precise amounts of radiation targeting the affected area. He told me he would be careful and that there would be no mistake in the calculations. He let on that he was actually related to me as his sister was married to my brother-in-law's nephew. He appeared very reassuring to a very frightened me. He had a doctorate degree in physics.

I began my treatment, going three to four times a week to the hospital for 3-D conforma radiotherapy. The NWC meetings were in full swing around that time, but I did not tell any of my colleagues that I was undergoing radiotherapy treatment. I was quite afraid that I might end up without any hair, in which case they would have found out anyway. I also continued to play golf. Only my wife and close relatives knew of my condition.

One day, I met a former Member of Parliament Chan Chee Seng in the same room while preparing for radiotherapy. He was suffering from the same condition but was able to joke about our circumstances. He said, "You and I enjoy a great privilege. We strip completely naked in front of three young women nurses each time we are here and we do not get punished for it!" Mr Chan was a very healthy and good-looking man. He was a positive thinker.

Both he and I went through our treatments unscathed, and we fully recovered; my hair was even intact, to boot. The radiologist was delighted. The oncologist and the urologist too were delighted.

However, over the years, I have been still under the care of Professor Foo Keong Tatt and Dr Terrance Tan over the non-metastasis of the prostate problem. So far, so good.

Over the subsequent years, my preoccupation with economics has erased my memory of my health scares. However, my wife has an ingenious way of getting me to remember. She said, "Two of our grandchildren were born on the day of your health crises: our grand-daughter Shimei when you underwent your heart bypass, and our grandson Shiwei when you first went for your radiotherapy treatment. From their ages, you know your two health crises." I agreed.

Asthmatic attacks

Perhaps more worrisome as far as my health is concerned is my asthma as it has developed into a chronic condition. Yet I was blissfully unaware that I was prone to it for years, nay, for decades.

It first surfaced when I was in Kiel, Germany in 1991 on a sabbatical. I was then 59. I was attached to the Institute of World Economics. Where I was staying was unfortunately very dusty, triggering my first attack. I had difficulty breathing as my airways were blocked. I had never used any kind of asthma medication before and the doctor who treated me recommended the use of a puffer or inhaler, a kind of device which is used to inject a dose of medication to help open up my airways.

From Kiel, after the sabbatical was over, my wife and I went to Copenhagen in Denmark to visit our second daughter, who was working as a journalist there.

We visited a museum which used so many chemicals that it triggered my next attack. This time it was so serious that I ended up being in a hospital for three days. The episode, however, was an eye-opener on how hospitals there were run. There was only one class of patients and visitors were welcomed with coffee, tea and fruit. The doctors had a good bedside manner, holding my hand every time they visited as if reassuring me. And the wonder of it all was that I was not even charged for my stay as I was considered a bona fide visitor who was in trouble.

Back home, I also experienced another attack caused by dust generated from a neighbouring house undergoing extensive renovations. I was rushed to hospital where thankfully, I was able to recover under the good care of Professor YY Ong.

Presence of aneurism

Some time ago, during one of my regular yearly medical check-ups it was discovered that I had an aneurism in an artery or vein — I cannot remember which — close to my right kidney. Aneurism is the enlargement of the artery or vein.

I was warned by my doctor that sooner or later surgery would have to be carried out. He also pointed out that since the aneurism was too close to the kidney, there was a possibility that I could lose the kidney as well. I was fearful and could not sleep for days. I thought I should seek a second opinion.

But as things turned out the specialist who was attending to me emigrated shortly after for the UK. When I went back a few months later, I found that a new specialist had been assigned to me. After undergoing an MRI (Magnetic Resonance Imaging) scan and other tests, he concluded that the aneurism was stable and what he called 'watchful waiting' was recommended. This meant going back every six months for tests.

Believe it or not, there was no change in the nature or severity of the aneurism after several years. The specialist recommended doing nothing in the meantime despite the risk of the aneurism erupting.

The specialist was reassigned elsewhere and I was asked to see a third specialist who after another MRI scan, told me that there was no imminent danger of my aneurism bursting. In fact, the danger was receding as the walls around the artery were getting stronger. If ever it got worse, the specialist, Professor Tan Seck Guan, said he would recommend surgical treatment. To this date, nothing has happened. And though I have been comforted by the fact that the aneurism has remained stable and constant over the years I am mindful of the possibility of it bursting and causing bleeding. I continue to see the specialist each year. Each time, he would give me the comforting diagnosis that the aneurism was stable, and no further action on his part was required, except to see him again in a year's time.

So I had three flirtations with death after which I think I became more religious, often saying 'Hallelujah' and 'Praise be to God' these days whenever things turn out unexpectedly well. I also started to attend church more regularly. Notwithstanding all my health problems, I appear healthy, happy and cheerful most of the time. Praise be to God.

But I take measures nevertheless to prevent reoccurrences. For instance, I play golf regularly to keep fit and to help prevent asthmatic attacks, I take a puff on the inhaler twice a day and I bring it with me on my travels.

The asthma is under control while the prostrate problem has been, hopefully, eliminated. The other two — the aneurism and the possibility of a heart attack — are not as predictable but I hope they are under control as well. I do have a piece of paper listing my aneurism condition in case I get into trouble. I am supposed to bring it with me when I travel but I do forget sometimes to carry it — I am living on hope. Similarly, I live on hope that my heart problem does not become a problem, especially when I trek hills and mountains or play golf in remote places such as Iceland.

I am deeply thankful that I live in Singapore where medical facilities are well-developed and medical specialists are available. My life has been prolonged by them. God bless them for their expertise.

I would like to round off this chapter with four more lines from Whispering Hope:

Then when the night is upon us,
Why should the heart sink away?
When the dark midnight is over,
Watch for the breaking of day.

CHAPTER 21

REFLECTIONS AND RECOLLECTIONS

A Brigadier-General's farewell couplet

My son-in-law Hsien Yang came to see me one day, living a stone's throw away from my house. "Dad, as you know, I will be retiring from the army soon. My colleagues have planned a farewell party for me. I am thinking of a souvenir to be left behind. Can you suggest one?"

Yang was educated in Chinese, from nursery school to A-levels before going to Cambridge as a President's Scholar and SAF Scholar. I suggested a Chinese scroll with the following extremely well-known old Chinese couplet: "人生自古谁无死, 留取丹心照汗青". Loosely translated, in the special context, it means "fear not death in the defence of your country".

I hope the couplet is still hung in our army headquarters.

My timely prayer

On my second visit to Israel, this time with a group of church friends, I found myself in the most holy of holy places to Christians, on the Mount of Beatitudes. Tan Wah Tong, one of my travelling companions was with me. In the still quietness and holy environment of the place, I started to pray, praying for the good health and speedy recovery of two of our very dear and important leaders: Mr Ong Teng Cheong, then the Republic's President, and Mr Lee Hsien Loong, who was then a young budding political leader. Both were diagnosed with lymphoma. Loong's was said to be much more life-threatening than President Ong's. After my prayer, I turned to Wah Tong, "Wah Tong, you are the witness, the Good Lord appeared to have answered my prayer that Loong's lymphoma would be cured." Both of us were very delighted. It did later come to pass that against quite big odds, Loong was cured of his much-frightened attack of lymphoma. He later emerged, as expected, as one of the greatest leaders of Singapore, following in ability and devotion, the great footsteps of his very gifted father, Mr Lee Kuan Yew, the founding father of the Republic of Singapore.

Mrs Lee Kuan Yew

Mrs Lee Kuan Yew arranged for an appointment with me and my wife in our house at Caldecott Close, then known as Jalan Piala. "Ah, you are so fortunate to have four children. Harry and I have only three, Fern is your eldest and Yang is our youngest. Do you share in my view of the marital success of such a family birth-ranking combination?" she asked. Neither my wife nor I ever thought of birth-ranking in the family and marriage. So, I replied, "As long as they love each other and care for each other till the end of life, there should be no problem." "Yes, you know both Fern and Yang come from a very stable family. They should be able to have a happy family as we have in both cases." My wife and I agreed. We discussed about arrangements for the marriage. I only insisted that they had to be married in church — Barker Road Methodist Church. She agreed. The marriage ceremony was held there in 1981 with Reverend Dr Kang Ho Soon as the presiding pastor.

Years followed. Whenever there was a call from Mrs Lee to me or my wife, she always referred to her husband as Harry or Kuan Yew. We tried not to use these terms. I would prefer, when occasions warrant, to call Mr Lee as Prime Minister Lee or Senior Minister Lee or Minister Mentor Lee. And we always refer to Yang's mother as Mrs Lee, not Geok Choo, in part because they were about 10 years older than we were.

Who am I?

Looking back at my life, I have often asked myself, who really am I?

For a start, with gusto, I can sing seven national anthems in four languages — quite a rare feat. There was first "God Save the King" in English. Then, during the Japanese Occupation I was taught to sing in Japanese the Japanese national anthem, "Kimi Ga Yo". After the end of the Second World War, I was taught in school to sing "God Save the Queen".

It was during this same period that I also learnt to sing in the market place in Malacca the national anthems of both the People's Republic of China (mainland China) and the Republic of China (Taiwan), in Mandarin.

After the independence of the Federation of Malaya on 31 August 1957, I learnt to sing on my own its new national anthem, "Negara-ku", in the Malay language. Then, when Singapore separated from Malaysia on 9 August 1965 and had its own national anthem, "Majulah Singapura", I learnt to sing this too in Malay when I moved back to Singapore.

In fact, when I first arrived in Singapore in 1951 from Malacca to study at the University of Malaya, I already knew how to sing five national anthems in three languages — English, Japanese and Chinese.

All this thanks to the rapidly changing circumstances of the times in British Malaya. We were then taught to call ourselves Malayans.

Before the Second World War, when I lived in Bandar Hillir in Malacca, I went to a government school nearby where English was the medium of instruction. Whenever there was a flag raising ceremony, we all sang "God save the King".

Then came the Japanese Occupation, which lasted almost four years. During the first two years, I was sent to a Chinese school, Pei Fong. We were also taught Japanese and learnt to sing the Japanese national anthem and other Japanese patriotic songs that I can still remember.

Today, whenever I watch the Olympic Games on television and hear the national anthem that I knew being played when an athlete won a gold medal, be it "God Save the Queen", "Kimi Ga Yo", "March of the Volunteers" or "Negara-ku", I would be hit by a wave of historical nostalgia of childhood and bygone years.

After the war and before the Malayan Emergency was declared in 1948, another popular song that was sung in all Chinese schools in Malaya including Singapore was the national anthem of the then Republic of China (from 1912 to 1949) after the overthrow of the last imperial dynasty in China.

When China later split in 1949 with the Communists taking over mainland China while the Kuomintang retreated to the island of Taiwan, that song was retained as the national anthem of Taiwan. Called "三民主义", loosely translated as "Three Principles of the People," the anthem focuses on how the hopes of a nation can be achieved through the three principles that are "of the people, by the people and for the people."

Then there was another patriotic song that began with "起来! 不愿做奴隶的人们!" (Arise, we who refuse to be slaves) which was also referred to as the "March of the Volunteers". The song was a battle cry for the Chinese volunteer armies that were opposed to the Japanese invasion of Manchuria in the 1930s. It was meant as an anti-Japanese song imploring the Chinese to wake up and not be slaves and a conquered people. It was a rousing and touching song.

This song was also sung among the Mandarin-speaking Chinese diaspora throughout Southeast Asia. When the People's Republic of China was formed by the Communists in 1949, this song was adopted as its national anthem. The rousing song was recognised not just as an anti-Japanese cause but also as an inspiration to the Chinese populace to wake up from their long stupor and depressing backwardness.

These two Chinese national anthems reflected the tremendous changing forces taking place in China and in East Asia. There was a tumultuous awakening movement among Asians against Western and Japanese imperialism. It was also a movement against feudalism. And a new way of thinking — against backwardness, deprivation and for freedom — was setting in.

For instance, during the initial decades after the war, my New Year cards and letters would end still with the urging "祝你进步", which means advancement. It signifies praying for progress and advancement and the need to "act that each tomorrow find us further than today," as the 19th century American poet, Henry Wadsworth Longfellow, used in his immortal poem, "A Psalm of Life".

When the Federation of Malaya became independent from British rule, I learnt to sing the newly created national anthem "Negara-ku". I particularly love the words, "Tanah tumpanya dara ku" which means "Land where my first blood began to flow from my mother's womb". What a beautiful way of saying "Land of my birth"!

I had to learn the lyrics which were put to a tune that I was familiar with as this was the former "Terang Bulan" song I used to sing in Chinese when I was teaching in the Chinese school in Pontian Kechil in Johor in 1953 during my long vacation as a second-year undergraduate in Singapore.

The Chinese version is a translation of an Indonesian/Malay song called "Terang Bulan", starting with the line "Bright moon shines over my village".

So, can you imagine, even though the Malayan national anthem was created in 1957, I had in effect been singing it, albeit with different lyrics, four years earlier. It just shows how our society was very complex and confusing and rapidly changing, hopefully for the better.

Then, when Singapore became independent in 1965 after my move back here with my family, I had the privilege of learning my seventh national anthem, "Majulah Singapura" (Onward Singapore).

I hope I have enough national anthems to last me a lifetime; I do not wish to learn new ones. My last must be "Majulah Singapura".

I was born a British subject. When Malaya was occupied by the Japanese, I became a Japanese subject. When the British returned, I was a British subject again. When the Federation of Malaya became independent from British rule, I became a Malayan citizen by birth. When I moved back to Singapore, and Singapore became an independent sovereign state, I became a Singapore citizen by application. Do I have a choice in my nationality? I now live happily in a Little Red Dot called Singapore which was part of British Malaya that I was born into and grew up. I spoke, thought and dreamed in Chinese when I was a child and a boy. Now, and for many decades already, I speak, write, think and dream in English; a great metamorphosis in language usage and in language skill.

I seem to be a tri-cultural person. From the chess games I have enjoyed playing, first from childhood, Malay chess, then Chinese chess and as an undergraduate, English chess or Western chess. I have been an expert in none though. And chess nonetheless can be too taxing on the tired intellect; good, however, particularly for those old people afraid of getting dementia and the young for the training of the mind, and, of course, for enjoyment for all ages.

And from the food I eat and enjoy eating, I am 100 per cent global: Chinese food, Japanese food, Korean food, Thai food, Malay food, Indonesian food, Indian food, Turkish food, French food, Italian food, Spanish food, American food, and all the variants in all the types of food, and I must quickly add of wine as well. And I keep reminding myself that gluttony is a sin, and thus I keep my food consumption under control, though occasionally, in practice, not perfect control though.

Lastly, as to the question of who am I, my simple answer is that I am a human being living with my family in Singapore, influenced and tempered by the political, cultural, religious and economic currents of my time, and thank goodness not completely swept away by them and still surviving happily, and grateful to God for life itself, and the countless blessings besides.

My philosophy of life

Do we need one? I sometimes ask myself this question. If I were to answer it in one sentence, I would say that I would like to live a life worthy unto God and worthy unto man.

However, when I was a little boy in Malacca, my father used to teach me two Chinese words that keep reminding me of life — 勤俭. 勤 means hard work or anti-sloth, while 俭 means thriftiness. Simply put, the combination means "do not spend beyond your means", that is, do not get into debt. Taken together, they also mean do not gamble in any game of chance. Depend on your ingenuity and hard work to earn a living.

These are not exact translations but these two characters often reflect the attitude of Chinese immigrants in Southeast Asia.

These two in combination reflect what I would call the Confucianist ethic that is similar to Max Weber's Protestant work ethic coined in 1904 as described in his famous work, *The Protestant Ethic and the Spirit of Capitalism.*

When I left Malacca to study in Singapore, I realised that I would be separated from my family — my father, my two sisters and two younger brothers.

I was faced with a dilemma of whether or not I should leave. If I did not, I would be caught in a trap of poverty and backwardness. The Malacca government scholarship was the deciding factor. There was no university in Malacca and I was very determined to give myself a university education. To me, that was the only road to the future that I wanted — higher education. I thus went to the University of Malaya, then in Singapore, in 1951.

Years later, when ruminating on the past, I often think of one of former British prime minister Margaret Thatcher's quotes: "When you hold back the successful, you penalise those who need help."

I also learnt that if the mountain does not go to Mohammad, Mohammad must go to the mountain. Since there was no university in Malacca, I had to go elsewhere, to a bigger city, in this case, Singapore, which for us then was not a foreign country. In our mind, we were going to our own university, a Malayan university, as Malayans in Malaya.

In fact, Singapore then was considered a prime city in Malaya. But little did I realise that after Singapore separated from Malaysia in 1965, after being part of the Federation of Malaysia in 1963 together with Sarawak and Sabah, my father and siblings and their families would become Malaysians and myself Singaporean. It became a divide to me that was a painful thing to accept. But we had no choice. I could understand why the then Prime Minister Lee Kuan Yew cried on television when announcing the separation of Singapore. But life must move on. We had to move on as separate sovereign states.

I must also add that when the separation was announced, I knelt down to thank God that at long last the Good Lord would give a place to people of Chinese origin in Southeast Asia where they would not be discriminated strongly against like the Jews in Europe during the Second World War. One must remember that China then under Chairman Mao Zedong, was ultra-communist, and wanted to spread the communist ideology to Southeast Asia, including the Federation of Malaya and the British Colony of Singapore.

Coming back to my decision to leave Malacca for Singapore to study — it all stemmed from my love for the world of learning. I always liked to be an educator and I wanted to teach right from childhood. Joining the Civil Service here after graduation was but an interregnum. I have remained in the world of learning ever since I left the Singapore Administrative Service in 1959. That was 56 years ago.

I have worked in three of the greatest universities in Asia — the then University of Malaya in Pantai Valley, the University of Singapore (now National University of Singapore) and Nanyang Technological University (NTU). Indeed, QS World University Rankings 2015/16 has just classified the University of Malaya as by far the best university in Malaysia and one of the best in Asia. And NUS and NTU the 12th and 13th best universities in the world. NUS and NTU rank as the first and second best universities in Asia.

My philosophical outlook has remained the same throughout my life. It is best summed up in three stanzas from Longfellow's A Psalm of Life:

Lives of great men all remind us
We can make our lives sublime,
And, departing, leave behind us
Footprints on the sands of time;

Footprints, that perhaps another,
Sailing o'er life's solemn main,
A forlorn and shipwrecked brother,
Seeing, shall take heart again.

Let us, then, be up and doing,
With a heart for any fate;
Still achieving, still pursuing,
Learn to labor and to wait.

Guiding principles in my life

I will name only seven guiding principles that have helped me in my life.

One, we can always learn from one another.

Two, one should not worry about things one cannot change.

Three, health is wealth.

Four, invest in human capital.

Five, be positive in outlook.

Six, be of good cheer.

Seven, be strong and never say die.

Turning point in my life

There were of course many turning points. Perhaps the most important was my decision to take my whole family back from Kuala Lumpur to Singapore. That was a very tough decision.

That was in early 1969 — without my coming back to Singapore, the latter half of my life would be totally different. I came back in early March 1969, three months before the racial riots broke out in Malaysia. The Singapore environment too had become completely different, being then an independent republic.

So, I had to replant, re-root myself in Singapore. I would not know what I would be doing in Malaysia if I had not returned to Singapore — there is no point in speculating. The Malaysian Government under the prime ministership of Tun Abdul Razak did try to get me back as a cabinet minister. My old friend Professor Hamzah Sendut, then the new Vice-Chancellor of the new second Malaysian university in Penang, did try to get me back as his first dean of the Faculty of Humanities and Social Sciences. I decided not to move back. That was a difficult decision too.

The stages of my life

Remarkably, the first 80 years of my life can be divided into four convenient parts and each by coincidence, would last for about 20 years.

Part 1, the first 20 years, would be my childhood years in Malacca. I suppose one could call that period my early formative years. They were also very turbulent and challenging years, because they also covered the civil wars in China, the Second World War and the Japanese Occupation of British Malaya.

Part 2, the next 20 years, can be divided into two sub-parts, each spanning 10 years. The first decade covered the period when I came to Singapore to study for a degree and then worked in the Civil Service. The two events are important turning points in my life too. I also got married during this time and had two children. This was another important turning point. In the second sub-part, I moved to Kuala Lumpur to the University of Malaya at Pantai Valley to teach for eight years, during which time, I also obtained an MA in Economics. The next two years were spent at the University of Oxford studying for my doctorate degree. I completed my MA and PhD while being a member of the staff of the University of Malaya at Pantai Valley.

So, that summed up the first 40 years of my life, the formative years, all spent in Malacca, Singapore, Kuala Lumpur and Oxford; the four cities that are all so dear to me.

Part 3, the next 20 years began when we returned to Singapore in 1969, coming back with two more additions to the family, Lynn and Ron. I was then 37, still full of ideas and idealism. This 20-year summer period in my life also marked my appointment as dean of the Faculty of Arts and Social Sciences at the then University of Singapore and also as substantive head of the Department of

Economics and Statistics. It was during this time of my life that I took on the much-valued work as chairman of the National Wages Council, and also as chairman of the Skills Development Fund Advisory Council. Both were honorary public service appointments. So, in the twinkling of an eye, 60 years had passed. I was to retire from my beloved university, also my alma mater. Most unexpectedly, I then started a new academic life at NTU.

Part 4, or the next 20 years after this, I have been with the Nanyang Technological University first as a full Professor, later as the Albert Winsemius Chair Professor of Economics until my retirement as Emeritus Professor in 2012, at the age of 80. I thus became an academic holding two Emeritus Professorships of two universities, living on my past savings, as these are also honorary appointments.

Research and publications

It was during the 40 years of my life back in Singapore that I wrote most of the books and articles that have been published. I have written 28 books, 38 chapters in various books, 71 conference papers, 50 journal articles and articles in 37 diverse academic publications. I have been quite productive in research and publications, quantitatively at least, under the "publish or perish" policy of the two great universities.

Of these, a few are particularly worth mentioning. They include the two A-level economics textbooks which have run into third editions and many reprints in each edition. They are widely used as textbooks at college level not only in Singapore but also in Malaysia. One book, *Elements of Economic Theory*, was even adapted for use in Pakistan. One book went into braille in Malay in Malaysia. The two books were published by Oxford University Press. Both the books have also been translated into Malay and Chinese.

Also significant was the *Report of the CPF Study Group*, which is a classic study of our Central Provident Fund system, and *Policy Options for the Singapore Economy*, which appeared in 1998. Some of my contributions to public policy formulation in Singapore can be found in these two volumes. *Policy Options* was translated into Japanese in two volumes by two eminent Japanese professors. A group of Singaporean parliamentarians presented 60 copies of the book to the Canadian Parliament in Ottawa.

Also of particular importance to me was my book on *Development and Underdevelopment* published by Longman in 1991. It is a highly academic book, which explains my EGOIN theory and my case study of the Japanese and Taiwanese economic development experience, based on my stay in these two countries whilst on sabbaticals.

When I joined NTU at 60, there were other new book titles of note. One was *Southeast Asia: The Long Road Ahead* which made its first appearance in 2001. It has since gone into three editions.

The most recent book is *Singapore's National Wages Council: An Insider's View* which was published in 2013. Professor Bhanoji Rao in his review of the book states thus, "In 1965, the just born city-state had a per capita GDP of US$516. In nominal terms, it rose by 100 times to US$51,709 in 2012. In this accomplishment, the most crucial role was played by the country's only resource — manpower. Guiding the pricing of that resource, ably and humanely, was the task carried out by Prof Lim as the NWC Chairman."

I will mention only two journal articles of recent vintage I particularly like. They are: "The World Bank Spence Commission Report and the Trinity Growth Theory", *Singapore Economic Review*, Vol. 55, No. 1, Special Issue edited by Dr Pradumna Rana on the Asian Economic Integration, 2010, pp. 1–10, and "The Great Depression, the Great Recession and the Next Crisis", jointly with Dr Sng Hui Ying in *World Economics*, Vol. 12, No. 3, September 2011, pp. 163–190.

As for my unpublished conference papers, one of my favourites is "The Trinity Growth Theory: A Theory of Wealth and Poverty", Keynote Address at the 13th International Conference of the East Asian Economic Association (EAEA), 19 October 2012, Grand Copthorne Waterfront Hotel, Singapore. And lastly, one of my favourite articles on the Singapore economy appearing as a chapter in a book is, "Transformation in the Singapore Economy: Course and Causes", Chapter 1 in Chia and Sng (eds), *Singapore and Asia in a Globalised World*, World Scientific, 2009, pp. 3–23.

Before I stop, I must add that while in Kuala Lumpur, I produced a very valuable book, at least to the Malaysians, on *Economic Development of Modern Malaya*, among other publications. The book was published by Oxford University Press.

Writing by me on others

My writings have not only focused on economics but also on people. For instance, I was given the honour of writing the forewords in Ambassador Wee Mon-Cheng's book *Economic Diplomacy in the Land of the Cherry Blossom*, Mrs Lim Tay Boh's biography on her University of Singapore's Vice-Chancellor husband Professor Lim Tay Boh, and Dr Daisaku Ikeda's book to commemorate the 50th anniversary of the independence of Singapore.

I was also given the honour by NUS to be the university's Public Orator on the conferment of honorary doctorates on Dr Lim Kim San, Dr George Bogaars, Dr Puey Ungphakorn, Dr Chen Wen Hsi, and Dr Affandi. NTU too asked me to prepare and deliver the convocation address to welcome Professor Su Guaning as the new President of NTU.

When Dr Toh Chin Chye passed away, on my own initiative, I wrote an article as an obituary in his memory and honour, published in TODAY. I was among those who were given the honour to deliver an anecdotal eulogy by the then Secretary-General of NTUC, Lim Swee Say, on the late Mr Lee Kuan Yew at the former Conference Hall of NTUC at Shenton Way at Mr Lee's memorial service in March 2015.

Writing by others on me

There have also been writings by others about me. The first remarkable piece was by Dr Melanie Chew in her well-regarded book *Leaders of Singapore*. She wrote about me in a full chapter under the sub-title "Creating a Nation" together with the Republic's founding leaders like Mr Lee Kuan Yew, Dr Goh Keng Swee, Mr S Rajaratnam, and Mr Yusof Ishak (our first head-of-state). That was in 1996.

Years later, in 2012, I was also given coverage in a monumental study called *Southeast Asian Personalities of Chinese Descent*. The chapter on me was authored by Professors Hank Lim and Lim Tai Wei. The book was edited by Professor Leo Suryadinata.

Prior to this a student in my Mayors' Class (马誉峰) also had a chapter on me in his book on Singapore. That was in Chinese. Also in Chinese with photos was a long article on me, "The World is a Better Place Because of You" as the book title. It was written by Ms Han Xinyu (韩昕余).

Lately, I have been honoured by a concise biography on me by Alvin Chua for the Singapore National Library (Singapore Infopedia) series on selected personalities of Singapore.

Yes, the list is incomplete, if I do not add the latest (2016) audio-visual production on me by two very bright NTU Communication Studies final year students for their final year joint project. The students are Wong Ding Jie and Krystal Foo, and their product is entitled, "A Man of Economics — A Brief Encounter". I am told their work will be deposited in the NTU Library.

Of course when NUS and NTU each conferred on me an Emeritus Professorship, the Public Orator too had a write-up on me, basically justifying the conferment. The NUS Public Orator was the dean, Professor Ernest Chew. The NTU Public Orator was the provost, Professor Freddy Boey. I also appeared on Singapore television as one of "A Few Good Men of Singapore". That was in 2007.

When Soka University in Japan in 1998 conferred on me an honorary doctorate degree, the conferment speech was by Dr Daisaku Ikeda, the founder of the university. His speech on me has now appeared in his book (2015) commemorating the 50th Year of Independence of Singapore.

Lastly and finally, my work in the NWC and my publications of the Trinity Growth Theory consisting of the EGOIN Theory, the Triple C Theory and the S Curve Theory have resulted in at least three successful PhD theses. One NUS PhD thesis was by Dr Rosalind Chew on NWC, one NTU PhD thesis by Dr Sng Hui Ying on the S Curve Theory and the other NTU PhD thesis by Dr Mona Chew on the EGOIN Theory. Another successful ANU PhD thesis, by Dr Paul Chan, was inspired by my earlier research publications on the rubber and tin industries and export taxation.

The university's integrity

One cannot judge a book by its cover, nor can one judge a university just by the beauty of its campus. If one judges a university by its campus alone, then NTU must rank as one of the most beautiful in the world.

However, a university must be judged by the integrity in student and faculty management. By the integrity of student management, I refer to the way students, both undergraduate and graduate students, are admitted into university, and the way the university marks and awards grades to them. In the case of NUS and NTU and the early University of Malaya (MU) at Pantai Valley, I had had first-hand knowledge of their *modus operandi*. Their integrity on student education and management was at the highest, based solely and only on students' merit, without any consideration given to race, religion, gender, caste or class or connection. The universities, NUS and NTU at least, still maintain this very enviable and meritocratic standard of impartiality and integrity.

What about faculty and staff? Both NUS and NTU had, and still have, the highest possible score. For decades too, I had the privilege of being a part of the selection, assessment and promotion mechanism and can therefore vouch for the university's integrity at NUS and NTU and during my eight years at MU in Kuala Lumpur. At MU, I even had the privilege of serving as a faculty-elected member of its University Council.

I have been truly privileged to be associated with, and to be a part of, the three universities, and in the case of NUS, as an undergraduate as well.

In conclusion

As to which of the 20 years of my life are more important and challenging, it is difficult to say. Each period had its challenges and its own problems and solutions.

Life has its sorrows and joys. But life moved on, from day to day, from year to year and from decade to decade.

It was after I returned to Singapore in the second half of the 40 years of my life that my four children got married and seven grandchildren were born. That rounded up the sum total of my life. I love all of them, and their spouses, very dearly.

I am a joyful person by nature and get very happy very easily. Friends say they can hear my shouts of joy when I manage to achieve a simple task such as most unexpectedly driving a golf ball into a hole. I appreciated the adoration of my students whenever they gave me a standing ovation at the end of my series of lectures whether at the University of Malaya at Pantai Valley or at the National University of Singapore or at the Nanyang Technological University. Whenever a book or an article is out, I jumped for joy, probably at my own creation. I sing very often in coaches with friends journeying in different parts of the world, enjoying the beauty of the earth and the beauty of the sky.

I tried my best to raise my children with the important and indispensable help of my wife. I have come to learn that family love is and should be unconditional. "Love one another" is the best adage of mankind and it must begin at home.

Finally, at age 84, I hope that I have lived a life that is worthy unto God and worthy unto man. And I would like to add and worthy unto my wife: N^2, whom I have loved dearly from the start.

Long live our world, without end. Praise be to God for that.

CLOSING POEM

And, departing, leave behind us
Footprints on the sands of time.

Footprints, that perhaps another,
Sailing over life's solemn main,
A forlorn and shipwrecked brother,
Seeing, shall take heart again.

Lines from "A Psalm of Life",
Henry Wadsworth Longfellow.

LIST OF PUBLICATIONS
(LIM CHONG YAH)

(1) Number of refereed journal articles	51
(2) Number of conference papers	74
(3) Books and Monographs, and Chapters in Books	
(i) Number of books and monographs	29
(ii) Number of chapters in books	39
(4) Other Publications	39

(1) JOURNAL ARTICLES (1–51)

1. "A Re-Appraisal of the 1953 International Tin Trade Agreement", *Malayan Economic Review*, Vol V, No. 1, April 1960, pp. 13–24.
2. "Export Taxes on Rubber in Malaya — A Survey of Post-War Development", *Malayan Economic Review*, Vol. V, No. 2, October l960.
3. "Some Aspects of Price and Fiscal Stabilisation in Malaya", *Ekonomi*, Vol. I, No. 1, 1960.
4. "More Equal Distribution of Income and Economic Growth", *Ekonomi*, Vol. I, No. 1, 1960.
5. "Export Duties: Direct or Indirect Taxes?", *Ekonomi*, Vol. II, No. 1, November 1961.
6. "The Malayan Rubber Replanting Taxes", *Malayan Economic Review*, Vol. V, No. 2, October 1961.
7. "K. K. Kurihara and the Purchasing Power Parity Theory", *Ekonomi*, Vol. III, No. 1, December 1962.

8. "Post-War Economic Development Malaya: A Preliminary Study", *Ekonomi*, Vol. IV, No. 1, December 1963.

9. "The Malaysian-Singapore Currency Split: An Appraisal", *Ekonomi*, Vol. VII, December 1966.

10. "West Malaysian External Trade, Fluctuations and Growth", *Kajian Ekonomi Malaysia*, Vol. IV, No. 1, June 1967.

11. "West Malaysian External Trade, Fluctuations and Growth", *Kajian Ekonomi Malaysia*, Vol. IV, No. 2, December 1967.

12. "Changes in Organisation and Management in the Industrial Sector in Singapore", *Malaysian Management Review*, Vol. 5, No. 2, August 1970, pp. 26–31. Also appeared in *Suara Universiti*, Vol. 11, No. 5, January 1971.

13. "Teaching and Research in the Social Sciences in Singapore", *Review of Southeast Asian Studies*, Vol. I, No. 1, March 1971.

14. "Singapore's Position in the World Economy", *Review of Southeast Asian Studies*, Vol. I, No. 4, December 1971.

15. "Singapore's Economic Growth and ASEAN Co-operation", *Asia Research Bulletin*, 31 December l975.

16. "Singapore and ASEAN Economic Co-operation", *United Malayan Banking Corporation Economic Review*, Vol. XII, No. 1, 1976, and ASEAN Business *Quarterly*, Vol. III, No. 1, 1979. Also in *Proceedings of the Conference on ASEAN: Problems and Prospects of a Changing World*, East-West Seminar, Tokyo, Japan, and the Institute of Asian Studies, Chulalongkorn University, Bangkok, Thailand, 1976. Republished in *New Directions*, Vol. III, No. 1, March 1976.

17. "Some Facts and Fallacies of the Singapore Economy", *Journal of Economic Development and Social Change in Asia and Pacific*, Vol. II, No. 2, 1977.

18. "ASEAN: Economic Co-operation and Economic Reality", *UMBC Economic Review*, Vol. XIV, No. XIV, No.1, 1978. Republished in *Review of Southeast Asian Studies*, Vol. VII, December 1977; *New Directions*, Vol. IV, No. 4, 1978, and *Thailand Business*, December 1978.

19. "Economic Development and the Quality of Life in Singapore", *Commentary*, Vol. III, No. 2, December 1978.

20. "Progress with ASEAN Industrial Projects", *ASEAN Business Quarterly*, Third Quarter 1978, Vol. 2, No. 3.

21. "ASEAN's Industrial Projects: Significance and Feasibility", *Asia Pacific Community, A Quarterly Review*, No. 2, Fall 1978.

22. "A Comment on P. J. Drake: The Economic Development of British Malaya to 1914: An Essay in Historiography with Some Questions for Historians", *Journal of Southeast Asian Studies*, Vol. 10, No. 2, September 1979.

23. "ASEAN's Internal Advances and External Unity", *Asia Pacific Community, A Quarterly Review*, No. 6, Fall 1979.

24. "Economic Restructuring and the Trade Union Movement in Singapore", *The Singapore Employer*, Vol. II, No. 2, January 1980.

25. Review article on R. M. Sundrum's "Development Economics: A Framework for Analysis and Policy", *Singapore Economic Review*, April 1983.

26. "Report of the Central Provident Fund Study Group", Chairman of Group, *Singapore Economic Review*, Special Issue, Vol. XXXI, No. 1, April 1986, 108 pages.

27. "The Causes of Development", *Singapore Economic Review*, Vol. XXIX, No. 2, October 1984.

28. Review article on Staffan Burenstam Linder's "The Pacific Century: Economic and Political Consequences of Asian-Pacific Dynamism", *Singapore Economic Review*, October 1986.

29. "Trade in Manufactures: A Singapore Perspective", in Special Issue of *Tonan Ajia Kenkyu* (*Southeast Asian Studies*), Vol. 25, No. 3, December 1987, Kyoto, Japan.

30. "Obituary on J R Hicks, A Personal Recollection", *Singapore Economic Review*, Vol. XXXIV, No 2, Oct 1989, pp. 1–8.

31. Lim Chong Yah and Tay Boon Nga, "Shelter for the Poor: Housing Policy in Singapore", *Asian Development Review*, Vol. 8, No 1, 1990.

32. "The Schumpeterian Road to Affluence and Communism", *Malaysian Journal of Economic Studies*, Vol. XXVII, June and December, 1990, pp. 213–223.

33. "Economic Theory and the Economic Reality" *Accounting and Business Review*, Vol. 1, No. 1, Jan, 1994, pp. 1–9.

34. Review article on Lester Thurow's "Which Nations Will Dominate the World", *Accounting and Business Review*, Vol. 1, No 2, July, 1994, pp. 261–273.

35. "Japan and East Asia in the Pacific Century: The Economic Dimension", *The Journal of the Institute of Asian Studies*, No. 17, March, 1996, pp. 77–95.

36. "The Trinity Growth Theory: The Ascendancy of Asia and the Decline of the West", *Accounting and Business Review*, Vol. 3, No 2, July 1996, pp. 175–199.

37. "The Low-Income Trap: Theory and Evidence", *Accounting and Business Review*, Vol. 4, No. 1, January 1997, pp. 1–19.

38. (I) "NWC: Targets and Goals", *Accounting and Business Review*, Vol. 4, No 2, July 1997, pp. 165–185.

39. (II) "NWC: The Politics of Consensus", *Accounting and Business Review*, Vol. 4, No. 2, July 1997, pp. 187–199.

40. (III) "NWC: Issues and Initiatives", *Accounting and Business Review*, Vol.5, No. 1, January 1998, pp. 1–22.

41. "From Recession to Recovery in East Asia: A Non-IMF and Non-World Bank Explanation", *Accounting and Business Review*, Vol. 7, No. 2, July 2000, pp. 145–161.

42. Lim Chong Yah and Lee Chee Tong, "An Examination of Labor Productivity Growth and Structural Changes in the Singapore Labor Force", *Asian Economic Journal*, Vol. 16, No. 3, 2002, pp. 267–283.

43. "Macroeconomic Management: Is Keynesianism Dead?" *Singapore Economic Review*, Vol. 48, No. 1, April 2003, pp. 1–12.

44. "New Growth Theory and the Ascendency of China", *Nanyang Business Review*, Vol.2, No. 2, July 2003, pp. 68–74.

45. "China in the World Economy", *Nanyang Business Review*, Vol. 4, No. 1, 2005, pp. 7–14.

46. "Economic Theory and the East Asian Region", *Singapore Economic Review*, Vol. 50, Special 50th Anniversary Issue (2005), pp. 495–512.

47. Book review on Henri Ghesquiere's "Singapore's Success: Engineering Economic Growth", Singapore: Thomson. *Singapore Economic Review*, Vol. 52, No. 1, (2007), pp. 135–136.

48. "The International Monetary Fund and Exchange Rate Crisis Management", *Singapore Economic Review*, Vol. 52, No. 3. Special Issue edited by Dr Paul Yip on the Exchange Rate Systems and Policies in Asia, Dec 2007, pp. 285–294.

49. "The World Bank Spence Commission Report and the Trinity Growth Theory", *Singapore Economic Review*, Vol. 55, No. 1. Special Issue edited by Dr Pradumna Rana on the Asian Economic Integration, 2010, pp. 1–10.

50. "The Great Depression, the Great Recession and the Next Crisis", jointly with Sng Hui Ying, *World Economics*, Vol. 12, No. 3, September 2011, pp. 163–190.

51. "Economic Growth and Exchange Rate: A New Road Ahead for Indonesia", *Singapore Economic Review*, Vol. 60, No. 2, June 2015, pp. 1550010-1–1550010-6.

(2) CONFERENCE PAPERS (1–74)

1. "Southeast Asia: The Challenges of Economic Independence". Keynote Address, 5th National Conference, Australian Institute of International Affairs, MELBOURNE, 10 May 1975.
2. "Singapore and Asean Economic Co-operation". Regional Conference of Asean: Problems and Prospects in a Changing World, Chulalongkorn University, THAILAND, 19 December 1975.
3. "Some Aspects of ASEAN Economic Co-operation — the Singapore Perspective", jointly with Francis Chan, Chia Siow Yue and Amina Tyabji. Conference on ASEAN Economic Co-operation, JAKARTA, 27–29 October 1977.
4. "The Role of Large Scale Industries in the Industrialisation Joint Venture Activities" in "The 5th Asian Roundtable Report", The Asian Club, JAPAN, 1978, pp. 49–51.
5. "Policy and Perspective Outlook by Host Countries on Japanese Joint Venture Activities" in The 5th Asian Roundtable Report", The Asian Club, JAPAN, 1978, pp. 49–51.
6. "Obstacles to Economic Development in Southeast Asian and the New International Economic Order" International Conference on Progress in the Establishment of a New International Economic Order: Obstacles and Opportunities, Mexico City, MEXICO, 8 January 1979.
7. "Singapore and ASEAN Economic Co-operation". Institute of Developing Economies, TOKYO, 26 March 1979.
8. "Economic Restructuring and the Trade Union Movement in Singapore". NTUC Triennial Delegates' Conference, SINGAPORE, 8 November 1979.
9. "Singapore's Position in ASEAN Co-operation" in Joint Research Program Series, No. 14, Institute of Developing Economies, Tokyo, JAPAN. Also appeared in *Asean Business Quarterly*, Vol. 111, No. 1, First Quarter, pp. 9–19, and *Economic Bulletin*, 1979, pp. 17–21.
10. "Asean External Trade: Intra-Asean and Extra-Asean Co-operation" in "The 6th Asian Roundtable Report", The Asian Club, JAPAN 1979, pp. 70–83. Also appeared in *Asia Pacific Community*, No. 6, 1979, pp. 31–34 and "Malaysian Business", 1979, pp. 50–52.

11. "Development Performance and Experience in Singapore". The 14th SEANZA Central Banking Course, Hotel Royal, Singapore, organised by the Monetary Authority of Singapore, SINGAPORE, 30 September 1982.

12. "ASEAN-Australia Relation: A Perspective", jointly with Ow Chin Hock. The 53rd ANZAAS Congress, Perth, AUSTRALIA, 16–20 May 1983.

13. "Economic Interdependence: Perspective from Southeast Asia". FAEA-IEA Conference on Economic Interpedence: Perspectives from Developing Countries, MANILA, 23–27 May 1983.

14. "Trades in Manufactures: A Singapore Perspective". Korea Development Institute Workshop on Pacific Co-operation Task Force on Trade in Manufactured Goods, Seoul, SOUTH KOREA, 28 June–1 July 1983.

15. "Economic Development of Singapore Since Self-Government in 1959". British Association Conference on *The Economics of Human Betterment*, Sussex University, ENGLAND, 22–26 August 1983.

16. "Recent Economic Growth Among East-Asian Countries and Its Implications: A Summary Lecture". Dialogue Congress on Western Europe and North and Southwest Pacific, Albach, AUSTRIA, 6–10 July 1985.

17. "Changes in the Industrial Structure and the Role of Small and Medium Industries in Asian Countries: The Case of Singapore", jointly with Chew Soon Beng, Institute of Developing Economies, TOKYO, February 1985.

18. "Pax Americana and Thereafter: The Economic Dimension". Tokyo Colloquium, Yomuiri Research Institute and the Yomuiri Shimbun, TOKYO, 30 September–3 October 1987.

19. "Singapore's Development Strategy: An Interpretative Essay", jointly with Basant Kapur. First Conference of Asian Pacific Future on Direct Investment, Foundation for Advanced Information Research (FAIR), TOKYO, 19–22 April 1988.

20. "Foreign Investments and Economic Development in Singapore: A Policy-Oriented Approach", jointly with Soon Teck Wong. First Conference of Asian Pacific Future on Direct Investment, organised by the Foundation for Advanced Information Research (FAIR), TOKYO, 19–22 April 1988.

21. "Human Resource Development with Special Reference to Singapore". First International Human Resource Development and Assessment Centre Academic Conference, jointly organised by the China Human Resource Development and Assessment Research Centre and United Nations International Labour Office, SHANGHAI, 8–12 October 1988.

22. "Policy-Oriented Research in the Last Quinquennium on the Singapore Economy". Regional Collaboration Workshop on Monitoring National Research, organised by the Asian Development Bank, Manila, PHILIPPINES, 6–9 February 1989.

23. "Employment Policy and Strategy: A Search for Options". International Conference on Unemployment, Department of Economics, University of Cairo, EGYPT, 20–22 February 1989.

24. "The EGOIN Theory of Development and Underdevelopment". International Symposium on Development Strategies for Third World Countries, BEIJING, 18–22 April 1989.

25. "From a Basket Case to a Showcase State: A Case Study of Singapore". Asian NIEs Symposium, The Chinese University of Hong Kong, HONG KONG, 1991.

26. "East Asian Economic Co-operation and the New World Order", Seoul, SOUTH KOREA, August 1992, Opening Remarks as Vice-President, East Asian Economic Association.

27. "Will The 21st Century Be The Pacific Century?", Keynote Address, The 3rd Soka University Pacific Basin Symposium, SINGAPORE, September 1992.

28. "Singapore: The Steep Road Ahead". Paper presented to A-level Economics Teachers and Students at NTU, SINGAPORE, February 1993.

29. "Economic Theory and Economic Reality". Keynote Address, presented to A-level Economics Teachers at NUS, SINGAPORE, August 1993.

30. "East Asia in the Pacific Century". Keynote Address, United Nations Students' Association, NTU, SINGAPORE, July 1994.

31. "East Asia in the Pacific Century: An Uneasy Accommodation" Conference on *The Emergence of East Asia*, Hong Kong University of Science and Technology, HONG KONG, August 1994.

32. "Economic and Business Prospects in the Asian Pacific", Keynote Address, Stanford-NTU Executive Programme. (International Construction Management), The Beaufort, Sentosa, SINGAPORE, 4 September 1995. Similar address, *mutatis mutandis*, was presented at The Canon Asia Convention in Kota Kinabalu, Sabah, MALAYSIA, 26 September 1995.

33. "East Asia in the Pacific Century". Keynote Address, Coopers and Lybrand South East Asia Partners' Meeting, Four Seasons Hotel, SINGAPORE, November 1995.

34. "East Asia in the Pacific Century". Keynote Address, Coopers and Lybrand South East Asia Partners' Meeting, Four Seasons Hotel, SINGAPORE, November 1995.

35. "China in the Asia Pacific Century". Keynote Address, 6th ENDEC World Conference on Entrepreneurship, Shanghai JC Mandarin, SHANGHAI, 7 December 1995. Similar address, *mutatis mutandis*, was presented at Shanghai Jiao Tong University, SHANGHAI, 8 December 1995.

36. "The Trinity Growth Theory: The Ascendancy of Asia and the Decline of the West". Keynote Address, Ernst and Young Executive Seminar, SINGAPORE, 18 October 1996.

37. "Ascendancy of Asia and Decline of the West: Theory and Evidence". Keynote Address, 2nd Stanford-Nanyang Executive Programme, SINGAPORE, 25 August 1997.

38. "The S-Curve and the New International Economic Order". Conference on Patterns and Trends in International Relations in the 21st Century, Geneva, SWITZERLAND, 23–24 September 1997.

39. "Southeast Asian Exchange Rate Crisis and Currency Board System". Keynote Address, Currency Board System Symposium, SINGAPORE, 30 September 1997.

40. The Solution to the Asian Currency Crisis". Keynote Address, International Conference on The New Role of Government in a Market Economy, jointly organised by Osaka School of International Public Policy, Osaka University, JAPAN and Nanyang Business School, NTU, SINGAPORE, 5–6 February 1998.

41. "The NWC: An Experiment in Tripartism in Singapore 1972–1998". Keynote Address, International Seminar on Business-Government Deliberation Council organised by the Vietnam Chamber of Commerce and Industry and the Canadian Institute of Governance, HANOI on 28 April 1998.

42. "Foundations of Wage Guidelines in Singapore", SABRE Centre Staff Seminar, Nanyang Business School, NTU, SINGAPORE, 10 March 1999.

43. "Tripartite Negotiations on Wage Policy". Master in Public Policy Executive Programme, NUS, Orchard Hotel, SINGAPORE, 6 April 1999.

44. "East Asian Economic Crisis and Responses" 7th Meeting of the Council of International Advisors, NEC, JAPAN, 9 April 1999.

45. "Toward A Global Theory of Underdevelopment and Development" SABRE Centre Staff Seminar, Nanyang Business School, NTU, SINGAPORE, 16 April 1999.

46. "Wages Policy and Macroeconomic Crisis Management in Singapore". Department of Economics Graduate Seminar, NUS, SINGAPORE, 21 February 2000.

47. "From Recession to Recovery in East Asia". 8th Meeting of the Council of International Advisors, NEC, JAPAN, 14 April 2000.

48. "From Recession to Recovery in East Asia: A Non-IMF and Non-World Bank Explanation". 7th Pacific Basin Symposium, co-sponsored by Soka University, JAPAN and the University of Malaya, Kuala Lumpur, MALAYSIA, 28–30 August 2000.

49. "Welcoming and Keynote Address: Postmortem on the Asian Currency Crisis". 7th Conference of the East Asian Economic Association (EAEA), SINGAPORE, 17–18 November 2000.

50. "Marriage, Fertility, and the Household" Economics Executive Programme (EEP), Department of Economics, NUS, SINGAPORE, Orchard Parade Hotel, 14 May 2004.

51. "China in the World Economy" Public Lecture, Hainan University, Haikou, CHINA, 9 December 2004.

52. "Crises Management in Singapore" Invited Paper, Sunway College, Kuala Lumpur, MALAYSIA, 23 March 2005.

53. "China's Growth Momentum In The 'Opening Up' Process". International Conference on Political Economy, 16 July 2005, Xiamen University, Xiamen, Fujian, CHINA.

54. "Economic Theory and the East Asian Region". Singapore Economic Review Conference 2005, 4 August 2005, Pan Pacific Hotel, SINGAPORE.

55. "Government Institutions and Policy Options in Singapore's Economic Development Since Independence". IMF-Singapore Regional Training Institute, SINGAPORE, 18 Aug 2005.

56. "Crises Management in Singapore Since Independence (1965–2005)". Invited Paper, CPA Australia and ICPAS Meeting, 4 October 2005, Pan Pacific Hotel, SINGAPORE.

57. "The International Monetary Fund and Exchange Rate Crisis Management". Invited Special Lecture, The Launch of Philip Kotler Center for ASEAN Marketing Forum, The ASEAN Secretariat, JAKARTA, 24 November 2005.

58. "The Singapore Economy: The Right Options". Invited Special Lecture, Singapore Soka Association Youth Peace Conference, SSA Headquarters, SINGAPORE, April 2007.

59. "A Theory of Poverty in the S Curve Hypothesis: A Non-Mathematical Approach". Invited Paper, Singapore Economic Review Conference 2007, August 2007, Meritus Mandarin Hotel, SINGAPORE.

60. "Asian Economic Development in a Global Setting". Invited Panel Speaker, Temasek Forum on "Developing Asia in the 21st Century: Economic Prospects and Risks", The Atrium@Orchard, August 2007, SINGAPORE.

61. "Ten years after the meltdown in Asia: Are our economies more vulnerable or robust?". Invited Keynote Speech by NBS, The Asian Business Case Competition @ Nanyang 2007 Roundtable, Nanyang Executive Centre, NTU, October 2007, SINGAPORE.

62. "Transformation in the Singapore Economy: Course and Causes". NTU-MOE Student's Seminar 2008, NTU, 8 March 2008, SINGAPORE.

63. "The Asian Financial Crisis and the Sub-Prime Mortgage Crisis: A Dissenting View". NTU-MOE Teacher's Seminar 2008, Ministry of Education, 10 March 2008, SINGAPORE.

64. "The World Bank Spence Commission Report and the Trinity Growth Theory". 11th Conference of the East Asian Economic Association Conference (EAEA), November 2008, MANILA.

65. "The US Financial Crisis: the Moral Hazard Problem and the Two US Administrations". Invited Special Lecture by Dean, NBS, The Philip Kotler Center for ASEAN Marketing, Jakarta CMO Club, JAKARTA, December 2008.

66. "Transformation in the Singapore Economy: Course and Causes". NTU-MOE Student's Seminar 2009, NTU, March 2009, SINGAPORE.

67. "The Asian Financial Crisis and the Sub-Prime Mortgage Crisis: A Dissenting View". NTU-MOE Teacher's Seminar 2009, Ministry of Education, March 2009, SINGAPORE.

68. "Unpreparedness in the Great Recession". Invited paper, Singapore Economic Review Conference 2009, August 2009, Swissotel, SINGAPORE.

69. "A Case for Selective Capital Control". Invited paper, Workshop on *Exchange Rate Systems and Macroeconomic Policies in Asia: Lessons from Past Experiences and Outlooks amid the Global Economic Slowdown*, August 2009, Nanyang Executive Centre, NTU, SINGAPORE.

70. "The Aborted Great Recession and its Aftermath". 12th International Convention of the East Asian Economic Association (EAEA), 2–3 October 2010, Ewha Woman's University, Seoul, KOREA.

71. "The Great Depression, the Great Recession and the Next Crisis". Singapore Economic Review Conference 2011, August 2011, Mandarin Orchard, SINGAPORE.

72. "Does Singapore Need Economic Restructuring II or Another 'Wage Revolution'?". Economic Society of Singapore Distinguished Speaker Public Lecture Series, 9 April 2012, Orchard Hotel, SINGAPORE.

73. "The Japanese Economy: Past, Present and Future Viewed: From My Trinity Growth and Development Theory". Public lecture, Waseda University, 17 July 2012, JAPAN.

74. "The Trinity Growth Theory: A Theory of Wealth and Poverty". Keynote Address presented at the 13th International Convention of the East Asian Economic Association (EAEA), 19 October 2012, Grand Copthorne Waterfront Hotel, SINGAPORE.

(3) BOOKS, MONOGRAPHS AND CHAPTERS IN BOOKS

(i) Books and Monographs (1–29)

1. *Traffic Flows Through Port Swettenham Projected to 1975,* jointly with U.A. Aziz, S. J. Gilani and Jock Hoe, Kuala Lumpur: University of Malaya, 1964, 465 pages.

2. *Economic Development of Modern Malaya*, Kuala Lumpur: Oxford University Press, 1967. Reprinted in 1969, 387 pages.

3. *Money and Monetary Policy*, Singapore: Eastern Universities Press, 1969. (Reprinted in 1969) 42 pages. Translated into Chinese by Sin Chew Jit Poh, a Chinese Language daily in Singapore, for serialised publication.

4. *Elements of Economic Theory*, jointly with Lee Sheng-Yi and Chia Siow Yue, Kuala Lumpur: Oxford University Press, 1971, 250 pages. Translated into Chinese and Malay by Oxford University Press. Adapted for use in Pakistan. Second Edition, 1975, 401 pages. Third Edition, 1984, 527 pages.

5. *Pacific Regional Science Conference, Honolulu, 1969*, co-editor with Walter Miklius, Yukitide Okano, Anthony Pascal and Noboru Sakashita, Tokyo: University of Tokyo Press, 1971, 183 pages.

6. *The Singapore Economy,* co-editor with You Poh Seng, Singapore: Eastern Universities Press, 1971, 421 pages.

7. *Economic Structure and Organisation*, jointly with Chia Siow Yue, Bhanoji Rao and Ow Chwee Huay, Kuala Lumpur: Oxford University Press, 1973, 372 pages. Translated into Chinese and Malay by Oxford University Press. Revised Edition, 1977, 435 pages. *Went into braille.*

8. *Economics and Current Affairs*, Vol. I, Singapore: Sin Chew Jit Poh, 1978, 99 pages, in English and Chinese.

9. *Economics and Current Affairs*, Vol. II, Singapore: Sin Chew Jit Poh, 1979, 139 pages, in English and Chinese.

10. *Economics and Current Affairs*, Vol. III, Singapore: Sin Chew Jit Poh, 1980, 142 pages, in English and Chinese.

11. *Economics and Current Affairs*, Vol. IV, Singapore: Sin Chew Jit Poh, 1980, 161 pages, in Chinese.

12. *Economic Development in Singapore*, Singapore: Federal Publications, 1980, 149 pages.

13. *Economic Development in Southeast Asia*, Singapore: Federal Publications, 1981, 180 pages.

14. *Commentary on Economics and Current Affairs*, Singapore: Federal Publications, 1981, 162 pages.

15. *Learning from the Japanese Experience*, edited by Lim Chong Yah, Singapore: Maruzen Asia, 1982, 111 pages.

16. *Education and National Development*, Singapore: Federal Publications, 1983, 122 pages.

17. *Economic Restructuring in Singapore*, Singapore: Federal Publications, 1984, 117 pages.

18. *Singapore: Twenty-Five Years of Growth and Structural Change*, co-editor with You Poh Seng, Singapore: Singapore News and Publications Ltd., 1984, 392 pages.

19. *Resources and Growth in Singapore*, co-editor with Peter Lloyd, Kuala Lumpur: Oxford University Press, June 1986, 279 pages.

20. *Policy Options for the Singapore Economy*, co-authored with 25 others, Singapore: McGraw-Hill Book Co., Jan 1988, 499 pages. Translated into Japanese by two Japanese Professors.

21. *Development and Underdevelopment*, Singapore: Longman Publications, 1991, 250 pages.

22. *Eight Lectures on the Regional Economy*, Singapore: Nanyang Technological University, School of Accountancy and Business, 1995, 129 pages.

23. *Economic Policy Management in Singapore*, edited by Lim Chong Yah, Singapore: Addison Wesley, 1996, 450 pages.

24. *Wages and Wages Policies: Tripartism in Singapore*, author and joint editor, Singapore: World Scientific, 1999, 381 pages.

25. *Economic Essays by Lim Chong Yah*, (Editors: Hooi Den Huan and Koh Ai Tee) Singapore: World Scientific, 2001, 240 pages.

26. *Southeast Asia: The Long Road Ahead*, Singapore: World Scientific, 2001, 376 pages.

27. *Southeast Asia: The Long Road Ahead* (Second Edition), Singapore: World Scientific, 2004, 414 pages.

28. *Southeast Asia: The Long Road Ahead* (Third Edition), Singapore: World Scientific, 2009, 434 pages.

29. *Singapore's National Wages Council: An Insider's View, Singapore*: World Scientific, 2014, 397 pages

(ii) Chapters in Books (1–39)

1. "Malayan Economic Development" in Cranley Onslow (ed), *Asian Economic Development*, London: Weidenfeld and Nicolson, 1965, pp. 95–117.

2. "A Brief Note on the Finances of the University of Malaya", *UNESCO-IAU Study of the Role of Institutions of Higher Education in the Development of Countries in Southeast Asia*, UNESCO, Vol. I, 1967, pp. 477–489.

3. "West Malaysian External Trade, 1947–65" in Morgan and Spoelstra (eds.), *Economic Interdependence in Southeast Asia*, Madison: University of Wisconsin Press, 1969, pp. 203–237.

4. "Economic Trends in Malaysia", *Trends in Malaysia*, Singapore: Institute of Southeast Asian Studies, July 1971, pp. 1–9.

5. "The Economic Development of Singapore in the Sixties and Beyond", jointly with Ow Chwee Huay, in You Poh Seng and Lim Chong Yah (eds), *The Singapore Economy*, Singapore: Eastern Universities Press, 1971, pp. 1–42.

6. "The Singapore Economy and the Vietnam War", jointly with Ow Chwee Huay, in You Poh Seng and Lim Chong Yah (eds.), *The Singapore Economy*, Singapore: Eastern Universities Press, 1971, pp. 352–369.

7. "Monetary System and Banking Structure", jointly with Doreen Phua in You Poh Seng and Lim Chong Yah (eds), The Singapore Economy, Singapore: Eastern Universities Press, 1971, pp. 127 159.

8. "Trade Restrictions and Textiles Exports of Singapore: A Case Study", in English and Hay (eds), *Obstacles to Trade in the Pacific Area*, Ottawa: Carleton University Press, 1972, pp. 187–209.

9. "Economic Trends in Southeast Asia", in *Southeast Asia Today: Problems and Prospects*, Singapore: Institute of Southeast Asian Studies, July 1973, pp. 20–34.

10. "Mass Versus Selective Higher Education in Southeast Asia: The Responses of the University of Singapore", *The Growth of Southeast Asian Universities: Expansion versus Consolidation*, Singapore: Regional Institute of Higher Education and Development, 1974, pp. 119–141.

11. "Export Instability and Economic Development: A Brief Review", *Economic Stability Problems in Developing Countries*, Taipei: Tamkang College, 1974, pp. 142–160.

12. "Growth Without Inflation", in Bhanoji Rao (ed.), *Inflation and Growth*, Singapore: Stamford College Press, 1974, pp. 1–13.

13. "Southeast Asia: The Challenges of Economic Independence", in Edward P. Wolfers (ed.), *Australia's Northern Neighbours: Independent or Dependent?*, Australia: The Griffin Press, 1976, pp. 15–26. Also appeared in *Southeast Asian Affairs l976*, pp. 56–64.

14. "Means and Methods of Achieving Integrated Programmes in Higher Education in Singapore to Meet Basic Needs for Food", in Nasution and Virasai (eds), *Higher Education and Social Commitment*, Singapore: Regional Institute of Higher Education and Development, 1978, pp. 94–100.

15. "Economic Restructuring in Singapore", *PETIR 25th Anniversary Issue* Singapore: Central Executive Committee People's Action Party, 1979, pp. 260–271.

16. "The Role of Large-Scale Industries in the Industrialisation Process Minimising `Loss' of Culture in Southeast Asia", in Rolf E. Vente and Peter S. J. Chen (eds.), *Culture and Industrialisation*, Singapore: McGraw-Hill International, 1980, pp. 195–204.

17. "The Economic Development of the members of the Association of Southeast Asian Nations (ASEAN)", in Lozoya and Bhattacharya (eds.), *Asia and the New International Economic Order*, New York: Pergamon Press, 1981, pp. 174–188. Also appeared in *Asean Business Quarterly*, Vol. II, No. 4, 1978, pp. 9–17.

18. "Asian Newly Industrialised Countries and Japan: A Comparison", *Learning from the Japanese Experience*, Singapore: Maruzen Asia, 1982, pp. 49–55.

19. "The NWC As I See It", *Our Heritage and Beyond* Singapore: National Trades Union Congress, 1982, pp. 49–55.

20. "Development Performance and Experience in Singapore", *SEANZA Lectures 1982*, Singapore: Monetary Authority of Singapore, 1983, pp. 111–141.

21. "Singapore's Economic Development: Retrospect and Prospect" in Peter S. J. Chen (ed), Singapore Development Policies and Trends, 1983, pp. 89–104.

22. "The Transformation of Singapore in Twenty-Five Years" in You Poh Seng and Lim Chong Yah (eds.), *Singapore: Twenty-Five Years of Development*, Singapore: Nan Yang Xing Zhou Lianhe Zaobao, 1984, pp. 1–10.

23. "The Development of Singapore Since Self Government in 1959", in Kenneth E Boulding (ed.), The Economics of Human Betterment, London: MacMillan Press, 1985, pp. 105 131.

24. "Singapore: Twenty-Five Years of Growth and Structural Changes", *Singapore 1985*, Singapore: Ministry of Culture, 1985, pp. 3–28.

25. "Singapore : From High Growth Rates to Recession : A Personal View", *The Management of Success: The Moulding of Modern Singapore*, Singapore: Institute of Southeast Asian Studies, 1989, pp. 201–217.

26. "The Egoin Theory of Development and Underdevelopment", *Development Strategies For Third World Countries*, China: Chinese Association for International Understanding, March 1990, pp. 13–42.

27. "Taiwan's Economic Miracle: A Singaporean Perspective", *Economic Development in East and Southeast Asia — Essays in Honour of Professor Shinichi Ichimura*, Honolulu: Resource Systems Institute, East-West Centre and Singapore: Institute of Southeast Asian Studies, 1990, pp. 38–56.

28. "NWC Guidelines for Wage Increases That Keep Us Competitive", *30 Years On*, Singapore: NTUC, 1991, pp. 32–40.

29. "East Asian Economic Miracle: Framework for Understanding and Analysis", *The Development Experience of Singapore*. China: Institute for Asia-Pacific Economics Studies and Singapore: Asian Commerce and Economics Studies Centre, 1994, pp. 33–39.

30. "Southeast Asian Exchange Rate Crisis and Currency Board System" in *Currency Board System: A Stop-Gap Measure or a Necessity; Currency Board System Symposium 1997*. Singapore: Board of Commissioners of Currency, September 1997, pp. 22–28.

31. (I) "NWC: The Politics of Consensus", (II) "NWC: Targets and Goals" and (III) "NWC: Issues and Initiatives" in Lim, Chong Yah and Chew, Rosalind (Eds), *Wages and Wages Policies: Tripartism in Singapore*, Singapore: World Scientific, 1998, 381 pages.

32. "The International Monetary Fund and Exchange Rate Crisis Management" in Yip SL, Paul (ed), Exchange Rate Systems and Policies in Asia. World Scientific, 2008, pp. 1–10.

33. "Transformation in the Singapore Economy: Course and Causes", Chapter 1 in Chia and Sng (eds), *Singapore and Asia in a Globalized World: Contemporary Economic Issues and Policies.* World Scientific, 2009, pp. 3–23.

34. "The Asian Financial Crisis and the Sub-Prime Mortgage Crisis: A Dissenting View", Chapter 6 in Chia and Sng (eds), *Singapore and Asia in a Globalized World: Contemporary Economic Issues and Policies.* World Scientific, 2009, pp. 105–120.

35. "The Deepening Global Recession and the Great Depression Fear", Chapter 1 in Sng and Chia (eds), *Singapore And Asia: Impact Of The Global Financial Tsunami And Other Economics Issues.* World Scientific, 2010, pp. 3–13.

36. "Singapore Growth Model: Its Strengths and Its Weaknesses", Chapter 7 in Sng and Chia (eds), *Singapore And Asia: Impact Of The Global Financial Tsunami And Other Economics Issues.* World Scientific, 2010, pp. 123–132.

37. "The National Wages Council (NWC) and Macroeconomic Management in Singapore", Chapter 1 in Sng and Chia (eds.), *Crisis Management and Public Policy: Singapore's Approach to Economic Resilience.* World Scientific, 2011, pp. 3–17.

38. "Unpreparedness in the Great Recession", jointly with Sng Hui Ying, Chapter 2 in Sng and Chia (eds.), *Crisis Management and Public Policy: Singapore's Approach to Economic Resilience.* World Scientific, 2011, pp. 19–31.

39. "A Case for Selective Capital Control", jointly with Sarah Chan, Chapter 4 in Sng and Chia (eds.), *Crisis Management and Public Policy: Singapore's Approach to Economic Resilience.* World Scientific, 2011, pp. 51–62.

(4) OTHER PUBLICATIONS (1–39)

1. "The Teaching Profession and Nation Building", *Proceedings of the National Conference of Heads of Secondary Schools*, Malaysia, 1967.

2. "Education for National Development", *Proceedings of the National Conference of Heads of Secondary Schools*, Malaysia, 1967.

3. "The Contributions of Universities to National Development", *Kesatuan Bulletin*, Vol. 6, May 1971.

4. "Some Aspects of Development in the Faculty of Arts and Social Sciences, University of Singapore", *Kesatuan Bulletin*, Vol. XI, December 1972.

5. "Singapore and the World Economic Crisis", *Singapore and the World Economic Crisis*, Singapore: Ministry of Education and National Junior College, 1975. Republished in *Prospects*, Vol. III, No. 7, July 1975.

6. "An Overview on Productivity Agreements, Worker Motivation and Sharing the Gains of Productivity", *Productivity Agreements, Worker Motivation and Sharing the Gains of Productivity*, Tokyo: Asian Productivity Organisation, 1976.

7. "One Man's Week", *Business Times*, 24 October 1977.

8. "Limitation of Professionals in Fulfilling the Needs of a Developing Nation", *Proceedings of the Third Convention of the Singapore Professional Centre*, Singapore: Singapore Professional Centre, November 25–27, 1977.

9. "The Economic Impact of the Rubber-Growing Industry on Peninsular Malaysia and Singapore", *Singapore Rubber Centenary, 1877–1977*, Singapore: Rubber Centenary Committee, December 1977.

10. "Arts and Social Sciences: Retrospect and Prospect", *University of Singapore Campus News*, No. 4, January 1978.

11. "Where Singapore Stands: The 1978 World Bank Report", *The Mirror*, Vol. XIV, No. 42, 216 October 1978.

12. "The World's 800,000 Absolute Poor", *The Mirror*, Vol. XIV, No. 46, 13 November 1978.

13. "Singapore, 1929–1979", *Sin Chew Jit Poh 50th Anniversary Souvenir Magazine, 1929–1979*, 1979.

14. "ASEAN: The Package Deal, Poor, Inferior and Defective", *Malaysian Business*, March 1979 and April 1979.

15. "New International Economic Order: Attempting to Right Wrongs", *Malaysian Business*, May 1979.

16. "Market Research: Can You Afford To Do Without?", *Malaysian Business*, June 1979.

17. "Britain Today: The Making or Undoing of a Government", *Malaysian Business*, September 1979.

18. "The Future of Thailand: For Certain Not Another Kampuchea", *Malaysian Business*, September 1979, pp. 40–41.

19. "Development Concepts and Their Applicability in Southeast Asia", *Indonesian Business Association of Singapore Bulletin*, November 1980.

20. "Singapore and ASEAN Economic Co-operation", *Nihon Keizai Shimbum* (Japan Economic Journal), Tokyo, 10 July 1981.

21. "Towards An Association of Pacific Basin Nations: An Explanatory View", *Malaysian Business*, February 1980. Also appeared in *Asian Wall Street*

Journal, 3 January 1981 and *Pacific Economic Co-operation: Suggestions for Action*, 1984.

22. *Development, Trade and the Asia-Pacific, Essays in Honour of Professor Lim Chong Yah*, edited by Professors Basant Kapur, Euston Quah and Hoon Hian Teck, Singapore: Prentice Hall, 1996, 591 pages.(Thirty-eight contributors from 21 Universities).

23. Appeared in Melanie Chew, *Leaders of Singapore*, Part III, Creating A Nation. Singapore: Resource Press, 1996, pp197–206.

24. Completed book on "Southeast Asia: The Long Road Ahead" (Singapore: World Scientific, 2001), 376 pages. Book launched by President SR Nathan at Raffles Hotel on 11 May 2001.

25. Completed book on "Southeast Asia: The Long Road Ahead", Second Edition (Singapore: World Scientific, 2004), 414 pages. Book launched by Professor Su Guaning, President of NTU at NTU on 6 February 2004.

26. "How the IMF Can Stay Relevant", *The Straits Times*, 7 September 2006.

27. "Beijing Should Acquire Gold and Oil with Foreign Reserves", *The Financial Times*, 16 March 2007.

28. Appeared as one of four persons in Channel NewsAsia's 4-part interview series, *A Few Good Men*, Episode No 4 on 23 August 2007 as part of 2007 National Day's month programme.

29. "Modern-day Sir Galahads Who Can End the Global Distress", *The Financial Times*, 17 October 2008.

30. "Retrenchment In Singapore: Only As A Last Resort", *The Straits Times*, 20 November 2008.

31. *Foreword by Lim Chong Yah*, in Rana, Pradumna B. and Dowling, John Malcolm, *South Asia: Rising to the Challenge of Globalization*. World Scientific, 2008.

32. Completed book on "Southeast Asia: The Long Road Ahead", Third Edition. (Singapore: World Scientific, 2009), 434 pages. Book launched by Professor Su Guaning, President of NTU at Raffles Hotel on 22 May 2009.

33. *Foreword by Lim Chong Yah*, in Chia Wai Mun and Sng Hui Ying (eds), *Singapore and Asia in a Globalized World: Contemporary Economic Issues and Policies*. World Scientific, 2009.

34. "Dr Lee Boon Yang, "Tripartism and a Tale of Two Birdies", Speech by Lim Chong Yah in honour of Minister Lee on his retirement from politics at the Tripartite Golf Dinner, Sentosa Golf Club, 2 May 2009.

35. "Petrol Tax Can Wipe Out Fiscal Deficit", *The Financial Times*, 12 January 2010.

36. Three quotations on pages 49, 50 and 67 cited in book, "The History of Singapore: Lion City, Asian Tiger", Discovery Channel 2010, Wiley, 256 pages.

37. "Geithner's Plan for Adjusting Exchange Rates is Innovative", *The Financial Times*, 27 October 2010.

38. "A Personal Tribute to Dr Toh Chin Chye", *TODAY*, 10 February 2012.

39. "Time to Restructure Singapore for the Future", *The Straits Times*, 10 April 2012.

NAME INDEX

F

G

H

I

J

K

L

R

S

T

U

V

W

X

Y

Z

SUBJECT INDEX

D

E

F

M

N

www.ingramcontent.com/pod-product-compliance
Ingram Content Group UK Ltd.
Pitfield, Milton Keynes, MK11 3LW, UK
UKHW020351150926
8624IPUK00004B/111

9 789813 20304